**HABIT'S**

**PATHWAYS**

# HABIT'S

Repetition, Power, Conduct

Tony Bennett

# PATHWAYS

DUKE UNIVERSITY PRESS  Durham and London  2023

Designed by Aimee C. Harrison
Typeset in Garamond Premier Pro and Degular
by Westchester Publishing Services

Library of Congress Cataloging-in-Publication Data
Names: Bennett, Tony, [date] author.
Title: Habit's pathways : repetition, power, conduct / Tony Bennett. Description:
Durham : Duke University Press, 2023. | Includes bibliographical ref-erences and
index.
Identifiers: LCCN 2022060444 (print)
LCCN 2022060445 (ebook)
ISBN 9781478024989 (paperback)
ISBN 9781478020394 (hardcover)
ISBN 9781478027331 (ebook)
Subjects: LCSH: Habit—Political aspects. | Habit—Social aspects. | Politics and
culture. | Political culture. | Power (Philosophy) | Political socialization. | Political
sociology. | BISAC: SOCIAL SCIENCE / Sociology / Social Theory Classification:
LCC HM621 .B4525 2023 (print) | LCC HM621 (ebook) |
DDC 306.2—dc23/eng/20230419
LC record available at https://lccn.loc.gov/2022060444
LC ebook record available at https://lccn.loc.gov/2022060445

Cover art: Philip Guston (1913–80), *Painting, Smoking, Eating*, 1973.
Oil on canvas, 197 × 263 cm. Collection Stedelijk Museum Amsterdam.
© The Estate of Philip Guston, courtesy Hauser & Wirth.

# CONTENTS

## NOTE ON THE TEXT

There are, in some chapters, boxed texts outlining different Scenes of Habit associated with the positions taken by some of the most influential writers on the subject.

A good deal of the historical literature on habit that I discuss speaks of "man" as a generalized stand-in for the human without registering any differentiation of gender. I have retained this usage as part and parcel of the discourses under discussion rather than correcting it in the light of current critiques.

When I italicize passages in quoted texts I am, in all cases, following the original.

When quoting consecutive passages from the same source, I usually only give the author and date of the source following the first quotation and, thereafter, only the relevant page number. Where I quote a number of such passages from the same page, I give the page number after the last passage quoted.

Where I draw on earlier work I have published on habit, I indicate this in an endnote.

## ACKNOWLEDGMENTS

I have been interested in habit for quite some time in the context of both individual and collective research projects through which I have incurred many intellectual debts. My interest was initially prompted by my work on the history and theory of museums when, exploring the role played by anthropology in relation to the practices of museums in colonial contexts, I first came across the doctrine of survivals. This attributed the "backwardness" of "primitive peoples" to their perpetuation of an original set of habits marking their transition from a state of nature. As I have since learned, this doctrine has itself exhibited a remarkable capacity for survival in the continuing role it has played—well into the twentieth century—as an influential version of habit's conception as a form of uninterrupted repetition. I found out a good deal more about habit's colonial histories in a collective project—Museum, Field, Metropolis, Colony: Practices of Social Governance, funded by the Australian Research Council—that I convened shortly after joining the Institute for Culture and Society at Western Sydney University in 2009. It was in examining the role of museums in practices of colonial governance across a range of national contexts that I first came across John Dewey's work on habit and its relations to the Boasian tradition in anthropology. My thanks, then, to my coresearchers in this project—Fiona Cameron, Nélia Dias, Ben Dibley, Rodney Harrison, the late Ira Jacknis, and Conal McCarthy—for the insights I gained from the immensely collaborative spirit in which our research was conducted. I owe a special debt to Ira Jacknis for the generosity with which he shared his unparalleled knowledge of the work of Franz Boas.

Around the same time that I first became interested in museums, I developed an interest in the sociological tradition that went under the heading of "the critique of everyday life." Prompted initially by the influence this tradition had exerted on the currency of resistance theory in cultural studies, I was led to a different appreciation of its construction of the relations between habit and repetition by the feminist critiques to which it was subjected. My thanks, then, to Rita Felski and Lesley Johnson for first awakening my interest in the need for a more critical probing of the role of habit in this tradition and, indeed, in sociology more generally. And my thanks to Elizabeth Silva for the work we did together in pursuing this line of inquiry in the context of the Open University's National Everyday Cultures Program in the early noughties.

It was through this program that Elizabeth and I entered into a productive collaboration with Mike Savage, Alan Warde, and Modesto Gayo from the University of Manchester and David Wright from the Open University in the Cultural Capital and Social Exclusion project. Funded by the United Kingdom's Economic and Social Research Council (ESRC) over the period 2003–6, this project rekindled my interest in Pierre Bourdieu's concept of habitus and the intricacies of its relationship to the concept of habit. This was also true of the later project—Australian Cultural Fields: National and Transnational Dynamics, funded by the Australian Research Council—which, in probing the relations between cultural fields, cultural capitals, and habitus in Australia, allowed me to extend and deepen my acquaintance with Bourdieu's work on habitus. I am especially indebted to Greg Noble in this regard for constantly nudging me toward a more nuanced appreciation of the intricacies of this concept. But I owe a debt, too, to the other members of the research team: Michelle Kelly, David Rowe, Tim Rowse, Deborah Stevenson, and Emma Waterton from the Institute for Culture and Society at Western Sydney University; David Carter and Graeme Turner from the University of Queensland; Modesto Gayo from the Universidad Diego Portales in Chile; and Fred Myers from New York University.

The collaboration between the Open University and the University of Manchester in the Cultural Capital and Social Exclusion project led to a more extended collaboration between the two institutions in the ESRC-funded Centre for Research on Socio-cultural Change. I am grateful to Mike Savage, as the leader of this initiative, for involving me as one of the Centre's directors, for the opportunity this presented of developing a five-year program in collaboration with Patrick Joyce called Culture, Governance and Citizenship.

Working with Patrick and other colleagues in this theme, particularly Francis Dodsworth, contributed significantly to the development of my interest in the relations between habit and freedom associated with its enrollment in practices of liberal government. I am particularly indebted also to Nikolas Rose, with whom Patrick, Francis, and I collaborated in organizing an ESRC-funded program of workshops called Government and Freedom: Histories and Prospects. Apart from the stimulation of Rose's critical rethinking of the relations between government and freedom, the workshop program brought together many scholars who have made signal contributions to contemporary engagements with habit and from whom I learned a great deal. I record, in particular, my debt to the work of Mariana Valverde in this regard.

The same was true of the 2010 workshop I co-organized with Greg Noble and Megan Watkins from the Institute for Culture and Society, Francis Dodsworth, and Mary Poovey from New York University. This undoubtedly broadened my horizons regarding the scope of concerns encompassed by the concept of habit with probing contributions from Lisa Blackman, Nick Crossley, Simon Lumsden, and Melanie White. My thanks, too, to Clare Carlisle and Elizabeth Grosz. Although neither of these was able to attend the workshop in person, they contributed agenda-setting papers to the special double issue of *Body and Society* (19, no. 2–3) that came out of the workshop in 2013. Although the approach I take in this book differs significantly from those taken by Carlisle and Grosz, it is one I should not have been able to develop without the stimulation that their work has offered.

I am, however, more immediately indebted to the other members of the research team—Gay Hawkins, Greg Noble, and Ben Dibley from the Institute for Culture and Society and Nikolas Rose from King's College, London—for the Assembling and Governing Habits project. Funded by the Australian Research Council from 2017 to 2021, this examined different ways in which habits are assembled by, and made actionable on the part of, a range of governing authorities. Apart from giving me the opportunity to extend my reading of the literatures concerned with the relations between habit, power, repetition, and conduct, my approach to these questions was enormously enriched by this team of collaborators. I owe special debts to Gay for her work on the infrastructures of habit; to Greg for once again pushing me on the concept of habitus; to Ben for his critical engagement with the work of Gabriel Tarde and crowd theory more generally; and to Nikolas, whose work on the neurosciences and, before that, on the history of the psy disciplines has helped to shape my thinking on habit in many ways. I also owe particular debts to Gay for her critical reading of chapter 5, to Nikolas for his assessment of chapter 6, and to Greg for his critical review of chapter 7. And a special thanks to Ben for reading a draft of the whole book and for the comments on many points of detail, as well as on the book's overall argument, that he offered. And my thanks to the many participants in the two workshops organized by the project for the insights I derived from their contributions. I have also, in the case of Carolyn Pedwell, learned much from her work on those aspects of habit's histories in which we have shared a long-term interest. I am also grateful to Ian Hunter and Susan Zieger for their comments on an early draft of the introduction, and to Ian and Susan for their critical reading of chapters 4 and 2, respectively. I am also indebted to Susan for her work on various aspects of the relations between habit and the histories of addiction and slavery on which I draw in parts of the book.

Special thanks, too, to Kenneth Wissoker from Duke University Press for his exceptional guidance and support in shepherding my initial proposal and then my text and its revisions through Duke's commissioning and review processes. These had some unexpected but, in the end, productive ups and downs, and I am grateful to Ken for guiding me through them. My thanks, too, to Ryan Kendall and Kate Mullen for their supportive advice and assistance through these two stages. And my particular thanks to Ihsan Taylor and Brian Ostrander for their helpful guidance through all stages of the production process. I especially appreciate the rigorous copyediting of my manuscript at the outset of this process.

I am also grateful to the three anonymous reviewers commissioned by Duke University Press for their thoughtful and probing comments on the book's conception. These prompted me to rethink aspects of the structure I had proposed for the book and to be clearer, both in my own mind and for the reader, regarding my aims. I am especially grateful for the encouraging spirit in which reviewer 1 and reviewer 3 responded to the manuscript and proposed productive lines of revision. I am grateful, too, to Simon Chambers for his assistance in tidying up various technical aspects of the text.

Finally, even though it's getting to be something of a habit, I acknowledge my incalculable debt to my partner, Sue, for her support throughout the writing of this book, and for her critical reading of its various drafts. I doubt I should have kept on track otherwise.

# Introduction

HABIT HAS BEEN A SUBJECT of intellectual debate and political contention—and usually both together—since its initial conception in the Western tradition of classical philosophy. In being reinterpreted across a succession of intellectual traditions—Christian theology, early modern philosophy, and the empirical sciences, from eighteenth-century physiology to the contemporary neurosciences—accounts of what habit is and what it does have invariably formed a part of how it should be acted on in order to be guided or directed to particular ends. These questions have also prompted a further set of issues concerning whose habits should be acted on, by whom, and with what authority. There have been many periods in which such matters have been more or less settled and when, accordingly, the debates over habit's meaning and direction have been relatively muted, just chugging along in the background. But there have also been times when habit has become a hotly disputed topic as both the terms in which it should be understood and what should be done to or with it are sharply contested.

Ours is such a time. While subject to variable interpretations, habit has always been understood to constitute, as a part of its definition, a form of unthinking repetition. As such, habit is now, and has been for some time, at the forefront of a whole set of politically urgent questions. The exigencies of climate change put the role of unthinking repetition on the line in a variety of ways ranging across our daily travel routines and forms and degrees of energy consumption. A related set of ecological concerns flag the significance of the unthinking repetitions that often characterize practices of littering and waste disposal more generally. Then there are the unthinking habits of white privilege that have become key matters for concern in critical race theory, just as feminist thought and queer theory have sought to disrupt the unthinking repetitions that underpin dominant forms of gendered behavior. In a different register, the increasing presence of automation has generated a range of concerns centered on the roles played by unthinking repetitions across human and machinic forms of action: the role of automation in new forms of labor discipline, for example, alongside the development of new ways of collecting and acting on our habits through computational forms of governance. The list could and, as my argument unfolds, will be extended. What matters for now is just to note the extraordinary range of contemporary political concerns that foreground questions of habit and are responsible for the marked upswing of interest in the topic that has been evident over the last three to four decades. This upswing of interest has been characterized by marked disagreements as habit's repetitions have been cast in a multitude of different roles, some negative and disabling, others positive and generative, in being conscripted as both the target and agent of different political projects.

My primary purpose in what follows is to contribute to the current debates regarding these contested theories of habit and their practical implications by placing them in the context of habit's longer histories and disputations. I do so by pursuing two main lines of argument. The first is to propose a set of principles for interpreting the relations between habit's intellectual and political histories that will illuminate how habit has been implicated in the exercise of varied forms of power. This involves considering the different ways in which habit has been interpreted across a range of discourses, and how the capacities that have been attributed to it have informed the practices of different institutions and apparatuses. The different constructions that have been placed on the relations between habit and repetition are of pivotal significance in this regard. These vary from habit's conception as a mechanism through which the repetition of the same is reproduced to its interpretation as an aspect of the processes through which repetition, when viewed as a dynamic force, generates difference. There is, articulated across these contrasting views of habit, a related set of differences: between habit's conception as a chain or fetter and its conception as a liberating force giving rise to a capacity for freedom. In interrogating the relations between these different accounts of habit, I argue that what is at issue in habit's varied histories are a set of contests between different authorities—ethical, scientific, theological, and philosophical—regarding the means by which conduct should be governed and the ends to which its governance should be directed.

My second line of argument brings this perspective into a critical dialogue with what is arguably the most influential account of habit in contemporary critical theory: the tradition that, taking its cue mainly from Gilles Deleuze's *Difference and Repetition* (2004), has rehabilitated habit. In disputing the view of habit as a negative form of repetition that held sway in the early postwar period, this tradition has restored earlier understandings according to which habit serves as a positive mechanism in enabling change and transformation at both the individual and societal levels. This rehabilitation has largely taken place through a revival of interest in a distinctive lineage of French thought—Maine de Biran, Félix Ravaisson, and Henri Bergson are its main representatives—on which Deleuze drew. This lineage adopted a critical relationship toward the interpretations of habit that had been proposed, from the late eighteenth century and into the nineteenth century, across a range of new scientific disciplines: physiology, psychology, evolutionary biology, and neurology, for example. In doing so, it drew on earlier conceptions of habit—those associated with selected aspects of both Christian theology and early modern philosophy—in order either to rebut or to lend a different inflection to the programs for the governance of conduct that followed from the accounts of habit that these disciplines had proposed.

The intersections between these two sets of concerns define the historical coordinates—the relations between "habit then" and "habit now"—of my inquiries. The intellectual histories I consider are mostly limited to the contentions over habit's conception that occurred across the nineteenth and early to mid-twentieth centuries but tilted toward the issues at stake in the debates over "habit now." However, I also look back to some earlier episodes in habit's histories in view of their bearing on these later developments. These include the role that habit played both in medieval monastic culture and in the broader forms of pastoral government that were brought to bear on the laity by the Catholic Church, as well as the challenges to these associated with varied forms of dissent. They also include John Locke's account of the part played by habit in the constitution of the liberal subject in view of its long-standing influence on subsequent conceptions of habit's role in facilitating the acquisition of new capacities.

In addressing these aspects of habit's intellectual histories, I constantly have in view their relations to how habit has been put to work politically. I intend *political* here in its broad sense, referring to the uses to which habit has been put across a spectrum of institutions whose practices are involved in the direction and governance of conduct, rather than limiting it to the role of state actors. While the rehabilitation of habit that has followed in the wake of Deleuze's *Difference and Repetition* has not denied these political aspects of habit's histories, it has rarely paid them systematic attention. As a counter to this, I draw chiefly on Michel Foucault's work to foreground the respects in which interpretations of habit have always constituted operative parts of machineries of power. In doing so I discuss how the practical consequences of the place that habit has been accorded in such entanglements have varied historically across the different types of power that Foucault distinguished while, at the same time, taking account of the respects in which these have overlapped and influenced one another. This requires a consideration of the ways in which the positive accounts of habit associated with its role in the constitution of liberal subjects have been accompanied by limitations that legitimize habit's conscription as a mechanism for varied forms of the illiberal governance of others. This has been, and still is, true across relations of class (the factory system, the current algorithmic governance of labor); gender (the differentiation of gender roles according to different degrees of susceptibility to habit's repetitions); and race (from the role of habit in the ordering of slave labor to its role in the biopolitical underpinnings of colonial forms of governance).

In opting to pursue these concerns through the concept of "habit's pathways," I was guided, initially, by Sara Ahmed's use of the concept of pathways in *What's the Use? On the Uses of Use* (2019). This alerted me to the possibilities of using habit's pathways as a point of entry into the interacting intellectual and political histories constituted by the varied ways in which different authorities have treated habit as a means of acting on the conduct of specific populations in order to lead or direct them, or induct them into leading themselves, along specific trajectories. While I had come across pathway metaphors in the literature on habit in my earlier reading on the subject, I was surprised at how productive the concept proved when rereading key texts in the field. This was partly because of the virtual omnipresence of pathway metaphors, but more significantly because of the roles they have been accorded in the strategies through which leading writers on the subject have differentiated their positions from those of others. Such readings of habit's pathways—of their form and direction, of who should be led along them, of who should be left just where they are, and who should do the leading—constitute the summative signatures of different theories of habit. I shall, then, be concerned with habit's pathways for the insight they offer into how competing authorities have vied with one another in their interventions into habit as a discursive and institutional site for contending political figurations of the relations between repetition and conduct.

My purpose in pursuing these lines of inquiry is not to propose a new version of habit's pathways. I shall rather suggest a way of thinking about habit that is both more limited and more expansive than particular constructions of its pathways: more limited in that it does not prescribe a course for the direction of conduct; more expansive in that it provides a means of engaging with the role habit has played, and continues to play, in struggles and contestations over the conduct of conduct.

So much for a rough overview of my concerns. However, it will be worthwhile to flesh out these bare bones of the argument by looking at some examples of habit's pathways, and how I propose to navigate them, before offering a road map to the route I take through the following chapters.

## Navigating habit's pathways

In *An Inquiry into Modes of Existence*, Bruno Latour sings the praises of habit as "the patron saint of laid-out routes, pathways, and trails" (2013, 265). Imagining a "lost hiker who has to hew out his own path," and who has therefore to hesitate at every step, wondering which way to go, Latour casts the relief such a hiker feels on coming across "a trail already used by others" as a moment of encounter with "the extraordinary blessedness of habit: he no longer has to choose . . . he knows what to do next, and he knows it without reflecting" (265). Without habit, he continues, "action would no longer follow any course. No trajectory would ensue. We would constantly hesitate as to the path we should take" (266). Latour is by no means alone in drawing on the imagery of routes, pathways, and trails to identify habit's positive qualities. Indeed, he acknowledges his debt to William James, who, in his *Principles of Psychology* ([1890] 2007), also counted habit's unthinking repetitions as a blessing in enabling the acquisition of new competencies via the physiological legacy of the grooves they inscribe in the passages of the nervous system.

Although the pathway analogy has been regularly invoked in the accounts of habit developed in Western intellectual traditions, it has not always been interpreted so positively. Sigmund Freud, for one, was skeptical. While welcoming in theory the order produced by the mechanism of "repetition-compulsion by which it is ordained once and for all when, where, and how a thing shall be done so that on every similar occasion doubt and hesitation shall be avoided," he argued that this was constantly frustrated by an "inborn tendency to negligence, irregularity, and untrustworthiness" that only constant and laborious training could overcome (Freud 1994, 25). The blessedness Latour attributes to habit can equally prove to be a curse for others. Helen Ngo thus interprets the bodily habits of white racism that are "called upon readily and effortlessly in navigating encounters with the racialized 'other'"—flinching, turning away, crossing the street, panic—as ones whose ease arises from their unchallenged rehearsal as parts of a repertoire of responses that has become sedimented in white corporeal schemas (2017, 23). And the value that, in the passage I have cited, Latour places on the elimination of hesitation is not universally endorsed either. Indeed, for Pierre Bourdieu, it is precisely the moments of hesitation that are introduced when routinized practices coded into the habitus are interrupted by "'blips'—critical moments when it misfires or is out of phase"—that open up the possibility of marking out a new path for conduct (2000, 162).

Nor are the directions in which habit's pathways point always forward looking. If, for Latour and James, habit's pathways facilitate an onward journey, they have just as often been invoked to describe circuitous routes that bend back on themselves to return to their point of departure. It is this conception that Georges Perec invokes in his account of somnambulism exemplified by the "robotic actions" of "a man asleep": "It is one ceaseless and untiring circumambulation. You walk like someone carrying invisible suitcases, like someone following his own shadow. A blind man, a sleepwalker. You proceed with a mechanical tread, never-endingly, to the point where you even forget that you are walking" (2011, 187). The endless repetitions of habit's pathways may equally inscribe a backward trajectory for those obliged to tread them. It is the potential reduction of the workingman to an animal that thus informs the account offered by James Phillips Kay (later James Kay-Shuttlewoth) of the mechanization of labor in the early development of the factory system: "The dull routine of a ceaseless drudgery, in which the same mechanical process is incessantly repeated, resembles the torment of Sisyphus—the toil, like the rock, recoils perpetually on the wearied operative. The mind gathers neither stores nor strength from the constant extension and retraction of the same muscles. The intellect slumbers in supine inertness; but the grosser parts of our nature attain a rank development. To condemn man to such a severity of toil is, in some measure, to cultivate in him the habits of an animal" (1832, 8).

In other accounts, habit's pathways describe a descending spiral. This was the case in late nineteenth-century conceptions of addiction in which the loosening of the controlling force of the will associated with drunkenness described not just a downward course for the individual but, when transmitted via hereditary mechanisms, a degenerative pathway for succeeding generations (Zieger 2008, 204–5). This stood in contrast to the positive force that was attributed to habit's pathways in post-Darwinian evolutionary thought, as the advances registered along habit's pathways by one generation were viewed as being passed on to the next as an accumulating "second nature" that both was informed by and contributed to the development of culture and civilization. But if this collectivized the yield of habit's pathways, it did so only for some peoples. For the anthropologist Edward Burnett Tylor, the rituals of "primitive peoples" constituted the withered "survivals" of earlier habits that had become so fixed through endless repetition that they had kept their "course from generation to generation, as a stream once settled in its bed will flow on for ages" (1871, 1:61).

The currency of the pathway as a metaphor for habit can, Clare Carlisle has argued, be traced back to Nicolas Malebranche's late seventeenth-century conception of how habits are formed through the connections that practice establishes between "traces" within the brain whose repetitions make easier their future performance. It is a metaphor, she argues, that "conveys a sense of the temporality of habit" (Carlisle 2014, 25). This is not said to dispute the evident spatial dimension of the pathways that Latour, for example, invokes. But even here, where pathways take the form of routes laid out across the land or grooves carved within the body's nervous system, a sense of time is implicit. Such pathways require repeated movement across their course in order to be maintained through time. But if, like a path, habit constitutes an unconscious archive of past practices in bearing the trace of their passage, it also, Carlisle argues, looks forward, anticipating the beckoning future of the second nature that is the outcome of the ease generated by its repeated actions. This is, however, only one of the forms of temporality associated with habit's pathways that—depending on the authorities that order and superintend those pathways, on the different directions in which they are made to point, and on who is assigned to travel along them—articulate past and present in a range of markedly variable forms. They might, as Carlisle suggests, beckon a future of increasing ease and grace. But they might equally well portend a graceless degeneration into vice and misery, or an unending daily grind of repetitive toil.

It is, then, the different directions in which invocations of habit's pathways point that serve as my points of entry into an analysis of habit's political histories as constituted by the varying ways in which discourses of habit, and the apparatuses in which these have been deployed, have formed critical components in the exercise of different kinds of power. My concerns in these regards are with those discourses in which habit is figured in the singular—with *habit*, which has a history of specific theoretical uses, and not *habits*, which has a looser and more colloquial usage—while also taking account of their overlaps and interrelations. I shall thus consider both habit's positive interpretations as an enabling mechanism that facilitates the acquisition and development of new dispositions, and those that stress its negative connotations as a disabling form of automatism. There is, on the one hand, a remarkable continuity to how these different interpretations of habit—usually presented as deriving from Aristotle's distinction between, respectively, *consuetudo* and *hexis* (or *habitus*)—have been caught up with one another in the subsequent development of Western thought. This was true, initially, of their usage in Christian theology and then in early modern philosophy but also, from the early eighteenth century onward, of the accounts of habit developed across a range of new empirical disciplines: physiology, psychology, sociology, neurology, and the neurosciences. On the other hand, the positions that these two aspects of habit have been assigned—as well as those that straddle the relations between them—and the roles that they have played relative to one another have proved to be remarkably pliable depending on the shifting discursive, political, and institutional contexts that have conditioned their deployment in the exercise of different forms of power.

### Excavating habit's histories

The range of such variations far exceeds the scope of any single study. My purpose is the more limited one of examining selected episodes in the overlapping political careers of these two aspects of habit's conceptualization. I can best outline the historical scope of my inquiries by means of the Google Ngram on the distribution of English-language texts addressing the subject of habit across the period from the sixteenth century to the present (figure I.1). This highlights three general tendencies. The first is the notable rise of

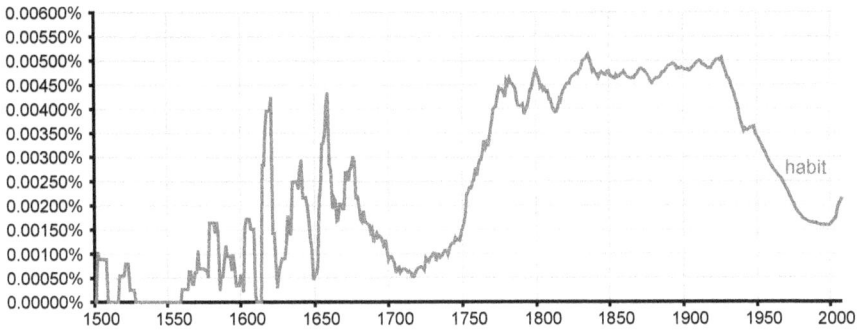

**I.1** Google Ngram, citations of *habit* in the English-language corpus, 1500–2008.

interest in the subject registered in the early to mid-seventeenth century with then, toward the century's end, a tailing off of interest bottoming in the early eighteenth century. The second is the steady ascent of interest, discernible from the mid-eighteenth century, leading to unprecedented levels of engagement with the topic toward the end of that century. And third, while high levels of interest are maintained more or less throughout the nineteenth century and into the early twentieth century, a steady decline is discernible from the 1920s through to the end of the century, when a slight lift in the level of engagement is evident.

In their commentary on this figure, Xabier Barandiaran and Ezequiel Di Paolo (2014) stress the respects in which, before the eighteenth century, theology and philosophy constituted the primary—indeed, virtually the only—disciplines engaged with the topic. While there had been a continuing interest in the subject within Christian theology from the period of the late Roman Empire and through the medieval period, it became a hotly contested subject during the Reformation when the roles habit had played in earlier directive forms of pastoral government were challenged by Protestant reinterpretations of the forms of agency it might be called on to perform in relation to more individualized forms of self-government. These concerns were paralleled by, and later gave way to, the varied roles that were accorded habit in the accounts of the formation and constitution of the self that were proposed in the founding texts of modern philosophy: those of René Descartes and John Locke, for example. The subsequent ascendancy of philosophy over habit's interpretation was unchallenged until the late eighteenth and nineteenth centuries when it was subjected to what were sometimes far-reaching reinterpretations prompted by new developments across a range of empirical disciplines: most notably, especially at first, physiology, psychology, neurology, and evolutionary biology, but also, as the century developed, sociology and psychoanalysis. None of these disciplines established a complete break with earlier philosophical and theological conceptions of habit; to the contrary, the conclusions they drew from the experimental evidence they produced were often overdetermined by the influence of preexisting conceptions of habit's place in the makeup of persons and the social consequences that followed from this. By the same token, however, philosophical accounts of habit have been obliged to consider its interpretations by these new disciplines, sometimes with a view to refuting or discounting them, but more often in order to find some accommodation between them and the legacy of earlier philosophical conceptions of personhood. It is this insertion of habit within a vastly enlarged intellectual terrain, one in which habit's conception was highly contested by competing intellectual authorities, that accounts for the consistently high levels of interest in the subject evident throughout the nineteenth century.

I will come back to the reasons for the declining interest in habit over the greater part of the twentieth century in chapter 1. Suffice it to say for now that my historical interests center principally on how habit was caught up in the intellectual to-and-fro between selected tendencies in nineteenth-century evolutionary thought, psychology, physiology, neurology, and sociology and parallel tendencies in philosophy. I shall also register how these exchanges were inflected in specific directions by the legacies of earlier periods of habit's conceptions in theology and philosophy. My concern throughout these historical excavations is to explore how the roles accorded habit along the pathways they uncover formed a part of the exercise of different forms of power over the direction of conduct.

These excavations are not ordered in the form of a chronology. My primary focus initially is with the nineteenth century, and it is from the perspective of the nineteenth-century debates that I look back at earlier moments in habit's intellectual and political histories to identify how these continued to reverberate within its later shifting political functions and uses. But I also, in a genealogical spirit, tilt my discussion of the political dimensions of habit's earlier histories toward a range of the positions habit occupies within the politics of the present, particularly as registered by the uptake of interest in the subject that has been evident since the closing decades of the twentieth century. This reflects the renewed attention that habit has received in the neurosciences; its increasing prominence across diverse currents of contemporary critical theory, particularly in feminist and critical race theory; and its increasing salience to matters of practical governmental concern ranging from climate change through waste management to urban transport flows in which questions concerning the relations between repetition and conduct are in play. Habit, in other words, is now a subject at issue across a range of contemporary intellectual tendencies and in relation to a wide range of governmental and political issues. The past-present relations I orchestrate, then, concern the light that previous contentions over habit might throw on its role across a range of contemporary debates.[1]

I pursue these questions via three main lines of argument. The first considers how conceptions of habit as a form of repetition that constitutes a pathway (or flow or course when aquatic analogies are invoked) have been related to the ways in which various kinds of authority (religious, philosophical, scientific) have sought to direct the conduct of selected populations. Such pathways might mark a positive developmental trajectory, ranging from Christian conceptions of habit as a pathway to virtue superintended by varied forms of pastoral authority, through to contemporary accounts of becoming in which habit is figured as a road to freedom that we are beckoned to follow under the guidance of philosophers. In other accounts—especially those in which it is tangled up with the concept of reflex action—habit marks a circuit, assigning its bearers to a treadmill of repetition whose effects are reinforced by coercive mechanisms: those of automated systems of production, for example. Or, where habit's pathways mark a spiraling descent into addictions, they also open up the prospect of return journeys along which their victims might be led back along the path to "normality" by therapeutic or medical authorities.

How these pathways are constructed—to come to my second argument—depends on how habit is placed in relation to other aspects of what I have called "architectures of the person" (T. Bennett 2011b): the senses, the will, reflexes, instincts, the nervous system, the brain, and consciousness. Habit is never figured by itself. What it is, the capacities or limitations that are attributed to it, how these might be acted on and by whom: these have all varied depending on how habit's relations to what have proved to be equally mutable components of personhood are construed. These aspects of habit's definition also have a crucial bearing on how it has been—in its variable singular forms—distributed across different populations and, relatedly, across the relations between humans and animals. Most usually reserved, in its positive definition, for dominant classes, races, and genders, it has been, in its negative forms, most usually associated with subordinate groups. This has often been part and parcel of their being approximated to "the animal," which has typically served as the foil in relation to which the ordering of habit's distribution across human populations has been effected.

My third strand of argument considers how these different aspects of habit discourses have operated in the context of different kinds of power. I take my cue here from the debates generated by Foucault's analysis of the principles informing the exercise of the main types of power that he distinguished: pastoral, sovereign, disciplinary, governmental, and biopolitical forms of power, as well as the operations of liberal forms of government. I shall also examine the different roles that habit has played in the circuits of capital across the different forms for the direction of free and enslaved labor associated with the factory and plantation systems, as well as its distinctive role in the dynamics of settler colonialism.

### The "wayward tradition"

In relating these historical lines of argument to contemporary debates, I explore their bearing on those versions of habit's pathways associated with its recent rehabilitation. The declining interest in habit in the twentieth century went hand in hand with a primary emphasis on its negative versions. This was particularly true, in postwar social and cultural theory, of the role accorded habit as a stifling and dulling form of repetition that characterized the internationally influential tradition in French sociology of the critique of everyday life. The marked increase in the degree of intellectual engagement with habit evident in the closing decades of the twentieth century and the early twenty-first century, by contrast, has been accompanied by a shift of emphasis toward its interpretation as a positive and enabling capacity. This has been prompted by a number of developments. The influence of Deleuze's reevaluation of habit—or, more accurately, the habit of acquiring habits—as a form of repetition that is generative of difference has been significant. This, allied with the influence of Ravaisson's work occasioned by the recent English translation of his *Of Habit* (2008), has given rise to a significant reengagement with what Elizabeth Grosz (2013, 219) has called the "wayward tradition" of habit theory. According to Grosz and its other advocates (Carlisle 2013a, 2014; Sinclair 2011a, 2018), this tradition—running from Maine de Biran (1929) through Ravaisson and thence, via Bergson (2004), to Deleuze—has given rise to a third view of habit in which the tension between its negative and positive definitions is reconciled by the conception of "the duality of habit," according to which its positive and enabling qualities depend on and flow out of its purely mechanical repetitions.

This rehabilitation of habit has undoubtedly been productive in prompting the need to rethink earlier terms of debate that had become somewhat ossified. My primary concern, however, is to explore how, in celebrating habit's pathways for their emancipatory possibilities, this tradition—just as much as the accounts of habit it is pitched against—constitutes a bid to bring conduct under the guidance of distinctive forms of intellectual authority. I pursue this line of argument in relation to the role that the wayward tradition has accorded the concept of indetermination as a moment when the determining power of causal forces is said to be temporarily suspended, thereby opening up the possibility for prereflective forms of habitual behavior to be redirected along the pathways of elected courses of action. This is a well-worn trope in the history of habit discourses, where it has usually been deployed as a means of marking a distinction between those who are said to have the capacity—through the operation of an interval of indetermination—to temporarily pause the force of causal determinations in order to bring their behavior under reflective review and redirect it, and those (variously, children, women, the enslaved, laborers, and Indigenous peoples) who have been denied this capacity. Its distinctive role in the wayward tradition consists in how it has enabled that tradition to both take on board the findings of empirical disciplines while also trumping them by invoking other forms of authority—usually philosophical or aesthetic—cast in the role of freedom's guides. The result is a structure that, in some of its formulations, revives aspects of the virtuous position that was accorded habit in medieval Christian theology, where it marked out a pathway, superintended by the pastorate, for humanity's progression toward salvation and grace while, in other formulations, invoking the authority of the mystic through which the authority of the pastorate was later challenged.

Habit has also been positively revalued as a result of the renewed attention accorded to the work of Gabriel Tarde (1903). Prompted largely by Latour (2002), this has focused on the positive role that Tarde accorded the habit-imitation nexus in the constitution of social life, in contrast to its condemnation as a negative and limiting force in the Durkheimian tradition of sociology. John Dewey's (2002) discussion of habit has also enjoyed a significant revival as a resource for recent progressive engagements with habit's pathways. In engaging with the Dewey and Tarde revivals, I examine how the versions of habit's pathways that informed their work resonated with the allocation of different populations to different stages along those pathways that characterized the contemporary racial discourses on which they drew. In the case of Tarde, I look at the two different pathways that are opened up by his account of, on the one hand, the role of genius in the development of germ capital and, on the other, the role he assigns the repetitions of automated labor. With regard to Dewey, I take issue with the tendency of a good deal of the recent literature to abstract what he said about habit from his parallel concern with the role of two other forces—impulse and intelligence—that he ranged alongside habit as the key determinants of human conduct. By probing his account of the pathways that emerge from the relations between habit and impulse, I show how these resonated with the values of American individualism in the stress he placed on the role of impulse as a drive to innovation, in contrast to the inertia that he invoked to account for the survival of savages in the present.

## A reader's road map

While the concerns I have identified run throughout the book, there are differences in the degrees of stress and emphasis accorded them in different chapters. In chapter 1 I elaborate more fully the theoretical and methodological settings I have outlined to this point. I do so initially by taking a closer look at the increasing interest in habit and its rehabilitation under the influence of Deleuze's positive reevaluation of repetition. My main concern, however, is to offer a more extended discussion of those aspects of Foucault's work that I draw on, placing particular store in his discussion, in *Punitive Society* (2015), of the historical transformation of habit's conception associated with the shift from its place in David Hume's account of the passions to its subsequent role in discourses and processes of normalization. In elaborating the implications of this argument, and its relations to Foucault's more general principles of archaeological and genealogical analysis, I take issue with a tendency of a good deal of the habit literature to attribute a distinctive force or power to habit. I contend, instead, that habit's political histories have been made up of the variable force that has been attributed to habit in the contexts of the different discourses and apparatuses in which it has been put to work in and across different regimes of power.

It is these histories that are my main concern in chapters 2 to 4, which, exploring various episodes in the history of "habit then," dig deeper into what I call the habit archive. Chapter 2 thus focuses on the role that disciplinary and biopolitical deployments of habit have played in shaping the circuits of capital constituted by the exploitation of different forms of labor. I revisit the debates occasioned by Eugene Genovese's (1976) differentiation of the forms of discipline associated with the plantation economies of enslaved labor from E. P. Thompson's (1991) account of the time-work discipline of the factory system. I also relate these concerns to Kyla Schuller's (2018) discussion of the role of sensibility in the racial and gendered aspects of sentimental biopower in the American School of Evolution. The chapter then considers those evolutionary versions of habit's pathways that have played a significant political role in settler-colonial societies in assigning "primitive peoples" to an endless repetition of the first steps along those pathways.

My concerns in chapter 3 initially center on the role that the discovery of the reflex arc in the late eighteenth century played in reconfiguring habit as a form of involuntary repetition disconnected from any controlling influence on the part of the mind, will, or reason. This was not the first interpretation of habit as a form of automatism. But it was distinctive in its inscription of habit's automaticity within a new conception of the body's neurophysiological architecture. By way of underscoring their distinctiveness, I review the respects in which these new conceptions of habit differed from, while also retaining aspects of, the role Locke assigned habit in relation to the dynamics of the association of ideas. Habit's role in these dynamics contributed to the construction of pathways along which the self-governance of the liberal subject might proceed. Nineteenth-century conceptions of "unwilled" habits, by contrast, figured habit as part of a negative dynamic of degeneration that could be countered only by acting on its conditioning milieus rather than through the reasoned direction of the will attributed to liberal forms of subjectivity.

In concluding chapter 3, I outline how those thinkers who drew on the new sciences of physiology, psychology, and sociology in the approaches they proposed to counter the downward dynamics of degeneration often took issue with the forms of authority over habit's pathways that had earlier been exercised by the Christian pastorate. But even where the authority of the pastorate was contested, its form was often replicated. This, I argue in chapters 5 and 6, is an aspect of habit's interpretation within the wayward tradition. As a prelude to these concerns, chapter 4 looks at the role accorded habit in Christian theology as a central mechanism in the governance of souls. It does so through the lens of Foucault's discussion of the role of "the conduct of conduct" in the forms of governance associated with "the archaic model of the

Christian pastorate" (Foucault 2007a, 110). In considering the place of habit within the techniques of pastoral government, I look at the role it played as a significant aspect of the stratification of social orders in medieval Europe. I then also consider the various forms of counterconduct that, in the late medieval period, disputed the role accorded habit in the techniques of pastoral government.

The rival authority of the mystic is given particular attention in view of the role this figure played in the work of Bergson. It thus forms a pivot into my concerns in chapters 5 to 8, where my focus shifts to the influence of habit's historical legacies on the contemporary debates constituting "habit now." Chapter 5 initiates these concerns by examining a range of positions that, rather than interpreting habit's pathways as describing a continuous course, stress the force of moments of interruption that, in stalling habit's repetitions, open up the prospects for unfolding pathways of becoming. In looking first at Bergson, I identify the respects in which, in displacing those versions of evolutionary thought that interpreted habit as part of a continuous path of progress, he installed a conception of habit's pathways that restored the power of spiritualized forms of authority to guide conduct across and through their ruptured course. I then go on to discuss the use that Grosz makes of Bergson's critical engagement with post-Darwinian social theory in her own reading of Darwin's work. In annexing the "nicks in time" that she attributes to the mechanisms of social and sexual selection to a feminist politics of difference, she interprets habit's repetitions as a mechanism of change that prepares us for a change yet to come. In reviewing what strike me as the shortcomings of Grosz's position, I draw on the lines of criticism developed by Walter Benjamin and Max Horkheimer in which they chastised Bergson for neglecting the role of institutional and discursive forces in shaping, regulating, and directing habit's repetitions.

In taking her cue from William James, Catherine Malabou likens habit's pathways to rivers or streams, currents carved in our neural passageways, and, like James, she is primarily concerned with the possibilities opened up when their course is interrupted by the operation of synaptic intervals. In contrast to the limited forms of plasticity that James attributed to such intervals, in *What Should We Do with Our Brain?* (2008) Malabou celebrates the radical possibilities that are opened up by the spaces, gaps, or cuts that she imputes to them. She has, however, since qualified this position in *Morphing Intelligence* (2019). My primary concerns in chapter 6 are twofold. First, I place the explosive possibilities Malabou initially attributed to neural plasticity in the context of broader debates concerning the implications of contemporary developments in the neurosciences for the position to be accorded our plastic brains in the relations between practices of social governance and practices of the self. I then consider Malabou's position in *Morphing Intelligence*, where, drawing on contemporary debates in the field of artificial intelligence and the work of Dewey, Jean Piaget, and Bourdieu, she distances herself from the Bergsonian legacy that informed her earlier work. No longer characterized by ruptural departures from its past course, the pathway in which habit is thus inscribed has an accumulating logic as intelligence converts past habits into projects oriented toward an extension of the continuum of life.

Malabou is not the first to see significant connections between the work of Dewey and that of Bourdieu. The subject was one that Bourdieu commented on. It is also one that has been taken up in recent forms of "habit activism," in which habit has been mobilized as a part of progressive feminist and antiracist politics. Shannon Sullivan's work has been especially important in the critical use it has made of Dewey's work in this regard. In chapter 7 I therefore orchestrate a three-way conversation: first, between Dewey and Sullivan via Sullivan's critical engagement with Dewey's work in her discussion of the habits of white privilege (Sullivan 2006); second, between the roles accorded different kinds of a socialized unconscious in relation to versions of habit's pathways that we find in the work of Sullivan and Bourdieu; and third, between the temporalities informing the pathways we find in Dewey and Bourdieu. In discussing Dewey, I consider how his account of the relations between habit, impulse, and intelligence constitutes a pathway that escapes the pull of what Dewey called the "routineer's road" to mark a course of innovation, but one that leaves behind those whose racial constitution has perpetuated the grip of an original and unmodified set of habits. Alert to the limitations of Dewey's work so far as questions of race are concerned, Sullivan looks instead to W. E. B. Du Bois's socialized version of the unconscious in examining the "transactional unconscious" that she argues governs the practices of white privilege. The pathway white subjects must travel to pull free from the habits of white privilege is consequently one that, like the Freudian unconscious, follows a course of tricks, evasions, and self-delusions. A similar set of tricks and evasions informs the different versions of habit's pathways that Bourdieu invokes in his account of the archaic habitus responsible for practices of male domination, in contrast to those whose habitus—characterized by blips, misfirings, and mismatches—opens up collective trajectories that break (relatively) free from the force of the past.

Finally, in chapter 8, I conduct four "probes" that, highlighting different ways in which the relations between habit, repetition, and power have been conceived in recent debates, prepare the ground for a way of thinking about habit capable of accommodating the contestations over how conduct should be directed that have been enacted across the different versions of its pathways I discuss. For my first probe, I go back to Latour's hiker to show how, in his broader discussion of habit, Latour repeats a key shortcoming that continues to haunt theories of habit: their oscillation between positions spread across the opposition between the conception of habit as an endless repetition of the same and its conception as a dynamic generator of new and free capacities, without paying due regard to the political rationalities informing the different ways in which habit has been enlisted in the governance of conduct. My second probe takes a closer look at the role that Deleuze accords exemplary forms of authority—those of the mystic—in guiding his own version of habit's pathways, in which it is the habit of contracting habits, enacted at the cellular level, that constitutes the basis for the formation of the self. I then look at the place that habit has been accorded in the operations of contemporary forms of digital automation and algorithmic governmentality. In doing so I also consider some of the synergies that have been developed between Deleuze's later work—particularly his account of "societies of control" (Deleuze 1992)— and Foucauldian governmentality theory in the roles accorded habit in post-disciplinary forms of power. To close chapter 8, I return to probe an issue I broach at the end of chapter 2 by considering the politics of habit associated with contemporary forms of "emergency governance" and their contestation through the strategies of "slow emergencies." I do so by reviewing the contentions occasioned by the coercive forms of habit management imposed on the habits of selected Indigenous communities in Australia introduced by the Northern Territory National Emergency Response Act of 2007.

These probes prepare the way for my discussion, in the conclusion, of a conception of habit as a form of determined indeterminacy that accounts for the diversity of the positions it has been accorded within the plural and contested politics of repetition that have been enacted across the histories of its different pathways. As to what I mean in referring to this as "the arbitrariness of habit," well, that's best left until we get there, except to say that it is a position I derive by extrapolating the implications, as I see them, of a passage in Bourdieu's *Pascalian Meditations* (2000).

# 1

# Powering
# Habit

HABIT AND REPETITION: two concepts that are inextricably, albeit variably, entangled with each other. In some uses, the two are simply equated or tied to each other in relations of mutual reinforcement. Habit—in its most common definition—is a form of mechanical repetition, both its outcome and its cause, perpetuated by and perpetuating repetition's stultifying effects through its reproduction of the same. In other uses habit is a mechanism that inflects the effects of repetition in new directions, paving the way for the development of new capacities. In the one case, habit is a limitation: a chain, drag, or fetter. In the other, it is a virtue, an essential aspect of processes of development that, in some formulations, lead to specific ends while, in others, they form parts of open-ended pathways of becoming, difference, and freedom.

The habit-repetition couplet is not, however, an exclusive one. Repetition is also associated with a range of other concepts that have different, albeit overlapping, histories: tradition and custom, for example. If these are sometimes equated with habit, they are just as often held to be distinct. David

Hume, for example, at times equated habit and custom, whereas, at others, in distinguishing them, he nonetheless posited a symbiotic relationship between them as forms of repetition that, since they were not reliant on any intervention of reasoning or the understanding, served as "the great guide of human life . . . that principle alone which renders our experience useful to us, and makes us expect, for the future, a similar train of events with those which have appeared in the past" (Hume 1975, 44). Later tendencies in English social and political thought, particularly those shaped by their engagements with evolutionary theory, tended to pull the two concepts apart, interpreting custom as a force that inhibited habit's potentially positive dynamics. And then there are those forms of repetition associated with anatomical, physiological, or psychological processes that take place independently of thought. Reflexes are a case in point, constituting a form of repetition inscribed in the body's subneural nervous system—the reflex arc—which, from its "discovery" in the late eighteenth century, contributed to the development of a conception of habit as a form of involuntary repetition giving rise to all manner of addictions.

These shifting coordinates of habit's use and the forms of repetition it instantiates relative to others have been accompanied by varying conceptions of its distribution across different forms of life. In some formulations, habit is a property common to humans, animals, and plant life and, more recently in the Deleuzian tradition, to the fluxions of matter. For Brian Massumi, although human habits might be socially and culturally contracted, they "reside in the matter of the body, in the muscles, nerves, and skin," where they operate as "the matter-hinge between nature and culture" through their connections with the habits forged by "the self-organizations of matter" (2002, 236–37). For the greater part of its history, however, habit has more usually been restricted to humans and animals, with variable lines of demarcation being drawn to distinguish its limited operations in animals from its more expansive human aspects. But the modus operandi of the habit-repetition couplet has also been differentiated, among humans, across the divisions between genders, races, and classes, and often in ways that echo their differentiation across the human-animal divide. Habit has thus functioned as a part of an "anthropological machine" that, in adjudicating the boundary between the human and the animal, has been implicated in the practices that differentiate human populations. Habit, finally, has also been associated with the forms of repetition attributed to automatic mechanical systems. But again, this has been so in varied historical forms with different implications. Attributed initially to René Descartes's conception of the body as an automaton modeled on hydraulic systems, such conceptions have since been applied in nineteenth-century understandings of the relations between the factory system and industrial labor as integrated automata and, more recently, in assessments of the role played by digital media in the automation of both labor and everyday forms of consumption.

These, then, are among the issues that need to be negotiated to engage with the variable forms of political work that habit has been enlisted to perform across its long and contested history. These have shaped a political career that has seen habit adapted to serve as a cog in diverse machineries of power in accordance with variable conceptions of the relations between habit and repetition superintended by a remarkable range of intellectual authorities: philosophers, theologians, physiologists, psychologists, sociologists, and neuroscientists, to name just a few. However, while drawing on its longer histories from time to time, I am mainly concerned with, first, the political histories in which habit has been implicated since the development of secularized ruptures with, or adaptations of, earlier theological accounts of habit associated with the early development of "modern philosophy," and second, with the accounts of habit proposed across a range of empirical disciplines from the late eighteenth century through to the present. But I shall also keep in view the interactions between these tendencies. This will involve considering, on the one hand, how empirical engagements with habit are often premised on pregiven terms of debate provided by one or another version of its earlier philosophical conception and, on the other, how later philosophies of habit have usually engaged with empirical inquiries into the subject in order either to discount them or to trump them by according them a limited validity that, in being taken on board, is integrated into a higher philosophical truth.

In this chapter I look first at how the relations between habit and repetition have been reconfigured in recent debates, focusing principally on how Gilles Deleuze's *Difference and Repetition* overturned the negative assessments of habit associated with its interpretation in existentialist thought and the tradition of the critique of everyday life. I then mine Michel Foucault's work both for what he had to say specifically about habit and for the light that his more general approach to the analysis of knowledge/power relations throws on the relations between habit's intellectual and political histories. In doing so I outline the respects in which what I take from Foucault in these regards brings together perspectives derived from his early archaeological approach to knowledge practices and his later genealogical analyses of the operations of different forms of power. I can best identify what I draw from these aspects of Foucault's work by distinguishing the directions in which I point them from the assumptions underlying the question that Clare Carlisle puts when she asks, "What kind of power does the force of habit generate? Is it a power of liberation or of bondage, of creativity or of domination, of freedom or of servitude?" (2013b, 52). Carlisle is not alone in putting such questions. As Mark Sinclair (2011b) shows, there is a continuing concern running throughout philosophical engagements with habit to identify the distinctive kind of force or power that it exercises. Rather than supposing that there is such a force, or that habit generates a single kind of power, the questions I put will ask how habit has been implicated in the exercise of different forms of power in view of the different forces that have been attributed to it in the discourses and the apparatuses through which its political histories have been enacted.

This prepares the way for a closer look at the variable interpretations of habit within and across the discourses composing the "habit archive." This involves a consideration of the implication of habit's dispersal across neighboring fields of discourse: those of custom and tradition, in which repetition is also invoked, and those associated with the other aspects of personhood (will, instinct, reflex) in relation to which habit's modes of operation have been identified in varying and mutable forms. This will prepare the way for a fuller identification of what is involved in bringing these concerns together to examine how conduct has been fashioned and directed along habit's pathways. I conclude the chapter by outlining the issues that need to be taken into account in applying this perspective to the distinctive forms of authority that have been put into play by those philosophical accounts of habit associated with the "wayward tradition."

### Reconfiguring the habit-repetition couplet

In his overview of the role accorded habit within different moments and traditions in the development of sociology, Charles Camic notes that it had been virtually written out of the history of sociology and scarcely figured at all as a matter of sociological concern at the time he was writing. While featuring in the accounts of social behavior proposed by the "founding fathers" of "classical sociology"—Émile Durkheim, Ferdinand Tönnies, and, albeit more ambivalently, Max Weber—its significance had progressively waned in early twentieth-century debates. And it had dropped out of the sociological lexicon more or less entirely in the postwar period when the interest it had registered in repetitive forms of social behavior was replaced by "a model of action that has alternatively been called purposive, rational, voluntaristic, or decisional" (Camic 1986, 1040). Camic attributes this, in good part, to the influence of Talcott Parsons's conception of social action as necessarily volitional and as therefore excluding habit, given its predominant conception as an unthinking form of repetition.[1] In doing so, he inadvertently treads in Parsons's footsteps by limiting his attention to those sociologists—such as Durkheim and Weber—whom Parsons had canonized as the founders of "the sociological tradition" that led to his own theory of social action. This elided the significance of the contending sociology that, with Gabriel Tarde as its leading champion, assessed habitual actions more positively in the role they accorded somnambulism—or unconscious imitation—as the basis of the social order (Tarde 1903) and that, courtesy of its subsequent rehabilitation by Bruno Latour (2002), is now a significant point of reference for contemporary sociological debates. With his eye focused chiefly on postwar American sociology, Camic also overlooks the role accorded habit within the critique of everyday life tradition, which had a significant influence on European sociological debates in the 1960s and 1970s.

For Henri Lefebvre, the leading exponent of this tradition, the everyday was the site and scene of repetition, of mechanical actions bound into a cyclical recurrence of time through which the rhythms of everyday life were integrated into the new "bureaucratic society of controlled consumption" of the postwar period (Lefebvre 1971). The everyday was, above all, not conscious of itself as such. The product of prereflective forms of immersion in the repetitive structure of habits, its horizons constituted the limit that critical thought must break with in order to make "the everyday" thinkable and politically actionable. But this was a possibility that was only open to some. Lefebvre ruled out women as too subjected to the habitual routines of everyday life to be capable of transcending them (Scene of Habit 1).[2] Lefebvre was also skeptical of the capacity that Georg Lukács had attributed to the proletariat for introducing a double-leveled consciousness into history. In becoming conscious of itself as both the supreme object of commodity production and an emerging self-conscious political force portending history's completion, Lukács had argued that the proletariat would become conscious of itself as both the subject and object of history.[3] While viewing this as no longer an option given the working class's absorption into the repetitions of controlled consumption, Lefebvre nonetheless retained the structure of modernist social theory that had underlain Lukács's account in looking to youths and students, whom he viewed as not yet integrated into the repetitive structure of the everyday, as the potential leverage points from which its glacial structures might be ruptured.

In this respect, Lefebvre's classic text *Everyday Life in the Modern World*, first published in 1968, resonated only too clearly with the expectations generated by the temporary fusion of students' and workers' movements that characterized that period. But these expectations had already been called into question a year earlier in Georges Perec's *A Man Asleep*, in which a student of sociology, probing the illusions of a life freed from the repetitions of habit, explores what Sianne Ngai calls "the tension between difference and repetition" (Ngai 2012, 140). Committing himself to becoming "unused to everything," Perec's anonymous sociologist sets about detaching himself from all the routines of daily life—such as "the habits of going to meet those with whom you rubbed shoulders for so long, of taking your meals, your cups of coffee every day at the place that others have kept, sometimes defended for you" (Perec 2011, 162). But the result, as Michael Cuntz observes, is that "when the veil of habit is torn apart, what appears behind it is not the new, true self nor a new, true vision of the world; there are only more habits, past habits whose eradication is tantamount to the complete loss of memory, or new habits he cannot avoid acquiring" (2016, 215). In shattering the modernist dream of an authentic life beyond habit, Perec reminds us that one of modernism's central illusions was, as Cuntz puts it, that it would distinguish itself from earlier societies by its "very exclusion of habit" (218).

The year 1968 was also when the French edition of Deleuze's *Difference and Repetition* was published. Although Deleuze had earlier, in his 1953 text *Empiricism and Subjectivity* (Deleuze 1991b), offered a positive account of habit, *Difference and Repetition* marks a more decisive moment in the rescue of habit from its condemnation in postwar French thought. This was not universal. Paul Ricoeur (2007)—continuing lines of inquiry flowing from the work of Félix Ravaisson and Henri Bergson—assigned habit a positive role in his account of the relations between the voluntary and the involuntary. The influence of Maurice Merleau-Ponty's (2002) phenomenological account of habit as embodied practice also carved out a role for habit, albeit a qualified one, in Pierre Bourdieu's account of the social dynamics of person formation.[4] And the habit-repetition nexus was a bone of contention in French feminist thought, polarized between Simone de Beauvoir's condemnation of repetition as, according to Rita Felski, "a sign of women's enslavement," and Julia Kristeva's positive estimation of it as "the key to women's experience of extra-subjective time, cosmic time, jouissance" (Felski 2000, 82). However, it was the critique of everyday life tradition allied with the condemnation of habit in existentialism—its condemnation as the key mechanism of the automatism of the "practico-inert" by Jean-Paul Sartre (1967)—that constituted habit's dominant cultural and political signature in the debates of the 1960s and 1970s.

Perhaps the most economical summary of the respects in which Deleuze's work disrupted this tradition is that which he provided in his introduction to the English translation of *Empiricism and Subjectivity*: "We start with atomic parts, but these atomic parts have transitions, passages, 'tendencies' which circulate from one to another. These tendencies give rise to *habits*. Isn't this the answer to the question 'what are we?' We are habits, nothing but habits— the habit of saying 'I.' Perhaps, there is no more striking answer to the problem of the Self" (Deleuze 1991b, x).

This has proved to be an influential formulation in the ongoing rehabilitation of the habit-repetition couplet that has characterized recent debates. In shifting the concept of repetition from what he called the "mechanics of quantity" (67) and considering it from the point of view not of the objects repeated but of the mind that contemplates such repetitions, Deleuze refashioned habit as a mechanism that situates the self in a present moment along a pathway shaped by the dynamic relations between the past and an anticipated future. Habit, as he was later to put it, "*draws* something new from repetition" (Deleuze 2004, 94). In doing so, it inscribes the self in a dynamic process constituted by the habit of acquiring habits, of moving on from one set of repetitions to another through a propensity for change that is internal to them.

*Difference and Repetition* did not immediately undermine the traditions it was pitched against. The tradition of the critique of everyday life remained influential through to the closing decades of the twentieth century and, indeed, elements of it are still in play in current engagements with digital culture. Jonathan Crary, for example, invokes Lefebvre's work alongside Deleuze's account of the "control society" to chastise a range of contemporary media apparatuses for effecting a "powerful habitual patterning" of behavior, giving rise to a "diffuse attentiveness and a semi-automatism" that results in "states of neutralization and inactivation, in which one is dispossessed of time" (Crary 2014, 87). But it was largely a spent force by the noughties roundabout the time when *Difference and Repetition*—translated into English in 1994—began to have an appreciable influence on Anglophone debates.[5] Since then, Deleuze's interpretation of repetition as, far from necessarily leading to a reproduction of the same, constituting an essential aspect of processes of differentiation has been worked through in the varied engagements defining Elizabeth Grosz's wayward tradition that have restored to habit the more positive assessment it had earlier enjoyed in selective strands of late nineteenth and early twentieth-century philosophy.

Although pointing in different—but occasionally overlapping—directions, current revaluations of the relations between habit and repetition also owe a good deal to the revival of interest in John Dewey's *Human Nature and Conduct* (2002), first published in 1922. While Dewey's insistence on habit as an active capacity that is not reducible to mere repetition was an aspect of his work that Bourdieu appreciated (Bourdieu and Wacquant 1992, 122), it has more recently served as a model for approaches that, shaped by the "material turn" in social theory, have stressed the need to deindividualize habits: to interpret them not as a set of mechanisms internal to the physiological and psychological makeup of individuals but as forms of conduct that are shaped and enacted across the relations between persons and material environments ranging from ecological systems to urban infrastructures.

I shall return to various aspects of these literatures in the following chapters. The perspective from which I do so is shaped by the light that a parallel "turn to Foucault" has thrown on the ways in which habit has been tangled up in the exercise of varied kinds of power. Foucault's work has thus been invoked in accounts of the role played by Saint Augustine's conception of habit in mediating the relations between Christian metaphysics and the political structures of sovereignty that characterized the inscriptions of imperial power in the kingdoms that followed the collapse of the Roman Empire (Heiner 2009). The significance of John Locke's conception of habit in divesting the authority of priestly mediations of its role in the governance of conduct in favor of new forms of secular and individualized self-rule has also been considered from a Foucauldian perspective (Crary 2001; Tully 1993). I have also drawn on Foucault's work in earlier accounts of the role of habit in biopolitical forms of government (T. Bennett 2004b, 2011b). But what did Foucault himself have to say about habit? In truth, not that much, and what he did say on the subject was usually as an aside to his main interests. Nonetheless, his occasional remarks, considered in the context of his more general concern with knowledge/power relations, provide a basis from which a broader set of theoretical and methodological precepts for engaging with habit's political histories might be extrapolated.

### The variable force of habit

There is one place where, as an exception to the qualification just noted, Foucault accords the concept of habit a central role in his concerns. In the final lecture of the course *The Punitive Society* that he delivered at the Collège de France in 1972–73, Foucault said that he had wanted the course to offer "the very first history of the power of habits, the archaeology of those apparatuses of power that serve as the basis for the acquisition of habits as social norms" (2015, 237). This was by way of pulling together the threads of his account of the respects in which the institutions of sequestration—prisons, reformatories, factory prisons, provident banks—constituted a form of power that operated to secure the conditions required for the capitalist mode of production. A "society of disciplinary power," as he put it, is "a society equipped with apparatuses whose form is sequestration, whose purpose is the formation of a labor force, and whose instrument is the acquisition of disciplines or habits" (237).

It is then, in shifting from the plural to the singular as he goes on "to consider this notion of *habit*" (237), that questions of knowledge enter into Foucault's account as he distinguishes its uses across the eighteenth and nineteenth centuries. In the former, he argues, with Hume primarily in mind, that habit had played a critical role in the development of modern political philosophy, providing a basis for criticizing conceptions of a political order founded on traditional obligations. By recasting such obligations as purely the effects of habit—understood, in the terms proposed by Hume's melding of habit and custom as the combined effect of nature and artifice, as "the habit of contracting habits" (238)—such accounts called into question their theological attribution to a source of transcendental authority. In doing so, they prepared the way for a conception of a social order based on contractual bonds voluntarily entered into by free and independent—in the sense of propertied—individuals. In nineteenth-century discourses, by contrast, habit loses these critical resonances. It becomes rather, Foucault says, what people must submit to; or rather, what *some* people must submit to. If the eighteenth-century critique of habit contributed to the development of a conceptual basis for the establishment of contractual relations, mediated by the state, between property owners, its nineteenth-century development reconfigured it as a set of attributes to be acquired by those without property, for whom it functions as what "binds them to an apparatus they do not own . . . to an order of things, an order of time and to a political order" (238). It fixes individuals to the production apparatus through "a play of coercion and punishment, apprenticeship and chastisement" (239), a process that operates through mechanisms of normalization. Habit, Foucault thus argues, came to be centrally inscribed in the series that produces modern society: "formation of labor power—apparatus of sequestration—permanent function of normalization" (239).

In developing this argument, Foucault complements the contrast it proposes between habit, discipline, and normalization, on the one hand, and a political order based on the principles of contract, on the other, with a further contrast: that between the public dramaturgy of sovereign power and a new form of power that, abandoning "all that visible, ritual magnificence," takes on "the insidious, quotidian, habitual form of the norm" (240). These relations between normalization, habit, and discipline give rise to a new form of political discourse in which the symbolic theatrics of sovereign power yield to the "discourse of the master . . . of he who supervises, states the norm, makes the division between normal and abnormal, evaluates, judges, decides: discourse of the schoolmaster, the judge, the doctor, the psychiatrist"; in short, "the normalizing discourse of the human sciences" (240–41).

Foucault returns to further develop these arguments in different aspects of his work that followed the 1972–73 course of lectures in pretty short order: *Discipline and Punish*, first published in 1975; his 1974–75 course of lectures,

*Abnormal*; *The Will to Knowledge*, the first volume in his *History of Sexuality*, initially published in 1976; his account of the relations between racism and biopower in his 1975–76 course of lectures, *Society Must Be Defended*; and his discussion of pastoral power in his 1977–78 course of lectures, *Security, Territory, Population*. In *Discipline and Punish*, it is the regulative effects of habit as repetition that he stresses. The "apparatus of corrective penalty," Foucault argues, works on "the body, time, everyday gestures and activities; and the soul, too, but in so far as it is the seat of habits." It does so with a view to producing "the obedient subject, the individual subjected to habits, rules, orders, an authority that is exercised continually around him and upon him, and which he must allow to function automatically in him" (1977, 128–29). A little later, commenting on the new disciplinary regimes introduced into the French army in the late nineteenth century, it is the role of the "automatism of habit" that he stresses as the crucial mechanism through which the "formless clay" of the peasant was transformed into the machinic regularity of the soldier (135).[6] And in generalizing the history of discipline as being concerned with those practices that seek to "regulate the cycles of repetition," it is the role of the timetable in instilling habits in monastic communities that Foucault turns to as the model that was later adopted "in schools, workshops and hospitals" (149). But Foucault is clear that, however much they might draw on techniques associated with earlier forms of domination, the relations between discipline and habit are historically distinctive. They differ from those associated with slavery because, he argues, they could dispense with its costly and inefficient appropriation of bodies;[7] they differ from "service" as a form of personal subordination to the "caprice" of the master; from vassalage as a highly codified and ritualized form of allegiance; and from the forms of individual self-mastery associated with monastic asceticism (137).

But if, as he claimed in *The Punitive Society*, discipline was able to dispense with the theatrics of sovereign power, this was a consequence of the degree to which normalizing judgment—the differential distribution of populations around the norm—was central to its exercise. While this is a theme of *Discipline and Punish*, it is more central to the concerns of *Abnormal*, where it acquires another dimension. Here, Foucault's attention focuses on the early nineteenth-century transition of criminal psychiatry from its association with the regime of monstrosity to that of abnormality as one that resulted in psychiatry's "questioning, analyzing, and measuring bad habits, little perversities, and childish naughtiness" (2003a, 110). There were two aspects to this shift. The first consisted in the productive instability that characterized the nineteenth-century discourse of the normal, produced by its oscillations between what Peter Cryle and Elizabeth Stephens describe as its normative and frequentist dimensions in functioning as both a standard to be obtained and a statistical regularity, "as somehow both 'ideal' and 'habitual,' or alternately one and the other" (Cryle and Stephens 2017, 49). The second consisted in the inscription of habit in a new regime of personhood as the passions of the classical age give way to a radically transformed field of objects bearing on the understanding of behavior produced by the new tendencies in psychiatric discourse. This field of objects consisted principally in the reframing of questions of abnormality that was effected by the emergence of instincts, alongside "impulses, drives, tendencies, inclinations, and automatisms," as the new conduits for the management of conduct, which displaced the role that had earlier been accorded to the passions in this regard. Compared with the "specific dynamics" of these new determinants of conduct, Foucault argued that "passions, and affects" had only a "secondary, derivative, or subordinate status" (2003a, 131).[8]

This shift in the problematic of abnormality from monstrosity to "the most elementary and everyday conduct" (132) prepared the ground for late nineteenth-century developments in psychiatry and eugenics, each of which sought to get a hold on instincts in different, albeit overlapping, games of knowledge and power. The primary focus of Foucault's attention is with the role that instinct played at the junction of the penal and psychiatric realms in enabling a meshing of their respective mechanisms of power. It did so, first, by nullifying the "legal scandal" (138) of a motiveless, and therefore unpunishable, crime; and, second, by providing a basis for interpreting an absence of volition as an index of pathology. This required that psychiatric analysis shift its focus from what the ill might think or be conscious of to the analysis of involuntary behavior. There was a new symptomatology in play here, one in which it was the automatisms of habit carried to excess that indexed a disturbance in the normal balance of the relations between the voluntary and the involuntary in favor of the latter. The second game of knowledge and power in which the instincts were implicated revolved around the role they played in evolutionary thought generally, but with a specific inflection in eugenics as an aspect of the mechanisms of inheritance through which habit's involuntary repetitions acquired an accumulating, transgenerational force. Where these two games overlapped most consequentially was in those discourses of degeneration in which what Foucault refers to as the interacting forces of deviation and automatism responsible for the downward paths of individual pathologies were translated into hereditable pathways describing a descending course for lineages subject to the collective pathologies acquired via a range of bad habits.

This aspect of Foucault's work has informed a wide-ranging body of studies—opened up by Mariana Valverde's (1998a) analysis of the pathologization of alcoholism as a "disease of the will" needing new forms of psychological and medical intervention—focused on the conception of a range of addictions as involuntary habits. I shall come back to these questions. For now, though, I want to turn to the third of Foucault's texts identified earlier—*The Will to Knowledge*—for the light it throws on how to broach the history of habit. In taking issue with the "repressive hypothesis," Foucault charts the multiplication of sexual discourses in the nineteenth century as indexing a new set of preoccupations with involuntary behaviors—alongside those he identified in *Abnormal*—in which "the sexual conduct of the population was taken both as an object of analysis and as a target of intervention" (Foucault 1998a, 26). But two other aspects of the more general processes into which Foucault inserts his discussion of sexuality suggest a broader canvas for a parallel history of habit.

The first comes toward the end of the book, where he argues that it was the problematic of life—the conception of man "as a specific living being, and specifically related to other living beings" (143)—that constituted the key epistemological divide between the nineteenth century and the classical episteme. This leads him to add a new set of forms of knowledge and intervention into the governance of the human body to those constituted by the "anatomo-politics of discipline" centered on "the body as a machine: its disciplining, the optimization of its capabilities" (139). These consist in the regulatory controls characterizing "a biopolitics of population" focused on managing the "processes of life": propagation, births, and mortality. These two tendencies constitute the twin poles of the new forms of biopower, which, in placing life simultaneously outside history, in its biological environment, and inside human historicity, penetrated by its disciplinary techniques and powers, marked a signal departure from the "murderous splendor" (144) of sovereign power. They did so not just by substituting the powers of normalization for those of sovereign power but in constituting a power "whose highest function was perhaps no longer to kill, but to invest life through and through" (139).

In *The Will to Knowledge*, Foucault links the concept of biopower to racism only tangentially. In *Society Must Be Defended*, he takes a different tack in arguing that, far from muting the power to kill, the biopolitics of population transmutes it into a new form that multiplies its lethal force: that of scientific racism, which introduces "a break into the domain of life that is under power's control: the break between what must live and what must die" (2003b, 254). The key discourses in which habit's role was refashioned in accordance with the racial dimensions of biopower were those associated with the reordering of the relations between human, animal, and plant life and the associated racial hierarchies, ordering the relations between "what must live" and "what must die," produced by the evolutionary tendencies in biology and the life sciences more generally.

In all these regards, the trajectory from *The Punitive Society* through *Discipline and Punish*, *Abnormal*, and *The Will to Knowledge* to *Society Must Be Defended* is one concerned with the relative eclipse of sovereign power by new forms of power. The early part of *The Will to Knowledge*, however, pulls in the opposite direction when Foucault asks: From where and when did the *scientia sexualis* developed in the nineteenth century come? Assuredly, he replies, not from nowhere. The scientific placement of sex into a discourse of the truth constituted a recoding of the earlier procedures of the confession as a discourse and a technology for the regulation of sexuality, a mutation in the history of Western man as a "confessing animal" (1998a, 59). A mutation, to be sure: the unitary medieval discourse of "the flesh and the practice of penance" was, he argues, "if not broken, at least loosened and diversified" (33) in being distributed across the wider range of discursive and confessional contexts of the *scientia sexualis*. But "not broken" is the key term here. And the same is true of those theological discourses of habit as a divinely infused virtue leading to the acquisition of grace, and of the role that Foucault accords these discourses in his analysis of the techniques of pastoral government. For these have continued to inform subsequent conceptions of habit. And not just explicitly Christian ones. To the contrary, their legacies have continued to shape subsequent scientific accounts of habit in the very course of their attempts to displace the forms of superintendence that religious authorities have exerted over habit and its exercise.

These are among the questions that concern Foucault in the account he offers, in *Security, Territory, Population*, of the distinctiveness of the forms of power associated with the development of the Christian pastorate and the influence of the forms and techniques of pastoral government on the subsequent development of governmental forms of power. As these are questions that I look at in more detail in chapter 4, I shall make just two observations here. These relate to his commentary on the sixteenth-century formulation of Guillaume de La Perrière—"Government is the right disposition of things arranged to lead to a suitable end"—which Foucault interprets as marking a moment of transition from the relations between pastoral and sovereign power in the medieval period to the later development of governmentality. The aspect of this discussion I want to stress is that, in teasing out how we are to read La Perrière's reference to "things," Foucault includes "men in their relationships with things like customs, habits, ways of acting and thinking" while, at the same time, stressing their interconnectedness with other orders of things "like wealth, resources, means of subsistence, and, of course, territory with its borders, qualities, climate, dryness, fertility, and so on," and with events "like accidents, misfortunes, famine, epidemics, and death" (Foucault 2007a, 96).

## Archaeological and genealogical perspectives

While clearly on his radar from time to time, then, it is not what Foucault said about habit as such so much as the general implications of the conceptual apparatus he proposed for understanding the political role exercised by different knowledge practices through their connections with different regimes of power that I take my bearings from in what follows. The main methodological precepts to be derived from the foregoing brief excursus through Foucault's work are the need to attend, first, to the ways in which habit functions in the context of the different discourses of which it has formed a part (theological, philosophical, psychological, sociological, etc.) and the forms of authority they organize; second, to examine how these discourses operate or are put to work within the apparatuses or *dispositifs* that construct habit as a point of entry into the regulation of the conduct of individuals, groups, and races and the ordering of the relations between these; and third, to attend to how these accord habit a different force and variable effects in the context of different regimes of power (pastoral, sovereign, disciplinary, governmental, biopolitical) as well as across the continuities and connections between them.

These methodological principles bring together the procedures for analyzing the operations of statements within and across discursive formations that constituted the distinguishing feature of Foucault's early "archaeology of knowledge" and the principles that, from *Discipline and Punish* onward, characterized his later concern to develop a "genealogy of power." There are differences in the points of stress and emphasis between these phases of Foucault's work. Foucault's conception of archaeology, as outlined in a range of texts in the 1960s and early 1970s, articulated a tension with existing sociological problematics insofar as it insulated intellectual and artistic practices from the influence of preexisting social relations (as mediated by an author's or artist's intentions, the spirit of an age, or a class-based world view) in favor of a focus on their action; on what, as Joseph Tanke (2009) puts it, they do. But this was never, for Foucault, an autonomous action of the kind we find in formalist schools of criticism. In lieu of those connections that are forged by relating discursive events to preceding conditions "via the general forms of language or . . . the individual consciousness of the speaking subject," Foucault argued that what has to be attended to are rather the articulations of statements, as events, to nondiscursive events—economic, social, political, technical—via the functioning of discourse "in the system of its institutionalization" (1998c, 309). It is now generally agreed that these concerns were carried over into Foucault's later genealogies of power.[9] While Foucault's archaeological project was centrally concerned with the internal rules regulating the operations of discourses, Gary Gutting (2014) shows that this did not preclude a concern with the relations between discourse and the nondiscursive practices of the institutional regimes that later came to define the center of his concerns, just as that later focus on the functioning of institutionally embedded forms of disciplinary and governmental power continued to be informed by the close attention he paid to the discursive properties of knowledge practices. The underlying thread connecting these two phases of Foucault's work was that constituted by their joint concern with the politics of truth (Deere 2014).

There is, however, a further and more sharply pointed political aspect to Foucault's conception of genealogy: namely, the brief it proposes for the spirit in which historical inquiry should be conducted. The classic text here is his 1971 essay "Nietzsche, Genealogy, History," in which he invokes the necessity of bringing a historical perspective to bear on attributes that are commonly perceived as ahistorical. The examples he gives are a series of attributes— sentiments, love, conscience, instincts—that, like habit, are often interpreted as having a singular force. Rejecting the "meta-historical deployment" of such "ideal significations" (Foucault 1998b, 370), Foucault argues that "if he listens to history," the genealogist "finds that there is 'something altogether different' behind things: not a timeless and essential secret, but the secret that they have no essence or that their essence was fabricated in a piecemeal fashion from alien forms" (371). Anticipating the position he would later develop more fully in *Abnormal*, he contends that a genealogical perspective disrupts our belief in "the dull constancy of instinctual life" as if it "continues to exert its force indiscriminately in the present as it did in the past" and, in its place, "depicts its wavering course . . . and defines its oscillating reign" (379–80). Genealogy, as a form of "effective history," rejects all of those constants—of instincts, feelings, behavior, the body—that "traditional history" treats as "sufficiently stable to serve as the basis for self-recognition or for understanding other men" (380). It is by thus introducing "discontinuity into our very being—as it divides our emotions, dramatizes our instincts, multiplies our body and sets it against itself"—that genealogy, an intellectual practice that "is made for cutting" (380), disputes the attribution of any singular force to any human attribute, including, as we have seen, habit.

Foucault later qualified his position on this matter in urging the need to attend also to the dialectic between continuities and discontinuities in the relations between different discursive regimes and their institutionalization in knowledge/power apparatuses. But he did so without ever losing his concern that genealogical analysis should cut into the politics of the present. It is in this sense, then, that, while I shall be concerned with the dialectic of continuities and discontinuities that governs the political histories of habit discourses, I shall also mobilize Foucault's genealogical perspective against the attribution of a singular force to habit that characterizes the wayward tradition. And I shall do so by muddying habit in the varied material and technological forms of power in which its variable histories have been implicated.

### Figures of habit

I shall return from time to time to further elaborate how I draw on and bring together these aspects of Foucault's work. For now, though, by way of illustrating my arguments to this point more concretely, I shall say a little more about the key figures of habit I have already discussed, and add one or two more, in order to identify how they have stood for the variable force attributed to habit and the manner of its exercise along different versions of habit's pathways. Here, too, of course, I am piggy-backing on Foucault's reference to "the hysterical woman, the masturbating child, the Malthusian couple, and the perverse adult" as the figures he invokes to identify the key "targets and anchorage points" for the "mechanisms of knowledge and power centering on sex" in the eighteenth and nineteenth centuries (Foucault 1998a, 103–5). But these were not static figures; rather, they were subjected to varied representations, with mutating connections to different social strata, in the course of the nineteenth century.

It is with similar aims in view that I shall approach the figures that have been invoked as stand-ins for habit's pathways. These include, in its positive definition, the association between habit and virtue represented by the monk's habit, each item of which, Giorgio Agamben (2013, 14) has argued, symbolized a particular virtue of the monastic way of life. Then there is the musician, perhaps the most frequently cited stand-in for the power attributed to habit's repetitions of facilitating the acquisition of new competencies. The earliest version of this figure that I have come across is that proposed by the eighteenth-century physician Robert Whytt in the contrast he posed between, on the one hand, the "young player upon the harpsichord," who is "at first very thoughtful and solicitous about every motion of his fingers," and on the other, the "masters" of the art, who "perform the very same motions, not only more dexterously, with greater ability, but almost without any reflexion or attention to what they are about" (Whytt quoted in Fearing 1970, 79).[10] And then there is the tennis player, Bourdieu's favorite example of the difference between a theoretical knowledge of the rules of the game and their practical mastery by those who, through training, come to be possessed by its regularities and are thus able to translate these into their play without any gap between conception and execution.[11]

Ranged against these are the figures representing habit's negative pathways, composed by the force of repetitions that lead to an endless reproduction of the same, a sliding descent into involuntary servitude, or powerless subjection to exploitation: the housewife, the slave, the factory worker. Such figures are often superimposed on one another through a series of metaphorical substitutions: as in the nineteenth-century discovery of the new condition of "alcoholism" as an involuntary habit—"an inability to control the thirst for stimulants"—whose cause was rooted not in drink itself but in a deficiency in some aspect of the physiopsychological makeup of those who became "slaves to the drink habit" (Valverde 1998b, 227); or in Engels's account of the factory system as enslaving the laborer by chaining him to the "despotic bell" that "calls him from his bed, calls him from breakfast and dinner" (Engels quoted in Marx 1970, 424). The nineteenth-century medicalization of habit also gave rise to a new set of figures, perhaps most notably those afflicted by the condition of neurasthenia. Marcel Proust invokes this figure in *Remembrance of Things Past* when the narrator compares his aunt Léonie to "certain victims of neurasthenia . . . who present without modification, year after year, the spectacle of their odd and unaccountable habits, which they always imagine themselves to be on the point of shaking off, but which they always retain to the end, caught in the treadmill of their own maladies and eccentricities, their futile endeavors to escape serve only to accentuate its mechanism, to keep in motion the clockwork of their strange, ineluctable, fatal daily round" (1966, 232).

And then there is the sleepwalker, whom we have already encountered in Perec's account of "a man asleep" and Tarde's take on somnambulism. This is a figure, however, that is perhaps most famously represented by Lucy Westenra in Bram Stoker's *Dracula*, her revival of her "old habit of walking in her sleep" making her companion Mina Murray uneasy for both the lack of self-control it suggested and, as an inherited trait—"Lucy's father, had the same habit" (Stoker 2011, 86–87)—a further step on the downward path of degeneration. And the sphere of popular culture burgeons with figures at various points on habit's downward slopes: alcoholics, smokers, drug addicts, gamblers, zombies, and couch potatoes, for example. It is to this bank of figures that Philip Guston refers in his 1973 *Painting, Smoking, Eating* that provides the cover image for this book and, albeit more controversially, in his earlier *Bad Habits* (figure 1.1).[12] This adds to the vices of drink and gambling the bad habits of white supremacy evoked by the Ku Klux Klansmen whose hooded figures also function as a demoralized contrast to the moralized clothing—the "good habits"—of monks, a contrast that is reinforced by the ambiguous play of associations between the slave owner's whip and the self-lacerating function of the monastic lash.

There is also, to anticipate a figure we shall encounter later, the blind man who, guided by his stick in his encounters with the material world, has been a central epistemic figure in Western thought in standing for the role of objects in validating experiential knowledge.[13] For Maurice Merleau-Ponty, however, the blind man serves rather as an emblem for the habitual processes through which we become used to objects, incorporating them into our bodily schemas as an expression of "our power of dilating our being-in-the-world, or changing our existence by appropriating fresh instruments" (2002, 166).[14]

To appreciate more fully the pathways that these figures have represented, often in different ways and with variable consequences, it's necessary to broaden the conception of the discursive fields within which they operate by considering how the concepts of habit that compose the "habit archive" are conditioned by two broader sets of relations: those between habit and other kinds of repetition, and those that situate habit in relation to other aspects of personhood.

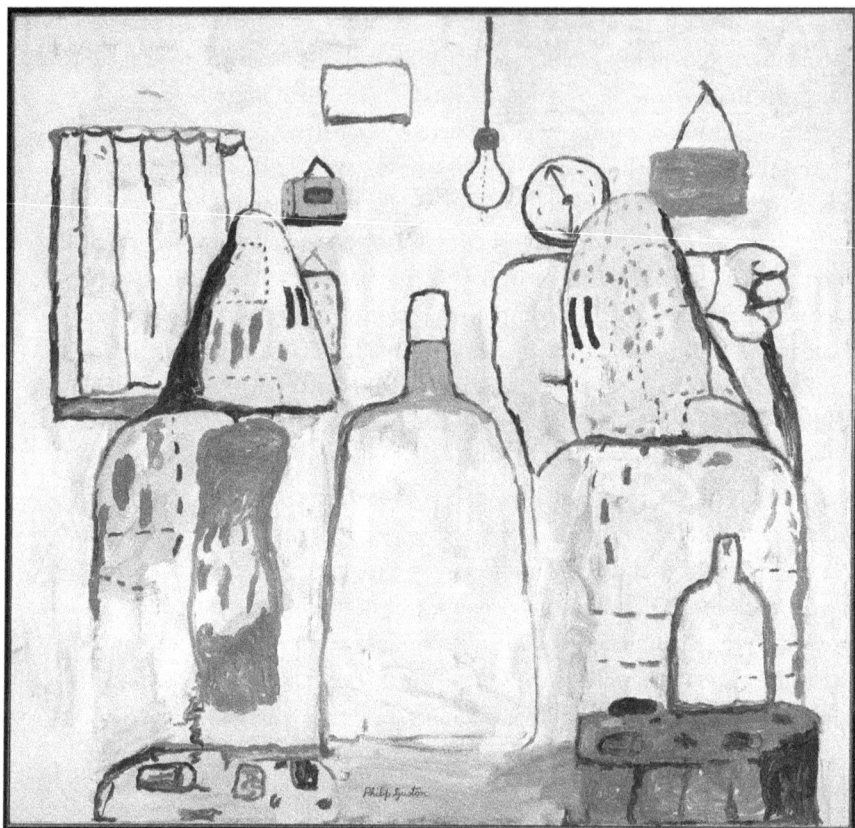

**1.1** Philip Guston (1913–1980), *Bad Habits*, 1970. Oil on canvas. 185.5 (H) × 198.2 (W) cm; 1,870 (H) × 1,998 (W) × 60 (D) mm (framed). National Gallery of Australia, Canberra. Purchased 1980. 1981.3050. Permission © The Estate of Philip Guston, courtesy Hauser & Wirth.

### The "habit archive"

The first set of issues is perhaps best illustrated by the mutable relations between habit and custom. The *Oxford English Dictionary* tends to merge the two when, after defining habit as an involuntary form of repetition, it goes on to equate it with "a settled practice, custom, usage." Yet the two concepts have often been sharply differentiated. Medieval Christian usage, maintaining the Latin distinction between *habitus* and *consuetudo*, distinguished habit from custom in order to mark a distinction between those who aspired to the forms of self-cultivation associated with the acquisition of grace and those—pagans, heretics, and layfolk—whose lives were regulated by custom: that is, by forms of routine training, akin to those applied to animals, that afforded no space for the more dynamic acquisition of dispositions associated with the mechanisms of habit (Miner 2013, 72–73). The relations between the two concepts have also been variably interpreted in the subsequent development of Western philosophical traditions. As we have seen, Hume tended to equate habit and custom as the key underpinnings of experiential knowledge. He also attributed a potentially progressive dynamic to their coupling in the capacity for transforming "unreflective custom" into "methodized custom" that he ascribed to their shared grounding in the dynamics of "common life" (Fosl 2013, 143). By contrast, John Stuart Mill, in distinguishing habit and custom, accorded the latter a considerable degree of power over the former in the role he assigned it in his conception of character. If, for Mill, the possession of character signified control over desires and impulses, he attributed the lack of character and the forms of self-control it engenders less to the grip of habit than to the despotism of custom, a despotism that, for Mill, is produced whenever the mechanisms of discussion—through which individual variations are able to become an active force in social life—are held in check.[15]

The two terms have also been interpreted in a number of different ways in the subsequent history of sociology. Émile Durkheim imputed a different force to habit, which he interpreted as a set of "organico-physical conditions" that the past has deposited in us that "chain us ... to our race," from that which he attributed to customs, which he viewed as being "imposed upon the individual only from without and by moral action" (1964, 30). This was, indeed, one of the issues at stake in the debates between Durkheim and Tarde concerning the role of imitation in social life. In Durkheim's view, the conformity associated with the forms of mechanical solidarity he attributed to "primitive societies" was not the result of the unthinking forms of repetition Tarde attributed to contagious forms of imitation but rather reflected some degree of volitional consent to tribal sources of legal and moral authority (Karsenti 2010). And for Ferdinand Tönnies, by contrast, habit was a liberating force—habit is "will which has become lord and master through practice" (1961, 34)—and, as such, opposed to custom, which he viewed as a conservative force invoked by varied forms of cultural authority to impede the assertion of the will and its conversion, through practice, into habit. Anthony Giddens added another chapter to the volatility of sociology's accounts of the relations between habit and custom. Interpreting the former as being shaped by modern forms of expertise whose force is limited entirely to their operations within the present, he argued that reckoning with the force of custom requires an "archaeological dig" that is also a process of "evacuation ... digging deep, in an attempt to clean out the debris of the past" (1994, 73).[16]

The clouded discursive field constituted by the overlaps and differences between habit and other forms of repetition is, then, one of the broader considerations to be factored into an analysis of habit's political histories. The second is the historically shifting web of associations that have conditioned habit's use and interpretation relative to the other attributes and capacities that, in different periods, have been viewed as crucial components in the makeup of persons. Habit thus needs to be considered as a part of what I have called "architectures of the person" (T. Bennett 2011b). This draws on Nikolas Rose's (1996, 301) discussion of the points of entry into the governance of conduct that are constituted by what have proved to be the highly pliable "spaces, cavities, relations, divisions" produced by diverse ways of partitioning the self and working on its varied parts that have been proposed by different authorities. The issues that this alerts us to are how the kinds of levers that interventions into habit provide for acting on and shaping our conduct depend on the distinctive configuration of its relations to other components of personhood. And, of course, the reverse is also true: where the levers for changing other aspects of conduct might be found, and what might be expected from activating them, also depends on how their place and function relative to habit are viewed within specific architectures of the person.

The relations between habit and the will have—since first being posed as antagonists by Saint Augustine of Hippo (Brown 2000)—been a relatively constant aspect of habit's definition. However, variations in the conception of how these stand in relation to one another span the full range from habit as the antithesis of willed and purposive behavior to its conception as essentially a product of the will. If Immanuel Kant is perhaps the most influential representative of the first view, pairing habit with the unwilled repetitions of nature (Scene of Habit 2), the second position is, as we have seen, one that Tönnies subscribed to. It is also one that we find, albeit given a different inflection, in the work of Dewey ("In any intelligible sense of the word will," he argued, habits *are* will" [2002, 25]) and Ricoeur ("effort is willed habit" [2007, 315]), while, for Herbert Spencer, the development of the will was the historical outcome of habit's exercise ("the cessation of automatic action and the dawn of volition, are one and the same thing" [1996, 614]). As we shall see, similar ranges of variation apply to interpretations of the relations between habit and

*Scene of Habit 2—The Instinctive Force of the Rule of Habituation*

In his *Anthropology from a Pragmatic Point of View,* Kant distinguishes physical anthropology's concern with "what nature makes of the human being" from his pragmatic orientation toward anthropology concerned with the investigation of what man "as a free acting being makes of himself, or can and should make of himself" (Kant [1798] 2006, 40). Habit consists wholly of natural or quasi-natural forms of conduct that, since they are driven by necessity, are devoid of moral significance. Since it "is a physical inner necessitation to proceed in the same manner that one has proceeded until now," Kant argues, habit "deprives even good actions of their moral worth because it impairs the freedom of the mind." Habit arouses disgust because "here one is led *instinctively* by the rule of habituation, exactly like another (non-human) nature, and so runs the risk of falling into one and the same class with the beast" (40). The only exception that is admitted to the rule that "all habits are reprehensible" (40) is where they testify to the power of intentionality to limit the force of nature, as in the adoption of mechanical culinary habits to offset the effects of old age. Far from being associated with virtue, habit is clasped together with instinct as a couplet through which the power of nature as necessity works and to which the power of culture—understood as the capacity for free self-shaping—stands opposed.

---

memory, desire, instinct, (un)consciousness, (in)attention, reflection, and an assortment of contrasting accounts of its place in the nervous system (Danziger 1982). Current developments in the neurosciences have led to a similar repositioning and revaluing of habit through the role attributed to the agency of a new set of neural actants with marked consequences for the ways in which habit is invoked in programs of governance and self-governance that work through the "managed mindfulness" of the brain's plasticity (Vidal 2009).

In deciding how to proceed in the midst of these definitional instabilities, I shall follow the lead of others who have grappled with similar difficulties in their approach to cognate concepts with similarly varied histories of use and interpretation.[17] Jonathan Crary (2001) thus warns his readers that, in order to engage with the history of the relations between attention and spectacle in contemporary industrial culture, he had avoided favoring any particular definition of attention in order to capture the variable effects produced by its operation within different discourses. Sara Ahmed (2014, 8) has similarly counseled that the history of the will can only be written by suspending any particular definition of the will in favor of an open-ended approach to the host of "willing associations" that have been established for it by its multivalent interpretations in the "willfulness archive." And Cryle and Stephens, in engaging with the shifting discursive registers that have conditioned the history of the category of "the normal," similarly refrain from proposing "a philosophical theory of normality" of their own (2017, 24).

There are good reasons for these hesitations. In *The Archaeology of Knowledge*, Foucault records that one of the first suppositions of the history of ideas he had to abandon in developing an archaeological perspective was that "statements different in form, and dispersed in time, form a group if they refer to one and the same object" (1972, 32). In place of this supposition, he argued that what might appear to be the same objects often prove not to be so when consideration is given to the modes of their dispersal across different discursive formations. The analytical focus this requires, Foucault argues, is not on the uniqueness of the object in question but "on the space in which various objects emerge and are continuously transformed" (32). It requires an engagement with "the interplay of the rules that define the transformation of these different objects, their non-identity through time, the break produced in them, the internal discontinuity that suspends their permanence" (33).

It is, then, with these considerations in mind that, while I shall, in concluding, offer an open-ended definition of habit that can accommodate its varied invocations across the relations of power, repetition, and conduct in which it has been implicated, I shall, in the meantime, avoid the temptation to sign up to any particular conception of what habit is or does. To do so would only inhibit the possibility of engaging with the variable ways in which it has been defined in being enlisted for different political purposes across different discursive formations. Habit does not, in and of itself, perform any political work. The work it performs is inseparable from the ways in which it, and its relations to other aspects in the makeup of persons and their relations to their environments, has been construed across a complex and varied, but interacting, set of discourses. I have already outlined some of the main kinds of political work in which, historically, habit has been implicated: its role in regulating the conduct of individuals; in demarcating the boundary lines between different groups; as a point of mediation between humans and machines; and in marking the distinction between human and nonhuman animals, for example. These are, however, not things that habit—as some pre-given attribute—accomplishes by itself; they are rather the outcomes of the ways in which different conceptions of habit have been fashioned by a historically diverse range of epistemological and moral authorities—ranging from the Catholic priesthood to today's advocates of "managed mindfulness"—as a means of acting on the conduct of individuals and groups, and the relations between them, through a historically diverse range of technologies.

## Habit, freedom, and the politics of "gapped time"

This, as I indicated at the start of this chapter, puts me at odds with those tendencies in philosophy that attribute a specific force to habit. From the perspective of the approach adopted here, the force that such accounts attribute to habit is to be considered just as much a part of habit's political histories as those histories arising from its conception within empirical disciplines and, indeed, especially so with regard to the ways in which philosophies of habit have both shaped and sought to trump empirical approaches. I shall, in developing this perspective, draw on those approaches to philosophical discourses that treat them as *paideia* rather than as *theoria* and as therefore to be assessed for the kinds of work on the self that they open up and superintend. Initially proposed by Pierre Hadot (1995), and subsequently developed by Ian Hunter (2001), this involves attending to the kinds of work on the self that philosophies propose, the spiritual exercises they enjoin as a means of translating these into practice, and the varied forms of intellectual or aesthetic distancing from—as well as the forms of work on—the conduct of others that they enjoin and enact.

In her discussion of the wayward tradition, Grosz proposes a contrast between those accounts of habit that take it as a point of entry into the ordering or regulating of conduct and philosophical approaches that rather inscribe habit—which she defines as "the rock to which the possibilities of personal identity and freedom are tethered"—as part of a benevolent pathway that sustains "the creation of a direction, a 'second nature,' an identity" (2013, 219). Where I part company with Grosz is, first, in the opposition between governing and freedom that subtends her approach. I do so in light of the doubt that Foucault cast over the validity of this distinction, contending instead, in *The*

*Birth of Biopolitics* (2008), that analysis must take into account how freedom is organized and produced as a key aspect of the relations between governors and governed. He placed particular stress on the need to take account of the limits that are placed on freedom's role in this regard in view of its differential distribution across the social body. In being accorded a role in the governance of some groups through their capacity for self-governance, freedom is withheld as a mechanism for the governance of others to whom, therefore, more coercive mechanisms are applied.[18]

This leads to a second difference regarding how to interpret the implications of the ways in which habit's trajectories have been shaped by the operation of what is sometimes referred to as the gap, sometimes as the interval, and sometimes as the stillness that is produced when the force of habit-as-repetition is stalled or paused in some way. In opening up a space of indetermination in which habit's unthinking repetitions might be reviewed and, as a consequence, made available to the possibility of being jettisoned in favor of the adoption of new practices, these moments of "gapped time" have played a significant role in accounts of processes of dis- and rehabituation. From the perspective I propose, this gap is not something to be simply celebrated as a necessarily liberating mechanism on the pathways of becoming. I shall rather probe the political history of this gap. This consists in the variable ways in which it has been interpreted and made actionable by a range of epistemological, moral, and aesthetic authorities with a view to directing how conduct should be reshaped once the force of habit-as-repetition has been temporarily suspended. If this gap had a significant career in late medieval Christian theology and early modern Western philosophy, it has since migrated to and informed the conceptions of habit that have been developed across the full range of modern empirical disciplines. In approaching this gap as a "circuit breaker" in which conduct can be potentially reshaped and pointed in new directions, these disciplines—the life sciences, sociology, psychology, the neurosciences—have, each in their different ways, proposed different techniques for intervening and acting within it. Equally, though, the various techniques that have been proposed for "minding the gap" (T. Bennett 2016) have also been accompanied by accounts of the social distribution of this gap—and the capacity for remaking habits that it confers—that has, in endowing some groups with this capacity, simultaneously denied it to others. In attributing to the mechanism of inhibition the power to pause the effects of a particular set of habits so that those "who are masters of themselves" might strike out on a new path, Théodule Ribot, following a long tradition in which the hypothetical universality of habit's generative capacities is always qualified, simultaneously denies this capacity to children, women, "savages," sufferers of abulia, and "unpolished men" ([1882] 1997, 17). It is in this regard that habit's positive and negative definitions have always been inescapably tangled up with one another.

It is these entanglements that I begin to explore in the next chapter through the position that habit is accorded in relation to those for whom its pathways lead to a series of dead ends or those who never get beyond its first steps. I start with this version of habit's pathways rather than those that interpret habit as a generative mechanism leading to the acquisition of a second nature in a spirit of calculated contrariness. If the generative pathway is the starting point suggested by the significance that Deleuze's famous aphorism—"We are habits, nothing but habits"—accords to the role of habit in the constitution of the self, the starting point I have opted for requires a counter-aphorism to cue how habit looks from the point of view of capital or that of the slave owner: "We impose habits, nothing but habits—is there any better way of accounting for how to dominate others?"

# 2

# Dead Ends and
# Nonstarters

IN SINGING THE PRAISES OF HABIT as "the patron saint of laid-out routes, pathways, and trails" (Latour 2013, 265), Bruno Latour—as I indicated in the introduction—draws on William James's interpretation of the path analogy. Likening the nervous system to "a system of paths between a sensory *terminus a quo* and a muscular, glandular, or other *terminus ad quem*," James argues that "nothing is easier than to imagine how, when a current once has traversed a path, it should traverse it more readily still a second time" ([1890] 2007, 107–8). In terms that have been echoed many times since, James counts the operations of habit in this regard as a blessing. Once its pathways are secured, the freeing up of attention that follows from the greater ease and familiarity of habit's actions means that "the upper regions of brain and mind are set comparatively free" (115). James, in turn, drew on the earlier formulations of John Locke, who, in what is perhaps the most frequently cited passage in the literature on habit, contended that "habits of thinking in the understanding ... of determining in the will, and of motions in the body," are, once settled by custom, "but trains of motion in the animal spirits, which once set a-going, continue in the same steps they have been used to; which, by often treading, are worn into a smooth path, and the motion in it becomes easy and, as it were, natural" (1965, 336).[1]

The imagery of habit's pathways is itself, then, quite a well-trodden path, albeit not always leading to the same outcome. Sara Ahmed, discussing the relationship between pathways and the concept of use, fills in some of the steps taken by the path analogy in the history of the life sciences that intervened between Locke and James, particularly its post-Lamarckian conception as an evolutionary pathway through which the transgenerational transmission of acquired capacities leads to an accumulating "second nature." But this transformation of previous effort, routinized through habit, into an accumulating inheritance is double-edged. Tracing the political career of the pathway analogy when translated into evolutionary interpretations of the currency of the blacksmith's arm—the strength acquired through its habitual exercise, in being inherited by the blacksmith's son, illustrating both the facility acquired through repeated use and the transmission of the effects of such use to future generations—Ahmed argues that the arm signifies "not only how a workload is eased *but how a workload is acquired*" (2019, 90).[2] Far from standing for a beckoning freedom, frequency of use—the well-trodden path—becomes a trap. For the blacksmith's son to inherit the effects of use is "*to inherit a workload*" (90). And, as Ahmed goes on to show in discussing Herbert Spencer's version of the blacksmith's arm, it is also to inherit a social position. The blacksmith, the laborer, the student, the clerk, the musician: habit's well-worn pathways mold their faculties into complete fitness for—but, by the same token, limitation to—their occupations.

James also viewed this as the other side to the potential for freedom arising from habit's pathways. Interpreting the brain's plasticity as destined to yield to an unremitting rigidity by the age of thirty, he saw those who had not by then bent habit's pathways to mark out their own chosen course as being chained to the destinies dictated by their inheritance. The ease of habit thus becomes a limitation that also operates as a conservative mechanism of social order:

It alone is what keeps us all within the bounds of ordinance, and saves the children of fortune from the envious uprisings of the poor. It alone prevents the hardest and most repulsive walks of life from being deserted by those brought up to tread therein. It keeps the fisherman and the deck-hand at sea through the winter; it holds the miner in his darkness, and nails the countryman to his log-cabin and his lonely farm through all the months of snow; it protects us from invasion by the natives of the desert and the frozen zone. It dooms us all to fight out the battle of life upon the lines of our nurture or our early choice, and to make the best of a pursuit that disagrees, because there is no other for which we are fitted, and it is too late to begin again. (James [1890] 2007, 120)

There is for Ahmed, however, something more involved in the relations between habit, frequency of use, and pathways than securing the distribution of persons across the relations between occupations and social positions. These relations also inscribe habit as a key mechanism in varied processes for managing the rates and forms of exploitation of labor. The well-worn path, the idea that use increases facility in prescribed tasks, becomes a justification for increasing workloads, for deepening the grooves that, in James's interpretation, repetition carves into the muscular and nervous systems. This echoes Michel Foucault's conception of discipline as a machinery that breaks the body down, rearranging its powers so as to increase them in terms of their economic utility while simultaneously diminishing those powers in exacting increased obedience from bodies that have become more "practiced" and more "subjected" (Foucault 1977, 138). Ahmed also reminds us that, at the time Spencer was writing, the circuits of capital were articulated across the relations between two asymmetrical systems for the use of labor: the enslaved workers of the cotton plantations in the southern states of America, and the factory workers of the English and American cotton industries (Beckert 2014).

These, then, are the matters that concern me in this chapter. I engage with them by addressing a range of figures standing in for negative conceptions of the relations between habit and repetition: the factory worker, the slave, the "primitive." I do so initially by revisiting the debates occasioned by Eugene Genovese's (1976) response to E. P. Thompson's classic essay "Time, Work-Discipline and Industrial Capitalism" (1991), first published in 1967. Genovese's primary purpose was to qualify the extent to which Thompson's account of the disciplinary effects of clock time associated with the factory system applied to the forms of discipline and labor routines associated with plantation slavery. In doing so he stimulated a debate—still ongoing—regarding the roles played by these different disciplinary regimes in those international circuits of capital defined by its flows across the relations between the factory and plantation systems. In reviewing these debates, I shall argue that the key questions concern not whether the role of habit in the anatamo-politics of

discipline was—as Genovese argued—*less developed* in the plantation economy than in the factory system but rather the *different logics* shaping its application across the relations between free and enslaved workers. This paves the
way for an examination of the role of habit in the mechanisms of biopower as
instanced by the different ways in which its pathways were inscribed in black
and white bodies in the distinctive evolutionary conceptions that dominated
racial politics in nineteenth-century America. I then consider the equally
deadly consequences of late nineteenth-century anthropological conceptions
of the failure of Indigenous populations—particularly in Australia—to advance much beyond their first faltering steps along habit's pathways.

## Machineries of production, discipline, and labor

In the *Grundrisse*, Karl Marx argues that the culmination of labor's adoption
into the production processes of capital consisted in its subjection to "an *automatic system of machinery*" that, "set in motion by an automaton, a moving
power that moves itself," casts the worker as "merely its conscious linkages"
(1973, 692). No longer an instrument through which the worker's activity is
transmitted to the object on which he works "and whose handling therefore
depends on his virtuosity," it is rather the machine that "is itself the virtuoso,
with a soul of its own in the mechanical laws acting through it" (693). In the
first volume of *Capital*, published roughly ten years later in 1867, Marx re-
hearses similar arguments while also aligning them with the set of historically
distinctive concerns clustered around habit that Ahmed identifies. For Marx
the ease with which the detail laborer performs his work provides no basis
for supposing it might lead to a beckoning freedom. To the contrary, it only
deepens his subjection to the power of capital. The laborer, he says, who "all
his life performs one and the same simple operation, converts his whole body
into the automatic, specialized instrument of that operation" (1970, 339). His
"continued repetition of the same simple act, and the concentration of his attention on it, teach him by experience how to attain the desired effect with
the minimum of exertion," and, like the blacksmith's arm, "the tricks of the
trade thus acquired . . . are accumulated and handed down" (339). This echoes
a tendency in earlier societies to "make trades hereditary . . . to petrify them
into castes . . . or ossify them into guilds" (339–40). But the consequence
of this ease and facility for the factory worker, he argues, is the loss of the
"knowledge, the judgement, and the will" exercised by the independent peasant, citing Adam Ferguson on the loss of mental capacities that accompanies

the habits of the factory worker: "Reflection and fancy are subject to err; but a habit of moving the hand or the foot is independent of either. Manufactures, accordingly, prosper most where the mind is least consulted" (Ferguson quoted in Marx 1970, 360).

And, as we have seen, for James Phillips Kay (later James Kay-Shuttleworth), surveying the conditions in Manchester's cotton mills in 1832, the "dull routine of senseless drudgery" that was the factory operative's lot, far from freeing him to develop new capacities, enforced his regression to "the habits of an animal" (1832, 8). This regression was, however, less a product of factory discipline as such than of a particular set of connections between the circulation of capital and of labor associated with a racialized conception of the degenerative influence inflicted by Irish workers on the respectable English factory operatives. The importation of labor from England's "sister kingdom" constituted the "introduction of an uncivilized race ... useful only as a mass of animal organization, which consumed the smallest amount of wages" and led only to the unwanted spread of their "barbarous habits," a contagion that has "demoralized the people" robbing them of all virtue (12).[3]

For Marx the powers that are lost by the worker through the imposition of factory discipline accrue to the power of capital in being converted into the "intellectual potencies of the material process of production, as the property of another, and as a ruling power" (Marx 1970, 339). Citing Andrew Ure's conception of the need to train factory workers "to renounce their desultory habits of work, and to identify themselves with the unvarying regularity of the complex automaton" of the factory, Marx interprets factory discipline as a form in which "the slave-driver's lash is taken over by the overlooker's book of penalties," endorsing Friedrich Engels's assessment that the factory enslaves the laborer by chaining him to the "despotic bell" that "calls him from his bed, calls him from breakfast and dinner" (424).[4]

For Jonathan Crary, Joseph Wright of Derby's 1782 painting *Arkwright's Cotton Mills by Night* serves as a visual emblem of this despotic bell. The "radical reconceptualization of the relation between work and time" constituted by the scene of a factory, its lights ablaze in the middle of the night, registered the new force of "productive operations that do not stop, of profit-generating work that can function 24/7" (Crary 2014, 61). If, as he argues, an Amazon warehouse represents the latest version of this process, Crary's concern is with both factory and warehouse as symbols of the increasing pressure capitalism brings to bear on those forms of sleep capable of functioning as a form of "suspended time" in which "there is a recovery of perceptual capacities that are nullified or disregarded during the day" (161). As such, Wright's depiction of the end of sleep constituted a marked contrast to the political restlessness attributed to the "withdrawal and apparent passivity" afforded by sleep that was praised by contemporary poets and artists like Percy Shelley and Gustave Courbet. The night could also serve as a symbol of another set of values for those artists, poets, and writers—like William Blake, Thomas De Quincey, and Charles Dickens—who, unable to sleep, transformed nightwalking, as Matthew Beaumont (2015) calls it, from its earlier associations with criminality and vagabondage into a countercultural activity, carving out a time against that imposed by capitalist modernity.

Although describing the slaveholder's lash as ceding place to the overlooker's book of penalties in the despotic temporality of the factory system, Marx draws on the imagery of slavery to different effect in discussing the impact of the factory system on power relations within the working-class household, casting the workingman as both slave and slave trader. As industrial machinery can dispense more and more with muscular power, then so more women and children—as "members of the workman's family" (Marx 1970, 394)—are brought under the "direct sway of capital" (394). No longer disposing only of his own labor power, the workingman "now sells wife and child. He has become a slave-dealer" (396).

The metaphorical transference of the language of slavery to scenes of industrial labor—and, indeed, to many other spheres of life—was rife at the time Marx was writing (Zieger 2008). All the same, his comparisons were not without point. The plantation economies of America's South and the Lancashire factory system have often been differentiated in terms of the consequences, for the latter, of the formal freedom of labor and the high rates of absenteeism and turnover of factory workers that this led to, in contrast to the problems of preventing, and recapturing, escapees that faced the slave owner (Delbanco 2019). Nonetheless, the opposition between coerced plantation labor and free factory labor was often exaggerated. Sydney Pollard, in his classic study of the forms of labor management associated with the early stages of the factory system, pointedly underlines the respects in which the disciplinary regimes of early factories, before the factory reforms that followed the Peterloo massacre of 1819, were often modeled on prisons. He also stresses the respects in which, chained to their husbands and fathers as much as to their factory managers, women and children were "not 'free' workers in any normally accepted sense" (Pollard 1965, 165). The early nineteenth-century development of the prison and factory also followed parallel trajectories. Pollard cites a range of contemporary sources recording how, as earlier attempts to combine traditional work customs with disciplinary habits gave way to the more singular imposition of the latter, difficulties were experienced in "training human beings to renounce their desultory habits of work, and identify themselves with the unvarying regularity of the complex automaton," or of urging on "the slovenly habits of workpeople ... a precision and vigilance unknown before" (183–84). Penal institutions underwent related transformations as earlier conceptions of the relations between prison and workhouse wardens and their inmates modeled on the reciprocal obligations of family life gave way to vocabularies reflecting the transfer of military discipline and drill from the army to the penal sector (Ignatieff 1978, 187–93).

It is against this wider context that we need to set E. P. Thompson's account of the displacement of earlier customary forms of labor regulation by the junction of clock-time discipline and the regimes of machinofacture. The validity of the historical contrasts between the different temporal regimes that underpin the broader aspects of Thompson's thesis has long been questioned (Glennie and Thrift 1996). However, I am only concerned here with the logic informing his more limited differentiation of the task orientation that he attributes to the organization of labor in peasant societies from the clock time imposed by the factory system.[5] In displacing the role of custom in variably regulating the temporalities of task-oriented labor regimes, clock time substituted the uniformity of labor's habitual regulation by the unvarying temporal regimes of machinofacture in which, since all time "must be put to *use*; it is offensive for the labor force merely to 'pass the time'" (E. Thompson 1991, 395). The pathways that were to be acquired by the "habits of industry" were clearly laid out in a late eighteenth-century assessment of the pedagogic role of the workhouse as being that of so accustoming children to constant employment that they would become "habituated, not to say naturalised to Labor and Fatigue" (Powell quoted in E. Thompson 1991, 387).

## Object, body, merchandise: The chains of habit and the using up of slave labor

For Genovese, neither the task orientation of Thompson's preindustrial peasant labor nor the clock time of the factory system applied to the conditions of plantation slavery. However much plantations resembled "factories in the field," their "preindustrial side ... threw up countervailing pressures": "The setting remained rural, and the rhythm of work followed seasonal fluctuations. Nature remained the temporal reference for the slaves. However much the slaveholders might have wished to transform their slaves into clock punchers, they could not, for in a variety of senses both literal and metaphoric, there were no clocks to punch.... Since the plantation economy required extraordinary exertion at critical points of the year, notably the harvest, it required measures to capitalize on the slaves' willingness to work in spurts rather than steadily" (Genovese 1976, 291–92). Genovese's assessment has since been either countered or qualified in a number of ways. Clock time, Mark Smith (1996, 1997) has shown, was more widespread among southern plantation owners than Genovese allowed. So was the interest in applying mechanically defined conceptions of time to the regulation of slave labor so far as was possible given the seasonality of their work and the thin spread of timepieces among enslaved workers. The forms of time discipline associated with factory work, which depended on the imposition of unvarying rhythms of work by mechanized systems of production and an internalization of a time consciousness on the part of the workforce, might have been undeveloped. But their place was taken, Smith argues, by what he calls "time obedience." This consisted in the inculcation of a respect for mechanical time among plantation workers that was enforced either through the threat of violence—the plantation owner's whip rather than the clock—or by the extension of "house-time," in which the work of domestic slaves was closely regulated by the clock,[6] to the field by the use of bells and horns to regulate both the rhythms and the productivity of labor. The development of a rigorous overseer system, finally, compensated for the lack of the automatic regulation of labor exacted by the mechanization of factory production.[7]

In more recent work, Caitlin Rosenthal (2018) has argued that, far from representing a less rigorous system of discipline and labor management than the factory system, the plantation economy anticipated the Taylorist system of scientific management that was not introduced into industrial manufacture until the early twentieth century. Rather than seeking to assess the degree to which the regulation of plantation labor approximated that of the factory system, Rosenthal focuses on the specific logic of the plantation system as itself a machinic system for the regulation of a labor force that was distinguished from the factory workforce in being both unfree and, for the slave owner, a capital asset as well as a source of labor.[8] These aspects of the plantation economy were reflected in the use of systems of accounting that differed radically from those of factories. If the latter recorded transactions—of daily attendance, rates of pay, and so on—with individual workers, this was because their freedom to leave enjoined the imperative of minimizing labor turnover in order to keep the factory machinery running without interruption. "Factory records," as Rosenthal puts it, "show how manufacturers tended machines despite unstable workforces and high turnover" (71). In the plantation system, by contrast, it was the enslaved, whose time was owned absolutely, who constituted the essential gears of its machinery; they were the commodity against which a plantation's output was measured and its yields calibrated in balance sheets that recorded output in aggregate terms, as so much per slave owned. And rather than recording daily or weekly rates of absenteeism of individual workers, the slaveholder's ledgers detailed changes in the overall numbers of slaves still on hand—the "Negro Account" alongside the "Live Stock Account" (57)—taking account of deaths and escapes, as a record of the changing value of the plantation's capital assets (Scene of Habit 3). Katherine McKittrick notes the operation of a similar form of calculation in the system of deadweight tonnage that underpinned the logic of the 1781 massacre of 134 slaves in the course of their transatlantic passage on the slave ship *The Zong*. It was the indiscriminate bundling together of all forms of cargo—human, animal, and inanimate—in the deadweight system that underlay the double rationality of this racial killing: eliminating black bodies from the ship by throwing them overboard as a means of both rationing its short water supply and, by measuring the weight of the jettisoned bodies, making it possible for the slavers to "collect insurance on their massacred human cargo" (McKittrick 2016, 10).

But there is another metaphor for habit that intersects with that of its pathways in the development of the slave economy and its role in establishing the infrastructures that connected plantations to one another and to their markets. It is that of the "chain of habit," which, like habit's pathways, has had a varied history. Associated initially with Augustine, the chain of habit—the "iron links" between previous actions forged by the force of memory—held one fast "not in another's shackles" but in a self-imposed limitation on the capacity of the will to initiate new, freely chosen actions (Augustine cited in Brown 2000, 165–68). However, chains, habit, and pathways were, as Susan Zieger has shown, brought into a very different, violent, association with one another in the relations between the coffle, or chain gang, and the development of America's roadways. While noting the longer history in which states of various kinds have used forced labor to build transport infrastructures, Zieger's concerns are with the tensions between the imagery of roadways as promising a beckoning freedom and the destiny of black men as "repeatedly

*Scene of Habit 3—The "Negro Account" and the "Live Stock Account"*

In the narrative of his life, Frederick Douglass recounts how, when his original master, Captain Thomas, died, he was required to return from Baltimore to the estate where he was born in Tuckahoe in order that he might "be valued with the other property." At this, he records, "my feelings rose up in detestation of slavery. I had now a new conception of my degraded condition. . . . We were all ranked together at the valuation. Men and women, old and young, married and single, were ranked with horses, sheep, and swine. There were horses and men, cattle and women, pigs and children, all holding the same rank in the scale of being, and were all subjected to the same narrow examination. Silvery-headed age and sprightly youth, maids and matrons, had to undergo the same indelicate inspection. At this moment, I saw more clearly than ever the brutalizing effects of slavery upon both slave and slaveholder" (Douglass 1845, 39–40). In the appendix to his narrative, Douglass also reflects on another system of bells, paralleling those regulating the rhythms of labor within the plantation but relating more specifically to the slave's status as property. In chiming in unison with each other, "the slave auctioneer's bell and the church-going bell" called the masters to market and to worship at one and the same time. Standing near each other, "the clanking of fetters and the rattling of chains" in the slave prison "and the pious psalm and solemn prayer in the church, may be heard at the same time" (102).

and violently merged with the road" (Zieger 2020). In both the plantation system and the post–Civil War reparation of America's damaged roadway system, the deployment of forced black labor in chain gangs constituted an early form of automatism that anticipated the disciplinary effects of the assembly line. In exacting precisely coordinated labor from its members, eliminating individual differences of rhythms and capacity as inimical to the demands of maintaining high collective work rates, the coffle "materially enacted the logistical mandate to move goods as efficiently as possible"; eliminating "spontaneous and irrelevant individual movements, it expressed an aspiration toward collective human automation." A vehicle for the circulation and accumulation of capital, the road can only "furnish this smooth, logistical mobility by consuming its laborers," who, "made to carve roads out of the landscape over and over again," are chained to habitual toil, their bodies used up by habit's pathways (Zieger 2020).[9]

It is with systems of calculation of this kind in mind that Achille Mbembe (2017, 79) argues that the development of the slave economy was shaped by a new form of governmental reason (he calls it mercantile reason) in which the black slave figured as "at once object, body and merchandise": that is, an "object-body" that was at the same time a "work substance" whose value flowed from its "physical energy." If this value flowed through the repetition without cease that was imposed on the enslaved, it was only when the slave as object-body was entirely worn out—used up, consumed, and exhausted by the owner—that death signaled the end of the slave's status as object and merchandise. If for the factory worker the dulling effects of habit's repetitions constituted a well-worn pathway that, far from nurturing a capacity for freedom and virtue, led to demoralization and a pending reduction to animality, habit's pathways led to the slave's eventual death and destruction as a capital asset. The demand for cotton from England's factory system, Ahmed reminds us, resulted, as Marx argued in *Capital*, in "the over-working of the negro and sometimes the using up of his life in 7 years of labor" as "a factor in a calculated and calculating system" (Marx quoted in Ahmed 2019, 94). Yet this, Frank Wilderson III argues, constitutes a shortcoming of Marxist accounts of slavery in conceiving the enslaved person as a subaltern structured solely by capital rather than being also subjected to the role of white supremacy (Wilderson 2003, 225). Commenting on the continuities between plantation slavery and America's current prison-industrial complex, he argues, as an African American, that "we were never meant to be workers. . . . From the very beginning we were meant to be accumulated and die" (238).

This was also because the slave started out on habit's pathways from a different point: one not of a pending animality of the kind faced by the respectable English factory worker exposed to the degenerative influence of Irish immigrants but of being already a lower form of humanity. To engage with the issues this raises requires taking account of a further aspect that Ahmed attributes to the path analogy. If, in post-Lockean accounts of habit, the stress is placed on the greater ease and familiarity that come from habit's repetitions so that "the more a path is used, the more a path is used," it also makes sense, she argues, to say that "the less a path is used, the less a path is used" (2019, 45).

This is true of the political histories of habit's pathways that have informed their relations to the racial coordinates of biopolitical governance. These are histories that have depended on a distinctive articulation of habit's operations across the relations between used and unused pathways.

## Breaking the law of repetitive addition: Habit, evolution, and self-selection

In her account of "sentimental biopower," Kyla Schuller accords habit a significant tributary role to the part played by sensibility in the organization of a distinctive racial politics in nineteenth-century America. This derived from contemporary conceptions of sensibility's relations to the nervous system, conceived as "a differentially pliable and agential entity in continuous interplay with its environment" (Schuller 2018, 3). Rather than resting on the principles of a fixed biological determinism, the varied strategies that were brought to bear on the management of differently raced bodies, in both the slave economy and its aftermaths, reflected the different levels of pliability and plasticity that were said to be acquired by white and black bodies as a result of the different degrees of "impressibility"—the capacity to respond dynamically to environmental influences—attributed to them. Like Ahmed, Schuller places particular emphasis on the role played by Jean-Baptiste Lamarck in translating Locke's conception of the greater ease and facility that come from habit's repetitions into the vocabulary of the life sciences, particularly in viewing the enhanced capacities that this gives rise to as being inheritable.

Ahmed takes her cue from the emphasis that Lamarck places on use in his first law of habit: "*A more frequent and continuous use of any organ gradually strengthens, develops and enlarges that organ, and gives it a power proportional to the length of time it has been so used*" (Lamarck 1963, 113). When conjoined with his second law, allowing that the "*acquisitions or losses*" resulting from the "*predominant use or permanent disuse of any organ*" are "*preserved by reproduction to the new individuals which arise, provided that the acquired modifications are common to both sexes, or at least to the individuals which produce the young*" (113), this makes the habits acquired by means of inheritance an accumulating "*second nature*" (114). It is the role that such habits play in shaping biological form that particularly attracts Ahmed's attention. Citing Lamarck's famed analysis of the giraffe's long neck as the result of the effort, sustained across generations, of straining to reach higher foliage, with the result that this habitual exertion gives the neck a shape and form it would not otherwise have obtained, she interprets the giraffe's neck as "a well-used path, *an effect of use that eases use*" (Ahmed 2019, 74).

Schuller's concern with the concept of impressibility developed in the American School of Evolution focuses rather on the respects in which it departed from the account of impressions offered by Locke and David Hume in which the sensation occasioned by the impression of an object on a sensory organ is "registered by the brain in the form of an idea" (Schuller 2018, 6–7). Rather than interpreting such impressions as the effects of external causes on passive subjects, the concept of impressibility "signals the capacity of matter to be alive to movements made on it, to retain and incorporate changes rendered in its material over time" (7). When viewed through the lens of Lamarck's account of the role of habit in the inheritance of acquired characteristics and conjoined to conceptions of cultural evolution as a set of civilizing processes laminated on top of those of natural evolution, the resulting attribution of a cumulative impressibility to the nervous system led to a conception of the civilized body as "the gradual outcome of its habit and surroundings, accumulating over the lifespan of individuals and the . . . evolutionary time of the race" (7). It is when Schuller goes on to say that the "more layers . . . civilization had impressed on the familial substrate over time, the more the individual possessed impressibility and the potential for further change—or rapid degeneration" (7–8)—that the pathway analogy comes into play. And the racial dimensions of the analogy become clear when the dual options of further change or degeneration, enhanced use or disuse, are complicated by the prospect that, owing to their lack of the capacity for impressibility, some bodies never got started out on habit's pathways or, if they did, were halted somewhere along their course.

This absence or relative lack of impressibility on the part of varied racialized populations effected a productive junction of biopower and disciplinary power in enabling the hyperexploitation of both free and unfree sources of racialized labor. The linchpin of this junction was the American School of Evolution's extension of Lamarck's interpretation of evolution as, in higher animals, a result of the effort exerted by the individual organism in adapting to a changing environment (the process exemplified by the giraffe's neck) into a rebuttal of Charles Darwin's account of natural selection. This rebuttal placed the individual organism in control of a conscious process of "intelligent selection" through which it negotiates its relations to its environment by selectively choosing, from among the repeated impressions that condition its development through habitual movements, those that are to be actively developed. Impressibility was thus both a condition and an effect of a capacity for a consciously managed process of development that shapes the physical form of both the organism and its descendants. The "sociobiological indeterminism" that attached to the body's plasticity meant that human bodies exhibited varying degrees of development depending on the degree to which conscious processes of striving, translated into the mechanisms of culture and civilization, have left their mark on bodies with varying degrees of impressibility.[10] "Racial status," as Schuller puts it, "thus indexed a hierarchy of impressibility" (2018, 41). If the plastic body of civilized races demonstrated a capacity for creative development owing to its high degree of impressibility, the underdevelopment of "primitives" was a testimony to their "unimpressibility," to the unyielding fixity, transmitted across generations, that was the result of their insensitive constitutions.

Schuller traces the origins of this conception to Locke's depiction of savages—alongside children, idiots, and illiterates—as among those who have only low degrees of impressibility. Since this means that they are only able to register ideas derived from those objects "which have made upon their senses the frequentist and strongest Impressions" (Locke 1965, 24), they are unable, by themselves, to set off on habit's pathways and, thereby, to develop through time. But the version of this argument that is central to Schuller's concern with American racial politics is that developed by Edward Drinker Cope, for whom habit's pathway, driven by the mechanisms of "intelligent selection," was the engine of evolutionary development.

Toward the end of his *Origin of the Fittest*, Cope, summarizing his "law of use and effort" (1886, 423), cites a passage from Lamarck to the effect that habits are not derived from the form of an animal's body but, to the contrary, as in the case of the giraffe's neck, it is the habits constituting its manner of life that shape its form. In higher forms of life, this process is driven by consciousness. In the case of humans, it proceeds through the organization of human character comprising the relations between the emotions, the intellect that reorders the experiences impressed on the emotions, and the will as the spontaneous power of the mind, which gives a direction to the intellect's ordering of the emotions and the actions this gives rise to. This mental structure is subtended by sensibility as the sensorily mediated impressibility of the body. It is the dynamic between sensibility and the actions of character that lies behind the initiation of new habits as, for Cope, necessarily the result of conscious effort.[11] This is a process that sets both individuals and, across generations, species down the familiar pathway along which habit contributes to the accumulation of new capacities: "When this machinery is completed, through the repetition of conscious stimulus, it works thenceforth without necessary intervention of consciousness. The consciousness may then be engaged in fresh acquisitions, accomplishing new organizations, thus accumulating a store of powers" (393).

It is via "the law of use and effort" that what Cope calls "the growth force"—through which external causes, in acting on the organism, are modified by that organism—interrupts the "law of repetitive addition" to initiate the generation of new, inheritable capacities. The growth force thus operates in a kind of dialectic between the physical and chemical causes that act on the organism and their transformation into vital forces by dint of the transformations of habitual uses through the exertion of effort. It is in relation to the effects of such uses that the blacksmith's arm makes its appearance in Cope's account, but this time as an inheritance to be superseded. "The hands of the laborer," he writes in summarizing the effects of repeated use on the muscular system, "are always bigger than those of men of other pursuits" (195), just as, he adds, are the "nails of the working woman" (24). If use thus regulates "the locality of new repetitions of parts already existing" (195), it is through effort that, among species, new bodily parts are produced and, among humans, that existing capacities are increased and new ones generated. If conscious effort is thus the root of new capacities, Cope also argues, "there is no determination of growth-force which may not become habitual" and "no habitual determination of growth-force which may not be inherited" (194).

In higher animals and in humans, it is their degree of impressibility that determines the extent to which they can exercise the capacity for "intelligent selection" (really self-selection) of the fittest: "Those in which impressibility is most highly developed will accumulate mental acquisitions most rapidly; ... they will be the most *intelligent* of their species. While others follow the old routine of once acquired and then inherited habits, those in whom consciousness most frequently recognizes events will *originate* new acts and new habits" (Cope 1886, 40). It will come as no surprise to learn that black peoples are placed at the bottom of Cope's hierarchy of impressibility. White middle-class women constitute its apex owing to their greater exposure to "music, color, or spectacle generally" (159), and to the timidity arising from their "irregularity of action in the outer world" and their greater immersion in cosseted luxury. But the concomitant low level of exposure to logic, a relative lack of ruggedness and sternness, imposes limits on "the 'woman stage' of character" (159). This is a stage that all men temporarily inhabit but eventually pass through by dint of their greater capacity for "discipline and labor" (159), and hence their superiority in both the intellectual and laboring worlds, albeit at the price of becoming emotionally inferior to women. But it is "savages" who are assigned to the bottom rungs of impressibility. Approximating apes in many of their physical features—prolongated jaws, deficient calf muscles, unusually long arms, all interpreted as representative of immature stages in the earlier development of Indo-Europeans—they are, as well as lacking intellect, deficient in all emotions save those of "power and fear" (387). The features that predominate among the "Negro" and the Mongolian, compared with the Indo-European, are those that are "retarded in man," whereas those that are underdeveloped are those in which "man is accelerated" (287–88).

Unaffected by the dynamics that arise from the "law of use and effort," lower races are stalled at the entrance to habit's pathways. The "plastic body of the civilized and the static flesh of blackness" constitute the opposite poles of the "animacy hierarchy" that defines the sphere of operation of sentimental biopower (Schuller 2018, 54). Where use is not dynamized by effort but remains caught in the law of repetitive addition, the result is an "automatism" that "represents a condition of 'lapsed intelligence' and diminished life" (235). If this provided a rationale for the black man's subjection to the rigors of slavery, it also, Schuller argues, linked Cope's theoretical position to his political interventions into the industrial politics of postemancipation America, signaling the adaptability of the racialized body to "the highly orchestrated and repetitive movements of industrializing labor" (14). In other contexts, however, the failure to enter into habit's pathways or to proceed beyond their early stages brought in its tow the threat of racial extinction.

## The persistence of the useless

In her discussion of George Eliot's *The Mill on the Floss*, Kristie Allen (2010, 840) underlines the significance of the contradictory pulls between the dynamics of habit as "cumulative character," through which the capacities of individuals and generations could grow and exceed those of their elders, and the flat and mechanical habits associated with animals, as enacted in the different life trajectories that Tom Dodson and Maggie Tulliver mark out relative to their parents. She also draws attention to Eliot's extensive use of channel metaphors to describe the flow of her characters' conduct and the course of their minds.[12] The basis for these metaphors was derived from the reworking of Locke's contentions regarding the relations between habit's pathways and the association of ideas proposed by late nineteenth-century physiological psychologists. The work of Eliot's partner, George Henry Lewes, was particularly influential in this regard. Lewes subscribed to post-Darwinian conceptions of habit's role in the production of a "second nature" in the form of an accumulating, transgenerational set of instincts. Over time, as he put it, "voluntary actions become involuntary, the involuntary become automatic, the intelligent become habitual, and the habitual become instinctive" (Lewes quoted in Otis 1994, 24). But in using the pathway metaphor, Lewes also added to it an embryonic neurophysiological dimension in his translation of those pathways into channels carved into the body's sensory and neurological structure by the force of repetition. For Lewes, however, these channels—conduits for, as Allen puts it, flows of "water running downhill, the paths of least resistance" (2010, 835)—also threatened to lead to a dead end as a consequence of the automatic ease of habit's unconscious repetitions. Where this was so, habit's pathways promised only to carve deeper and deeper channels in the body rather than freeing the person up for new, free, and creative acts. The latter required the intervention of the brain's capacity for "mental differentiation," which, in allocating different functions to its varied components, would fit it for "more energetic reaction and for new modes of reaction" (Lewes quoted in Allen 2010, 838). Only this would generate new capacities, the new steps along habit's developmental pathways, necessary for the cumulative structure of character to be realized.

Lewes's work was only one of many reworkings of Locke's formulations of habit's pathways in the context of the fusion of Darwin's theory of natural selection and Lamarck's account of the inheritance of acquired characteristics that proliferated in late Victorian England. Herbert Spencer's account of the processes through which reason and will came to be differentiated from the instincts through evolutionary processes in which habit and what he called "organic memory" played a generative role was perhaps the most influential of these (Spencer 1996). Responding to changes in its environment, which it experiences as external shocks, the organism registers frequent recurrences of the same shocks through habitual repetitions that prepare the way for the development of progressively more complex divisions in the nervous system and for the transgenerational transmission of the accumulating competencies this facilitates as a set of hereditable instincts. The relations between "conscious memory" and "organic memory" are centrally implicated in this process. Conscious memory comes into play when the connections between a particular set of psychic states induced by changes in the milieu are no longer coordinated through the automatic mechanism of habit; and it passes away when such coordination once again becomes automatic in being passed on as a part of an accumulated instinctual inheritance that is transmitted to the next generation via the organic memory carved into the body.[13]

This account of organic memory involved a significant recasting of the assumptions underlying Locke's empirical psychology. True, there are no innate faculties or ideas prior to experience, but this does not rule out the possibility of there being historical forms of innateness that are the somatic accumulation of the successive experiences of past generations that have come to be coded into the body as a set of compound instincts. Indeed, it is only this accumulating legacy of past experience that opens up the space and the time within which the higher faculties of reason and the will might emerge and be exercised. Except where this mechanism is halted or fails to get started. This was the case, for Spencer, with the "primitive" who, stalled at the start of habit's pathways, was condemned to a fate of "somatic and neural flat-lining."[14] The underdevelopment of the "brain of the uncultivated man as compared to that of the cultivated man" is thus accounted for in terms of "the routes taken by nervous discharges" being "less numerous, less involved, less varied in the resistance they offer," with the consequence that "the number of ideas that can follow a given antecedent is smaller and the degrees of strength with which they can present themselves are fewer" (Spencer quoted in R. Smith 1992, 149).

The reworking of habit's pathways that is involved here is more clearly developed in Walter Bagehot's (1873) account of "stored virtue," the term he uses in summarizing his conception of how the habits cultivated via the mechanism of drill come to be deposited in the nervous system.[15] This then functions as "the connective tissue of civilization" through which the skills acquired by one generation are transmitted to the next, with the consequence that their use is made easy and familiar as a set of inborn aptitudes. Another example of Ahmed's "use that eases use," the operation of this connective tissue acts as a divisive force in the respect that "the descendants of cultivated parents will have, by born nervous organization, a greater aptitude for cultivation than the descendants of such as are not cultivated," a tendency that "augments, in some enhanced ratio, for many generations" (Bagehot 1873, 8). But excessive use through repetition can also become a barrier to development if there is no development of mind and culture to add to the stock of virtue that might be stored and inherited. This is the problem and root cause, Bagehot argued, of arrested civilizations: their becoming trapped in an initial cycle of habit through which a foundational stock of virtue is acquired. The difficulty, as he puts it, is not that "of making the first preservative habit, but of breaking through it, and reaching something better" (53).

Similar consequences flowed from the translation of the metaphorics of habit's pathways into the late nineteenth-century anthropological doctrine of "survivals." This parted company with the mainstream of evolutionary thought in that its concern was with the survival not of the fittest but of the *unfittest*. Proposed initially by Edward Burnett Tylor, and endorsed and promulgated by an influential range of fellow "armchair anthropologists," this doctrine—the keystone, according to George W. Stocking Jr. (1987), of late Victorian imperial anthropology—complemented biological accounts of somatic and neural flat-lining like Spencer's with an account of "cultural flat-lining" that played a crucial role in the administration of Indigenous peoples, particularly in Australia. The aspect of this doctrine that is most relevant to my concerns here consists in the role it accorded rituals as part of a distinctive technique for deciphering the relations between past and present. This was derived via an analogy with Max Müller's "disease of language" theory, which argued that linguistic forms continued to circulate after their original meanings had been lost or had withered.[16] Expanding the argument by analogy, Tylor argued that rituals had also persisted through time in a similar "withered" form and might therefore validly be interpreted as remnants of the past in the present. In introducing his account of "survivals in culture" as old habits or customs that have become fixed, Tylor accounts for their durability in terms of their having been, once established, so little disturbed that they have kept their "course from generation to generation, as a stream once settled in its bed will flow on for ages" (1871, 1:61). Georges Didi-Huberman (2002) generalizes from this to characterize the time of survivals as a "spectral time," a legacy of the past that is disconnected from the present that has superseded it. The survival, in another of Tylor's formulations, "lies very much out of the beaten track of history" (Tylor quoted in Ratnapalan 2008, 135). As such, it also identified those aspects of "primitive cultures" that were to be surgically removed by colonial governance. Tylor was thus clear that his doctrine of survivals was intended to serve as a means of identifying those "streams of folly" that, persisting from the past, have to be eliminated in order to integrate "the savage" into the culture of the higher races (Tylor 1867, 92–93).

This was not because the persistence of rituals meant that the role of habit was too strong among "primitive" peoples. Their cultural backwardness derived rather from their failure to follow habit's pathways to their proper end, to translate the ease and familiarity arising from repeated use into a basis for new practices. This failure was most usually accounted for in the terms proposed by John Stuart Mill's concept of the "tyranny of custom" and its translation into anthropology by, among others, Baldwin Spencer and Frank Gillen (1899), whose work in the Australian context had considerable international influence.[17] It was, however, Henry Pitt Rivers (né August Henry Lane Fox), the English archaeologist and noted museum curator, who most clearly articulated its implications in terms of habit's pathways. In developing the reasoning underlying his interpretation of the tools and weapons of "primitives" as, like Tylor's rituals, survivals of earlier forms, Pitt Rivers presented his argument as an evolutionary confirmation and extension of Locke's critique of innate ideas. The logic of the development—of tools, weapons, rituals, ideas—is driven by the relations between the "intellectual mind capable of reasoning upon unfamiliar occurrences" and the "automaton mind capable of acting intuitively in certain matters without effort of the will or consciousness" (Fox 1875, 296). These are bound to each other by an evolutionary dynamic through which the accomplishments of the intellectual mind in earlier historical periods are passed on to subsequent generations as their inheritance of automated reason. The key mechanism shaping this dynamic is habit, which Pitt Rivers viewed as a form of conscious learning involving the intellectual mind but which then becomes routinized via repetition. It is through habit that the lessons of experience are passed on into the stock of instincts inherited by the next generation in accordance with the accumulative logic of habit's pathways, in which the completion of one habit-to-instinct cycle frees up the space for another such cycle, leading—through the inheritance of acquired characteristics—to an ever-growing set of instinctual responses constituting the automated mind.

The biopolitical implications of this position derive from the further argument that "the tendency to automatic action upon any given set of ideas will be in proportion to the length of time during which the ancestors of the individual have exercised their minds in those particular ideas" (Fox 1875, 299). This is the position accorded to the Australian Aborigine, whose "*persistent conservatism*" derives not from an excess of habit but from the failure of the dynamic mechanism of habit to kick in with sufficient vigor to build up an accumulated stock of what Pitt Rivers called "modified instincts," rather producing only a thin layer of these, which, due to their endless repetition over millennia, have acquired an unusually binding grip on their culture and conduct. The result was, as W. H. R. Rivers later put it in his pithy summary of the doctrine of survivals, "the persistence of the useless" (Rivers 1913, 293).

The role accorded habit's pathways in these formulations had different consequences for Indigenous peoples from those associated with either factory or slave labor, albeit ones still implicated in the circulation of capital.[18] Since the primary object of settler colonialism is possession of the land rather than the surplus to be derived from mixing Indigenous labor with the land, it aims primarily not at the disciplined training of Indigenous populations as a source of labor—although it does this too—but at their elimination.[19] It is in this respect that the role of habit, considered in its relations to the doctrine of survivals, played a significant role in establishing what Foucault called "a biological-type caesura within a population" that allows "power to treat that population as a mixture of races" (Foucault 2003b, 255). And it was this, in turn, that underlay those biopolitical programs of killing shaped by the evolutionary logic of dividing races between those who must live and those who must die that typified the practices of settler colonialism.

There were many aspects to settler accounts of the backwardness of Indigenous peoples: the fragility of their social and cultural forms, the morally and physically deteriorating consequences of their susceptibility to the "vices of civilization," and so on. It is, however, in the frequent reference to their inability to adapt, to their inertia, that the historical force of habit's pathways, and their racialization, was evident in the new twist it gave to earlier discourses of "unimprovability." This was now regarded as constitutive and irremediable, a result of the failure of Indigenous peoples to advance beyond the first step along habit's pathways constituted by their original differentiation from nature to take advantage of its generative possibilities. It was this that led to their subsequent lockdown into an endless cycle of repetitive copying unrelieved by an ability either to acquire new capacities or to initiate them through autonomous innovation. These two scenarios had different consequences with regard to the positioning of Indigenous populations on habit's pathways. With regard to the first scenario, only those who, through miscegenation, had acquired "mixed blood" were judged capable of being placed on a course leading to the acquisition of civilized habits. This conception provided the underpinnings for those assimilationist practices through which children of "mixed blood" were forcibly separated from their families and placed in custodial institutions whose instructional programs aimed to place them on a progressive pathway that would, as it was put in the Australian context, "breed out the color."[20]

The possibility of innovation associated with the second scenario was similarly regarded as having to come from elsewhere in a logic that was clarified in contemporaneous accounts of the connections between habit's pathways and early twentieth-century conceptions of the role of innovation in the circuits of capital. Gabriel Tarde's account of the role of repetition as a mechanism for the generation of difference is a case in point.[21] "Repetition," as he put it, "exists for the sake of variation" (1903, 7). As such, it takes three forms: the vibratory repetitions of matter, the organic repetitions of inheritance, and the imitative repetitions that, for Tarde, constituted the social. It is through the mechanism of imitation that the presocial forms of habit constituted by the force of repetitions inscribed in the body's nervous and muscular systems take on differentiated collective and social forms. These social forms of imitation are varied: fashion-imitation, obedience-imitation, custom-imitation, for example. Whichever the case, however, the dynamics of social life are propelled by the disruption of cycles of imitation that have become routinized by new ones initiated by moments of invention that are the product of flashes of individual genius. If, as Tarde puts it, socially speaking "everything is either invention or imitation," he likens the force of invention to that of a mountain and that of imitation to a river. This contrast serves as a stand-in for two different aspects of the course of history in which "the freakishness of a rock-bound landscape" interrupts "the conviviality of a park walk" (3). There is, however, a practice that serves as a counter to this logic. It is that of non-imitation, which, where it takes the form of "not imitating the neighbor who is in contact with us," is predicated on an antisocial logic: "The refusal of a people, a class, a town or a village, of a savage tribe isolated on a civilized continent, to copy the dress, customs, language, industry, and arts which make up the civilization of their neighborhood is a continual declaration of antipathy to the form of the society in question" (xix).

Where this nonimitation is practiced by original populations against the "extraneous and heterogeneous models" introduced by later arrivals, it serves only to enable the "harmonious group of home models to extend and prolong themselves, to entrench themselves in the custom-imitation of which they are the object" (xix). This theme is taken up later in the use that Tarde makes of the work of Tylor and, more generally, the archaeological perspective he attributed to the doctrine of survivals in characterizing "primitive savages" as being "like children" who "imitate for the mere pleasure of imitating" with the consequence that they have become locked into a "*self-originating* imitation" (Tarde 1903, 95): that of an initial repetition that introduced a difference that separated the primitive from nature. It is, however, a repetition that goes no further. Rather, destined to a repetition of this first difference that is never broken by the force of imaginative innovation, it traps primitive society "in the midst of a vast passive *imitativeness* which receives and perpetuates all its vagaries as the water of a lake circles out under the stroke of a bird's wing on its surface" (95). It is an unbroken repetition of initial difference, then, that can only be disrupted—moved on to a new cycle of "difference and repetition"—by the introduction of innovative differentiation from without.[22]

If this is a mechanism of diffusion that perfectly encapsulates the logic of settler colonialism, it is cut from the same cloth as Tarde's conception of the role that "germ capital" plays in the dynamics of capitalism. Latour and Vincent-Antonin Lépinay (2009) stress the respects in which Tarde's account of the role of genius in the generation of germ capital, and that of labor in translating the difference produced by each moment in the innovation of germ capital into a repetitive cycle of capital accumulation, represents a bifurcation of habit's pathways. If innovations depend on the capacity of genius to free the mind from the burden of repetition, that capacity is an effect of the energetic flow of neurons in carving new channels in the brain. And if it is this capacity that allows for new forms of capital "to be born and grow up," its generative powers derive not from "the slave's unpaid work nor the laborer's unpaid overtime" but from "the leisure of the free man of Antiquity or the modern 'bourgeois'" (Tarde quoted in Lépinay 2007, 535). But the path that labor is destined to follow is a different one. As the point of mediation between the discontinuity introduced by the invention of genius and its diffusion into a new cycle of automated routine, labor is "a continual stream of imitation, a periodic series of acts tied together, each of which had to be taught by others' example and strengthened by one's own repetition, by habit" (Tarde quoted in Lépinay 2007, 537).

## The circulation of temporalities

My purpose in this chapter has been to show how nineteenth-century conceptions of habit's pathways played a key role in securing the circulation of capital across different forms of exploitation and dispossession. These aspects of habit's political histories are, of course, by no means over and done with. The logic underpinning them—that of distributing different populations to different stages along the temporalities that characterize habit's developmental pathways—is still very much with us. In reviewing the literature on emergency governance, Ben Anderson, Kevin Grove, Lauren Rickards, and Matthew Kearnes identify how the temporalities associated with emergencies—such as pandemics—are fractured by the differential distribution of, on the one hand, anticipatory and, on the other, durative and repetitive temporalities across a series of social divisions, but particularly racialized ones.[23] The open-ended futurity of the anticipatory temporalities that beckon the liberal white subject along the redemptive pathways of self-governance that lead conduct along the road to a new normality beyond the emergency in question are predicated on the persistence of "the repetitive and durative temporalities of black and Indigenous subjects enduring the wake of slavery and genocide that denies these subjects the possibility of a future" (Anderson et al. 2019, 629). It is the interconnections between these two temporalities and the pathways they stand for that need to be stressed. White liberal subjectivities predicated on the anticipatory structure that projects a future of "growth, change, development and becoming" depend, discursively and materially, on techniques of racialization that suspend black and Indigenous subjects in "a durative temporality of decline, stagnation, decay, *and* a repetitive temporality of recurring plantation violence" (623).

The interdependency between these two different ways of conceiving and acting on habits and their distribution across different racialized populations is, then, one of the most vital issues posed by the politics of habit in the present. It is therefore one I shall consider more fully at various points in later chapters. For now, though, it will repay our attention to look next at the political histories associated with conceptions of habit's pathways taking the form of a descending trajectory in which each step on the downward road paves the way for the next one.

# 3

# Unwilled
# Habits

IN THEIR REVIEW OF RECENT RESEARCH into the role of the basal ganglia in processes of habit formation, Henry Yin and Barbara Knowlton (2006) interpret its significance as that of a meeting point for two different pathways. While one of these comprises the purely reflex repetitions enjoined by instinctual drives, the second and higher-level pathway exercises various forms of inhibitory control over such repetitions. These two pathways are controlled by two different learning systems: the former by the S-R system, in which stimulus-response bonds, strengthened through their use in forms of repetitive training, predominate; and the latter by the A-O system governed by goal directedness, in which calculations of the action outcomes that might follow from particular courses of behavior predominate. The first of these pathways is constituted by appetitive responses to external stimuli converted into habits through "overtraining"; the second is the locus of intentionality focused on the calculation of differential rewards. These are not presented as two hermetically separate systems. To the contrary, Yin and Knowlton's central concern is with the manner of their interaction, and the consequences that follow should they fail to do so properly.

While differing in its detail, this account of two different pathways inscribed in the relations between the body's sensory, muscular, and neurological structures is similar to that associated with nineteenth-century conceptions of the "reflex arc." These mediated the relations between involuntary actions, governed by the interactions between the body's sensory and muscular systems and the brain's lower centers, and voluntary actions, governed by the brain's higher centers constituted by the cerebrum. In his classic account of its history, Franklin Fearing identifies a number of features that, albeit weighted and inflected differently, have been more or less constant components of the definition of reflex action. These include the requirement that it should be involuntary; unlearned in the sense of deriving from an inherited mechanism; predictable and uniform, a necessary and invariable response to a given stimulus; unconditioned by consciousness; and with a shorter time lapse between the stimulus and the response than consciously conditioned reactions (Fearing 1970, 5). The historical discovery of the reflex arc was thus a major actor in the contrast Michel Foucault draws between the functioning of habit in the classical period, in which he accords pride of place to David Hume's language of the passions, and its later connections to the "impulses, drives, tendencies, inclinations, and automatisms" in relation to which "representations, passions, and affects" had a purely "secondary, derivative, or subordinate status" (Foucault 2003a, 131). This is not to suggest that the language of the passions disappeared entirely. Nor did the Lockean logic of the relations between habit's pathways and the association of ideas. These were, however, obliged either to give way to or to be pressed into varied forms of accommodation with the increasing significance accorded the body's neurophysiological systems in accounting for human aptitudes and dispositions.

If this entailed a rethinking of habit, it also entailed a rethinking of the will and of will-habit relations. In reflecting on the implications of recent developments in the neurosciences for current understandings of the will, Patrick Haggard (2008) argues that the dominant tendency has been to reject conceptions of "free will" as relying too much on dualist conceptions of mind-body relations in which the mind operates like a "ghost in the machine"—an immaterial presence that, although unaffected by the body's material properties, is nonetheless able to lord it over them—in favor of an account of voluntary action as an outcome of the interactions between different neural networks. In place of an "I" that, as the locus of a free will, superintends and directs brain-body actions, the challenge now is to chart the connections between so-called voluntary actions and the stimulus-driven responses of reflex actions. These are, Haggard argues, connections that take the form of a continuum rather than that of some linchpin between actions of different kinds—except insofar as, to the extent that they are not directly determined by any identifiable external stimulus, the more indirect forms of determination that apply to "voluntary" actions generate certain limited kinds of "freedom effect" derived from their distance from any immediate source of causation. This is, however, quite distinct from a conception of free will as the generative source of particular kinds of action.

I'll come back to recent reworkings of the relations between habit and freedom associated with current developments in the neurosciences in chapter 6. My concerns in this chapter are with the earlier, mainly nineteenth-century, reconfigurations of the relations between habit and the will prompted by the role attributed to the reflex arc in grounding new forms of automatism in the body's neurophysiological architecture. There is no single story to be told here. There were a number of different versions of the reflex arc and its relations to the operations of the brain, and these had different implications for understandings of the will.[1] In reviewing these accounts, I shall be primarily concerned to identify how the relations between habit and the will were reshaped in the context of different practices of government directed toward different populations. While in some accounts a positive construction of the relations between will and habit remained a significant aspect of practices of liberal governance, I am more concerned with the developments through which habit, in being disconnected from the will, was accorded a new status as characterizing actions that had become "unwilled." These called for quite different mechanisms of governance, ones that, rather than operating through a mechanism of the subject, worked through the manipulation of milieus.

I begin by looking briefly at the different accounts of mind-body relations and their bearing on the roles accorded habit in the work of René Descartes and John Locke, focusing mainly on the relations between the understanding, will, and habit in Locke and the role these played in the transition from sovereign power to the development of a self-governing liberal subject. I then outline how the discovery of the reflex arc and related developments in physiology and psychology challenged earlier conceptions of habit's pathways derived from Locke's account of role played by the association of ideas in fashioning the operations of the understanding. This often involved a reworking of the ease of action that Locke attributed to habit's pathways by interpreting this as an effect of the channels carved in the body's nervous and neurological systems by the force of habit's repetitions. I look next at how the relations between the will, habit, and practices of governing were reconfigured across a range of nineteenth-century concerns in which practices previously interpreted as willful acts were subjected to a historical process of being progressively "unwilled": most notably, varied forms of addiction. I then consider a further episode in the transformation of nineteenth-century conceptions of habit and their implications for processes of governance as attempts to buttress the power of the will relative to the debilitating force of "bad habits" gave way to forms of habit intervention focused on countering the debilitating influence of squalid urban milieus. This paves the way for a discussion of the problematic of degeneration produced by the interactions between medicine, psychology, and the new tendencies in evolutionary thought that marked the late nineteenth century. I pay particular attention here to the work of Henry Maudsley, who, while inscribing habit in a downward pathway, drew on Lockean imagery, albeit inverting it, in his account of how each step down that pathway made the next downward step easier. In concluding the chapter, I show how Maudsley took issue with the claims of priestly authority to guide the conduct of souls along habit's pathways in favor of the greater ability he attributed to psychology and the fledgling science of sociology to counter the forces responsible for inflecting habit's powers in a downward direction.

### Habit and the liberal subject

Descartes is frequently cited as the first to propose the concept of reflex action, albeit misleadingly so in the respect that, while he used the term, its associations in his work were different from its later usage. The responsibility for sowing the seeds of this confusion has been largely attributed to T. H. Huxley, who, in his essay on animals as automata, invoked Descartes's work in support of his own extension of mechanistic principles of explanation to encompass all forms of animal and human behavior. Describing humans as "conscious automata," Huxley (1874) contended that the relations between consciousness, will, and behavior should be understood as being caused by molecular changes of the brain substance.[2] This involved a conception of mind-body relations as uniformly automatic and mechanistic, whereas, for the greater part, the earlier history of reflex action had interpreted this as a localized stimulus-response system operating independently from the mind's conventional association with the brain's higher cerebral functions. Although not subscribing to the monism that Huxley attributed to him, Descartes's conception of mind-body relations was more complex than the straightforward dualism that he has often been accused of.[3] In his *Sixth Meditation*, he insists on the substantial union of mind and body in recording that he is "very closely joined to . . . and almost merged with" his body to such an extent that mind and body "compose a single entity" (Descartes 2011, 57). This is preceded, however, by his contention that his essence consists in the fact that he is "a thinking thing" and that, as such, he is distinct from his body and "can exist without it" (55). And it is followed by the assertion that the human body is "some kind of machine made from bones, nerves, muscles, veins, blood and skin so that, even if there were no mind in it, it would still have all the motions which it has at present and which do not result from the control of the will and, therefore, from the mind" (59). It was in thus proposing the relative independence of the operations of the body and the mind that Descartes served as a key point of reference for later conceptions of reflex action. His illustration of the modus operandi of reflex action via an analogy with the hydraulics of the Royal fountain systems has also been influential: "And, indeed, one may very well compare the nerves of the machine which I am describing with the tubes of the machines of these fountains, the muscles and tendons of the machine with the other various engines and springs which serve to move these machines, and the animal spirits, the source of which is the heart and of which the ventricles are the reservoirs, with the water which puts them in motion" (Descartes quoted in Fearing 1970, 20).

The political resonances of Descartes's account, however, consist less in its separation of the automatic forms of bodily action from the brain than in securing the autonomy of the brain from the potentially contaminating effects of the mechanical mediation of the body's relations with the external world effected by its pulmonary, muscular, and nervous systems. In this respect Descartes drew on contemporary neuroanatomical conceptions that, as Nima Bassiri puts it, modeled the brain's anatomical position on "the architecture of political absolutism" in its conception as "a castle or fortress that housed and safeguarded a sovereign mind or soul" (Bassiri 2016, 70). There are, in this respect, significant continuities between Descartes and Locke, particularly with regard to the metaphysics of interiority associated with their subscription to the currency of the camera obscura in producing a space for a nominally free subject whose relations to the external world were effected through what were envisaged as decorporealized visual practices (Crary 1996, 29–34, 38–43). In Locke's case, however, this metaphysics of interiority was connected to the production of a space for the exercise of new forms of liberal subjectivity operating through regimes of self-discipline effected by the mind's reflective introspection on its own operations.

The production of such an inner space, Étienne Balibar (2013) has argued, required that it be cleared from its subjection to Christian forms of spiritual authority associated with earlier conceptions of *conscienta* as a space pierced by God's gaze. This was accomplished by Locke's critique of innate ideas, conceived as spiritual implants in the mind, as a doctrine resting on the incoherent supposition that the mind might have ideas without being conscious of them. "But to imprint anything on the mind," as he put it, "without the mind's perceiving it, seems to me hardly intelligible" (Locke 1965, 11). The production of an inner space of liberal subjectivity also required its clearance from the forces of external causation. At the very start of his *Essay concerning Human Understanding*, Locke thus says that he will not "meddle with the physical consideration of the mind" or consider "by what motions of our spirits or alterations of our bodies we come to have any sensation by our organs; or any *ideas* in our understanding" or "whether those *ideas* do in their formation . . . depend on matter or no" (5). This conception of the mind as a self-reflective interiority fashioned its contents as consisting, first, of its interpretation of the sensations derived from experience of the external world acquired via the senses—conceived as neutral mediators of the relations between mind and matter—and, second, of the mind's "internal sense" constituted by its capacity for reflection on its own operations.

It is this capacity for reflection, considered in its relations to the will, and the bearing of both on the mechanisms of habit that are central to Locke's account of the parts played by different authorities in the conduct of conduct. This account is shaped by Locke's concern with how the liberal subject should negotiate the relations between such authorities in aspiring to the condition of liberty. This consists in "the power to act or not to act, according as the mind directs," and the power of the will "to direct the operative faculties to motion or rest in particular instances" (233). To be clear, it is not the freedom of the will that is at issue here since, if left to itself, the will is always impelled by the force of desires that are beyond its control. At a key point in his discussion of the role of the will as a distinctive form of power within the economy of the mind, Locke argues that what "immediately determines the *will*, from time to time, to every voluntary action, is the *uneasiness* of *desire*, fixed on some absent good." It is "this *uneasiness* that determines the *will* to the successive voluntary actions . . . by which we are conducted through different courses to different ends" (208). Should a man lack such *uneasiness* in being contentedly settled in a particular "relish of the mind," no action would be required from the will except the continuation of the mind's contentment. It is only the uneasiness generated by the desire for something that is absent that gives rise to willed action. And this is so irrespective of the virtue of what is desired. No matter how far a man might be intellectually persuaded of the virtue of pursuing the greater good of the common weal, "till he *hungers and thirsts after righteousness*, till he feels an *uneasiness* in the want of it, his *will* will not be determined to any action in pursuit of this professed greater good" (209). As his contrary example, Locke cites the case of the drunkard who, though aware that his habit might cost him his health and reputation, and lead to the loss of his estate, "yet the returns of the *uneasiness* to miss his companions, the habitual thirst after his cups at the usual time, drives him to the tavern" (209). Although acknowledging the pull of the greater good "in the intervals of his drinking hours... when the *uneasiness* to miss his accustomed delight returns, the greater acknowledged good loses its hold and the present *uneasiness* determines the *will* to the accustomed action; which thereby gets stronger footing to prevail against the next occasion" (209–10).

If willing is a driving force, then, it is itself driven and, as Sara Ahmed (2014, 72) notes in her discussion of Locke's remarks in *Some Thoughts concerning Education*, it may take the subject down the wrong path. If the mind is not "rightly disposed," the child might be led to the "repeated and willful neglect" of the "advice, direction, and reproof" offered by the father or tutor. Where this is so, the result is "a wrong bent of the will"—"a manifest perverseness"—that lies at the root of the child's disobedience (Locke 2007, 63). Freedom requires the intervention of the mind to suspend the operation of a particular set of willed habits. It requires that, in contrast to Bruno Latour's hiker, there *should* be a moment of hesitation—of stillness—before deciding on the path to follow. But not for everyone. As James Tully notes, Locke's prescriptions for the education of the children of the laboring poor urged an exclusive reliance on disciplinary measures: the new forms of military training being developed in the navy, the regimes of the workhouse, and compulsory apprenticeships enforcing "the activity of repetitious labor, from age three onwards, to fabricate an individual who is habituated to obedience and useful labor" (Tully 1993, 237).[4] In *Some Thoughts concerning Education*, Locke was rather preoccupied with the forms of training that private academies should develop in order to cultivate nonmechanical forms of comportment among the landed gentry and the occupants of liberal occupations. In prescribing the forms of training that a father from such a background should use in educating his son, Locke advocates the virtue of those forms of instruction that seek to instill prescribed codes of conduct through their repetition under the supervision of a tutor. But he insists on the need to do so gradually—not aiming to "settle too many habits at once" but one at a time—so that when "constant custom has made any one thing easy and natural to them, and they practice it without reflection, you may then go on to another" (2007, 45).

We can see clearly here how the relations between habit and repetition produced divergent pathways for different classes. If, in his critique of innate ideas, Locke sought to free conduct from the direction of Catholic forms of spiritual authority, his prescriptions regarding education were targeted at freeing the conduct of elites from the direction of two other forms of authority. First, in opposing such forms of training to earlier Renaissance practices of teaching via the memorization of rules, he sought to free conduct from both the unreliability of memory and its subjection to the traditional forms of authority produced by such a pedagogy. Second, he warned that while parents might exercise their authority directly or delegate it to tutors, they should take care to insulate their children from the contagious infection of their habits that would follow from their exposure to the influence of "unbred or debauched servants" (48).

This, then, is the kind of training that Locke advocates as preparation for the exercise of freedom later in life, an exercise that consists *not* in following the ease of action that results when custom "settles habits of thinking in the understanding, as well as of determining in the will, and of motions in the body" (Locke 1965, 336) but rather in the capacity of reflection to review the ends to which action is directed so long as it remains bound by particular relishes of the mind. For so long as particular uneasinesses have become settled in us as "acquired habits ... which custom has made natural to us," we are not free to contemplate directing our actions to some other end. We are rather tethered to "a constant succession of *uneasinesses*, out of that stock which natural wants or acquired habits have heaped up, [which] take the *will* in their turns; and no sooner is one action dispatched, which by such a determination of the *will* we are set upon, but another uneasiness is ready to set us on work" (216). Freedom is only possible on the condition that the mind suspend the uneasiness which prompts the operation of desire for some particular absent good—and to do so "before the will be determined to action" (218)—so as then to be able to examine the specific end to which such action is committed and weigh it against other possible ends. Only in this way can we effect a "perfection of our nature, to desire, will, and act according to the last result of a fair *examination*" (218). It is only when reflecting on what path to take, hesitating at the crossroads of conflicting courses of action, that freedom can be secured. Suspending the force of particular desires and the will to action they prompt requires a "*standing still*, where we are not sufficiently assured of the way," just as the process of examination is that of "*consulting a guide*" (219). Only when the will is put into action "*following the direction of that guide*" has it been subjected to the direction of a free agent.

In his account of Locke's work as "the first great modern doctrine of the individual subject" (Balibar 2013, 44), Balibar accords pride of place to the distinctive interpretation that Locke placed on the role of consciousness in the constitution of the self. His critique of innate ideas, premised on his contention that there can be no thought that is not conscious of itself as such, was central to his claim that consciousness constitutes what happens in a man's mind as belonging to him, as his property, and as therefore "that, that makes everyone to be, what he calls *self*" (Locke quoted in Balibar 2013, 9). What I have sought to highlight is the role that Locke's attribution of the mind's capacity to stall and take consciousness of its own operations, and the direction it then gives to conduct through the connections it fashions between will and desire within particular "relishes of the mind," plays in the dynamics of his account of the liberal subject. Of such a subject it might be said that he—for it was always he—is habits, nothing but habits, the habit of pausing and reflecting on old habits so as to acquire new ones: Is there any better definition of the liberal subject? But what happens when such a subject is anatomized?

### Anatomizing the liberal subject

In 1771 Johann August Unzer published his *Principles of Physiology*, which, although not using the term, proposed an early version of the logic of the reflex arc in severing the relations between voluntary and involuntary motion as sensory impressions are reflected away from the brain to their point of origin: "The impression is transmitted along the nerve upward to the brain; but ere it reaches there, it is turned from its course, and so reflected downwards, that it excites (as in internal impressions) the nerve of the other remote parts, or the nerve twigs or efferent nerve fibrils of the part receiving the impression; and this internal impression, which is nothing else than the reflected external impression, thus reaches the mechanical machine which has to perform the nerve-action" (Unzer quoted in Fearing 1970, 91). Unzer's work was one of the first accounts of "reflex action" based on the evidence derived from experiments in vivisection that showed that, in the case of frogs, cutting off their heads made no difference to particular forms of stimulus-response behavior. Its use of the vocabulary of "reflection," it should be noted, did not refer to the mind's capacity to reflect on its own operations but rather registered the influence of current preoccupations in optics with the laws of physics governing the behavior of reflected light (Leys 1980). The use of this vocabulary in relation to the reflex arc transposed such laws to the relationship between the body's peripheries (senses) and its center (the spinal cord), and its automatic reflection of impulses back from the latter to the former via the nervous system without any intervention of will or consciousness (figure 3.1). The formalization of the experimental evidence of vivisection and of clinical trials on humans into a theory of the reflex arc came later, most notably in the 1830s with Marshall Hall's conception of the "excito-motory" system as a nervous-muscular system that was structurally and functionally independent of the brain as the seat of consciousness and volition.

Although Unzer's reference to the "mechanical machine" implied a connection to Descartes's account of automata, his anticipation of the logic associated with the subsequent formalization of the reflex arc differed from

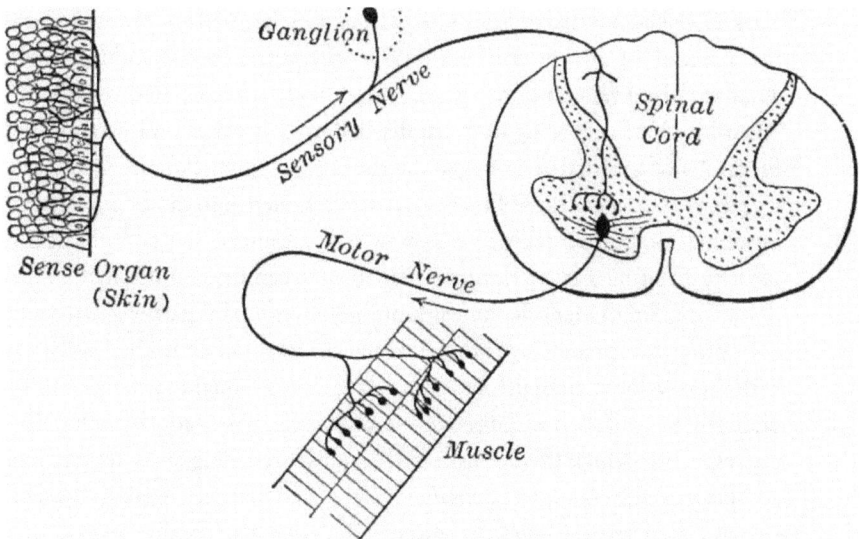

**3.1** The reflex arc. "The spinal cord is the seat of most of the reflex actions of the organs of the trunks and the limbs." From a textbook in general physiology and anatomy. Courtesy of The Book Worm / Alamy Stock Photo.

Descartes's in being based on experimental evidence rather than a purely philosophical conception of mind-body separation. Nonetheless, in some of its interpretations, the reflex arc continued to lend support to the conception of a set of automatic bodily processes operating independently of any controlling influence from the mind. In doing so, it also secured a conception of the continuing independence of the brain as the seat of the mind or soul, thus preserving its status as the locus of an autonomous and potentially free set of operations. The more general tendency, however, particularly toward the end of the nineteenth century, was for neuronal and physiological processes, brain and body, mind and matter, to be brought together on the same plane. This led to an anatomization of the liberal subject through the inscription of the capacity for self-governance in the relations between the body's neural, nervous, and muscular systems. According to such neurological conceptions of personhood, "person and brain became so conceptually linked that modifications to neural processes corresponded not to the loss but rather to the *modification* of self" (Bassiri 2016, 69). This was, however, a capacity for self-governance that could be destroyed should the relations between neuronal and physiological processes be severed or in some way disturbed, thereby impelling conduct on a perilous descent into habits unguided by any direction.

What was at issue here depended on the degree to which habit's pathways, inscribed now in the body's nerves and muscles, could be brought under the direction of the power of inhibition—the power to stop and think—as an anatomized version of the power that Locke had attributed to stillness. "By inhibition," according to T. Lauder Brunton, "we mean the arrest of the functions of a structure or organ, by the action upon it of another, while its power to execute those functions is still retained, and can be manifested as soon as the restraining power is removed" (Brunton quoted in R. Smith 1992, 7). In citing this as a classic late nineteenth-century definition of inhibition, Roger Smith identifies how inhibition functioned as part of a new set of discourses and apparatuses through which the forms of authority associated with the development of psychology and physiology sought to bring conduct under their regulation and direction. However, he places equal emphasis on the respects in which these constituted a somatic recoding of earlier forms of authority over the conduct of conduct. "Language changed: speaking loosely," he says, "spirit became mind, and mind became the upper brain; flesh became body, and body became the spinal nervous system" as earlier "religious, moral and political 'higher' forms of control" were reformulated in terms, "initially psychological, of the mind's control over the body and, later physiological, of the brain's control over the nervous system" (2–3). That said, the political metaphorics of inhibition proved to be both mobile and variable. In one set of uses, the power of inhibition as a form of hierarchical control exercised through the nervous system was likened to that of a higher spiritual or political authority exercising control over lower social orders. By contrast, late nineteenth-century conceptions of the exercise of psychological control over the nervous system that were modeled on the redistribution of forces within a closed-energy system played more to the tune of liberal conceptions of self-regulating technological or economic systems: the role of the governor on steam engines through which the flow of fuel is regulated to maintain a constant speed range, for example, or the self-correcting mechanisms of trade cycles. Interpretations of inhibition also varied according to whether it was used as a physiological term to refer to the action of body on body, as a psychological term to refer to the action of brain on brain, or as a psychological-physiological amalgam to refer to the action of brain on body.

A constant concern, however, was that, if the mechanism of inhibition failed to function properly, conduct would be let off the leash of the will as the automatisms coded into the body's nervous and muscular systems impelled habits on an unstoppable downward path. A host of new figures—the epileptic, the somnambulist, the hypnotized subject—functioned as stand-ins for involuntary and self-reinforcing forms of repetition marking a path of unstoppable descent failing the intervention of an authority (a clinician, psychologist, or psychoanalyst) capable of guiding the subject back along the pathway to psychic equilibrium. Combatting the forms of disorder associated with the severance of habits from the control of the will also introduced a new actor into the network of internal relations through which the economy of the subject's actions was organized. This consisted in the increasing importance accorded to the role of attention. Although the fuller development of this would come later, notably in the work of Théodule Ribot (1890), Smith accords a leading role to the new inflection lent to the concept of reflex action by W. D. Carpenter's concept of "ideo-motor" actions through which "an idea present in the mind automatically and involuntarily resulted in a corresponding movement" (R. Smith 1992, 43). This presented the potential for a descent into debilitating habits unless these were countered by the disciplinary training of ideomotor actions calculated to guide conduct along paths of ethical self-restraint. As a counter to this threatening lack of self-control, Carpenter envisaged the will as being obliged to operate through the mediation of attention. Only the volitional direction of the attention could determine which of the automatic functions associated with ideomotor actions would predominate, with the consequence that the "lack or misdirection of attention" could foster "an involuntary life of bad habits or worse" (43).

## Acting on habit: Buttressing the will, transforming urban milieus

These, then, are among the developments that produced a new place for habit in the architectures of personhood arising from nineteenth-century developments in physiology, psychology, and neurology. One manifestation of these developments was in the tendency for forms of behavior that had previously been regarded as the result of volitional activity to be reclassified—albeit not without contestation—as unwilled actions. These are among the issues that Mariana Valverde (1998a) addresses in her study of the different ways in which alcoholism has been conceived and combatted on the part different authorities. Focusing on the British context, Valverde contrasts nineteenth-century approaches to the regulation of drinking practices with earlier approaches to drunkenness that, concerned mainly with its manifestation in public contexts, treated it as a voluntary activity and, as such, to be addressed via legal measures—primarily short-term imprisonment—intended to deter offenders from recommitting the offense. And, as we have seen, drunkenness was just as much a willed habit for Locke as more virtuous habits. By contrast, the new condition of "alcoholism" revolved principally around its conception as an involuntary habit—"an inability to control the thirst for stimulants"—whose cause was rooted not in drink itself but in a deficiency in some aspect of the physiopsychological makeup of those who became "slaves to the drink habit" (Valverde 1998b, 227).[5] An addiction rather than a disease proper, its conception as a "disease of the will" differentiated it from diseases that affected everyone indiscriminately in both the etiology ascribed to it and the means of curing it. For since it derived from a deficiency of the will, its cure depended on forms of medico-psychological intervention that would buttress the will by enlisting the frayed capacities of the individual as a self-governing subject in supervised programs directed toward freeing them from the "drinking habit."

This, at least, was one response. A second, rather than seeking to cure excessive drinking through the mental effort required for flexing the will to bear on the task, recommended abstinence as the best means of shallowing the grooves that repetitive drinking habits had carved into the body's nervous and neural channels. And neither of these positions entirely displaced the activities of religious, temperance, self-help, and reform movements, which, in campaigns working through the coordinates provided by Christian or earlier liberal conceptions of personhood, sought to lead the drunkard back along the path to sobriety and righteousness.

There were also distinctive new cultural terms in which proposals for mobilizing the will to combat alcoholism were couched. Henry Cole (1875), the founding director of the South Kensington Museum, lamenting the weakened hold of religious institutions on the urban working classes, urged the opening of art galleries to take their place and, in so doing, to provide an alternative to the attractions of the pub or gin palace. Cole placed special emphasis on the ability of art galleries to contribute to this outcome without trespassing on the freedom of the subject. The work of John Stuart Mill was influential in this regard. In proposing the "habit of willing" as a means of breaking habits as a prelude to establishing new ones, Mill (1967, 550–51) urged the cultivation of this capacity as a means of overcoming the suggestion, associated with new accounts of the instincts, that being free and being subject to habits were contraries. Such conceptions had a significant bearing on questions of public policy given the prevailing conception of pauperism as a condition that could be avoided through the exercise of the will. When conjoined to the concerns clustered around Foucault's "Malthusian couple" (1998a, 105), this placed great stress on the need to equip workingmen with the ability to discharge the ethical responsibility that was placed on male heads of households to exercise prudential restraint in their conjugal relationships and in all other aspects of household management as the only means of preventing descent into poverty and starvation at the expense of the public purse. In echoing these concerns— "people that are allowed to get as drunk as they can, starve their wives and children, looking to others in the end to find coffins for themselves and feed them in the workhouse beforehand" (Cole 1875, 364)—Cole also registered the liberty of the subject as ruling out compulsory mechanisms for the regulation of drunkenness. In looking to art galleries as a potential solution, then, he drew on contemporary conceptions of the value attributed to art as a morally improving force that would incline the workingman to shun the gin palace or public house not because he had been compelled to do so but because the desire-will nexus that linked alcoholism to pauperism had been broken so that he would no longer *wish* to go there (figures 3.2 and 3.3).[6]

Although the currency of these conceptions continued into the 1870s, the assumptions on which they were based were radically undermined toward the end of the century. The moral economy underlying pauperism as "largely an

**3.2** C. Gregory, *Sunday Afternoon in a London Gin Palace, Drawn from Life*, in *The Graphic*, February 8, 1879, p. 130. Courtesy of Look and Learn.

**3.3** *Sunday Afternoon in a Picture Gallery, Drawn from Life*, unattributed engraving in *The Graphic*, February 8, 1879, p. 134. Courtesy of Look and Learn.

act of will ... associated with drink, improvidence, irreligion, and idleness" that Cole drew on gave way, Gareth Stedman Jones argues, to a conception of "chronic poverty" as something imposed on the working classes by the conditions of city life. Savage and brutalizing in themselves, these also placed the habits of the urban poor beyond the reach of liberal strategies of self-reform in impelling the poor "to escape the dreadful monotony of their conditions of existence by craving the 'cheap excitements' offered by the pubs, the low music-halls, and the streets" (Stedman Jones 1976, 286). There are many other aspects to how the relationships between habit and city life were reconfigured in the closing decades of the nineteenth century.[7] Those most relevant to my concerns here are those referenced by Thomas Osborne and Nikolas Rose in their account of the transition from practices oriented to directing how city populations might be able to govern themselves to practices oriented to governing them indirectly, behind their backs as it were, via action on the urban milieus that constituted the conditions of their existence. Comparing the varying "urban diagrams" through which the governance of city populations has been mediated across different forms of power, they trace how the tasks of governing city populations in Britain changed across the course of the nineteenth century. Initially "a motely of inventive projects intended to make urban existence the site of a certain regulated and civilized freedom" (Osborne and Rose 1999, 740), these evinced, by the end of the century, a concern with the "negative spiral of interaction between milieu and character" (743) suggested by the deteriorating conduct of the urban poor. Given that this assigned responsibility for such conduct to the effects of urban environments on the dispositions of the poor, remedial action needed to concern itself with reshaping such environments on the assumption that improvements in the moral character of the poor would follow as a matter of course rather than acting on character directly as a possible locus of voluntary self-reform. If, as Osborne and Rose put it, the city's poor had bad habits, the appropriate response was "not so much to act directly upon those habits themselves but to modify the city so as to induce the right kind of habits" (743).

This is not to say that questions of character were entirely displaced by such conceptions. To the contrary, as Stefan Collini (1979) and others have argued, account has to be taken of how the problematics of character associated with mid-nineteenth-century liberalism were altered by the historicization of character effected by post-Darwinian social and political thought. If Mill's account of the relations between will and character afforded a means through which habits might be directed along a path of voluntary self-reform, the historicization of these categories led to different populations being placed at different points along such developmental pathways as a consequence of the uneven distribution of the accumulated accomplishments required to follow their course. This involved something more than the temporal dimension that Osborne and Rose suggest in noting that the urban environment was often conceived as an engine for the generation of bad habits, "giving them impetus, exacerbating them, prolonging them, spreading them," as "bad habits engendered further habits" (1999, 743). It also opened up the prospect that the positive dynamics of habit's pathways might be put into reverse, leading, for some, not merely to their bad habits accumulating through time but to their—and their descendants—being dragged back through evolutionary time to successively lower layers of development. This, the prospect of degeneration—of not merely standing still or failing to get started on habit's progressive pathways but being dragged back along them—was another aspect of the accounts of habit associated with the tradition of organic memory discussed in the previous chapter. It was, moreover, one in which the progressive logic of Locke's account of the ease that follows from the repetitive association of ideas in the understanding still applied, albeit thrown into reverse, as each step along habit's downward pathways made the next one easier. This was now, however, a pathway that was inscribed in the grooves that repetitive action had carved in the body's nervous and neural systems, grooves that thereby came to be already etched into the physiological constitution of the next generation.

## Dissolution: Habit's descending pathways

In highlighting the significance accorded to the manipulation of urban milieus as an indirect way of acting on the conduct of city populations, Osborne and Rose's account echoes the significance that Foucault accords to strategies of governing through the management of milieus associated with the biopolitical orientations of modern forms of governmentality. His key formulations on this subject come at the end of his discussion of the governance of leprosy and plagues effected, respectively, by the territorializing logic of sovereignty as manifested in the power of separation imposed on the leper and the disciplinary forms of surveillance and control inflicted on plague-stricken cities. Foucault then goes on to identify the distinctiveness of the strategies that were later developed for managing pandemics, exemplified by smallpox, as consisting in trying "to plan a milieu in terms of events or series of events . . . that will have to be regulated within a multivalent and transformable framework" (Foucault 2007a, 20). Drawing on Georges Canguilhem's classic discussion, he identifies a milieu as the medium through which bodies interact with and upon one another.[8] When conceived as a field of intervention for acting on city populations, the practices through which governing via milieus is effected differ from those "affecting individuals as a set of legal subjects capable of voluntary actions" (sovereignty) and from those acting on "bodies capable of... required performances" (discipline), acting instead on "a population" as a "multiplicity of individuals... bound to the materiality within which they live" (21).

In summarizing the effects of the emergence of this new form of governance, Foucault argues that they consisted in the conjunction of the "'naturalness' of the human species within an artificial milieu" as a set of connections that is subject to the "political artifice of a power relation" (22). This substitution of the human species for earlier humanist conceptions of "mankind"—a process initiated toward the end of the seventeenth century—entailed a shift from the exercise of power over the "fine-grain of individual behaviors" (66) to a conception of the "general regime of living beings" as constituting "a surface on which authoritarian, but reflected and calculated transformations can get a hold" (75). This shift in the modalities of power is accompanied by a series of parallel, but equally critical, transformations concerning the widened range of variables bearing on the conduct of populations that governing practices must take account of. These go beyond the natural environment and climatic variations to include variations in material surroundings; in commercial activity and the circulation of wealth as well as that of diseases; in laws, customs, and educational practices; and, as the issues Osborne and Rose foreground in their discussion of the relations between milieu and character, ethical codes of conduct. They also include the different ways in which population is figured in a "whole series of knowledges" (76). Foucault places special emphasis here on the transformation of the eighteenth-century regime of classification focused on the identification of the external characteristics distinguishing different forms of life to a concern with "the internal organization of the organism" and thence to the varied conceptions—most notably those of Jean-Baptiste Lamarck and Charles Darwin—of the "constitutive or regulatory relationships" between the organism and "the milieu in which it lives" (77).

It was the accounts of such "constitutive or regulatory relationships" that were forged in the interactions between medicine, psychology, and evolutionary thought from the mid- to late nineteenth century that provided the conceptual incubator for the problematic of degeneration. I should, though, say "problematics of degeneration" since the specific forms of interaction between these disciplines varied between France and Britain. There were some generally shared characteristics: a conception of debilitating environmental conditions (slums, poor diet, disease) coming to be inscribed in the body through its nervous, muscular, and pulmonary systems and the translation of these into demoralizing codes of behavior; the role of habit in converting these environmental effects into a descending pathway of physical, psychological, and moral degeneration; the location of these processes within the body's nervous system, reflexes, and instincts, placing them beyond the reach of consciousness and its potential reforming influence; and the transmission of the degenerative qualities accumulated in a single lifetime to the next generation via the mechanism of inheritance. "The individual," as Laura Otis puts it, "not only inherited a 'burden' of nervous disease but also added to it through experience in an unhealthy environment, then transmitted the increased burden to descendants" (1994, 42). There were, however, significant differences between Britain and France in the positions accorded men and women in the transgenerational dynamics of degeneration. In France, Valverde argues, with Émile Zola's Rougon-Macquart novels primarily in mind, alcoholic men and degenerate women, although assigned different roles, were both held responsible for the downward path of degeneration. In Britain, by contrast (Valverde 1998a, 51–54), and as a marked departure from Cole's central concern with male drunkenness, it was women who, toward the century's end, were judged to be primarily responsible for the transmission of alcoholism as a hereditary taint (Scene of Habit 4). It was, consequently, women who were most targeted by the 1898 Habitual Drunkards Act, accounting for nearly all the compulsory admissions to inebriate retreats between 1899 and 1910 (Morrison 2017, 110–11).

The terms in which the problem of degeneration was posed in Britain were also distinct, in Daniel Pick's estimation, owing to the respects in which these reworked the relations between habit and the will associated with the classical liberal problematic of character. The most influential theorist in these regards was Henry Maudsley, whose work, as Pick summarizes it, was situated at "the confluence of a medico-psychiatric theory of *dégénérescence*, a Darwinian theory of evolutionary regression and a positivist theory of criminal inheritance, all of which in their turn flowed in a wider current of concern about the pathology of the city and modernity" (Pick 1989, 203). The reference to *"dégénérescence"* here is to Benedict Morel's *Traité des dégénérescence physiques, intellectuelles, et morales de l'espèce humaine* (1857). Conventionally

*Scene of Habit 4—Vampirism and Habitual Compulsion*

It is no accident that in Bram Stoker's *Dracula*, first published in 1895, it is Lucy Westenra's thirst for blood that crystallizes contemporary concerns regarding degenerative addictions. Susan Zieger interprets Dracula's blood drinking as "a crime of irrational, infantile repetition"—Dracula and his family, as she puts it, have to get up every day just for a drink—that was governed by a set of discourses that effected a systematic "othering" of a range of constituencies in the depiction of their "compulsive dependence on unreasoning habit" (Zieger 2008, 208). In one respect this othering referred to the forms of degeneracy attributed to the urban poor while also having a racialized aspect, Dracula's Transylvanian ancestry being widely interpreted as a coded reference to the racial inferiority attributed to the Irish. At the same time, the novel troubles this distinction in the parallels it floats between the allusions to the alcoholism represented by Dracula and his vampiric recruits, especially Lucy Westenra, and a series of distinctly modern forms of addiction associated with the rhythms and technologies of modernity. Zieger thus singles out the role played by a range of new media (the typewriter, recorded sound, photographs) as well as chemically induced sleep in the procedures through which Jonathan Harker, Minna Harker—his fiancée and, later, wife—and Dr. Van Helsing pursue Dracula. In constituting the mediations through which these pursuers connect with the vampire world, these technologies also routinize their activities in ways that align them with that world, "making their actions compulsive rather than volitional" (213). Jonathan Harker thus tellingly draws on the image of the groove as a synonym for "rut"—an image that had acquired a new currency through the association of the groove with new phonographic technologies of sound recording—in telling Dr. Helsing that the disturbance to his life occasioned by Lucy's sleepwalking had meant that, no longer knowing what to trust or what to do, the only course he could follow was "to keep on working in what had hitherto been the groove of my life" (Stoker 2011, 226). This was a course, however, that had been of no avail to him before Dr. Helsing's reassurances regarding Lucy allowed him once again to trust to the grooves of a life comprising the everyday routines of a white-collar worker. In these ways, Zieger argues, *Dracula* depicts addiction "as one of many compulsive, mechanized habituations and dependencies inhabited by white middle-class professionals, not just racially marked, deviant super-natural beings" (2008, 213).

regarded as the founding text of degeneration theory, this interpreted habit as the driver of the processes through which unhealthy deviations from the normal produced by the pathogenic conditions of one's milieu, and reinforced through repeated automatisms, led to regressive morphological and psychological adaptations that were passed on from generation to generation in a steady descent toward progressive decadence.[9]

Rather than simply adopting Morel's account of degeneration, Maudsley inflected it through the reworking of the role of habit derived from Locke's account of the association of ideas that, in a tradition running from Alexander Bain to Herbert Spencer, had relocated the principles of associationism from the mind to the body's physiological and neurological processes. Robert Young, in assessing the significance of the intellectual shifts effected by these two thinkers, argues that Bain's chief contribution consisted in the emphasis he placed on the significance of the body's motility and the effects it engendered. In contrast to Locke's passive sensationalism, which, taking no account of the effects of bodies in movement, focused solely on the impressions registered via the senses, Bain argued that "the exercise of active energy originating in purely internal impulses, independent of the stimulus produced by outward impressions, is a primary fact of our constitution" (Bain quoted in R. Young 1970, 15). This constituted, in Young's estimation, a key step in the transformation of associational psychology from an epistemological science into "a psychophysical science of feeling, knowing, and willing" in which "knowing was the result of experiences consequent upon doing" (R. Young 1970, 120).

It was, however, Spencer who brought Bain's perspective that experience derived from embodied forms of mobile behavior into a dialogue with evolutionary thought through which the principles of associationism were simultaneously corporealized, temporalized, and collectivized. Adaptations to changing environments accumulate through time to become naturalized responses to new environments through a mechanism for association located not in the understanding but in the repetitions generated by the nervous system. This was a mechanism that extended beyond the experiences accumulated by individuals in their lifetimes to the collective accumulation of experience on the part of different races. "By replacing the *tabula rasa* of the individual with that of the race," Young argues, "Spencer was able to retain the basic proposition of sensationalism while recognizing the inherited biological endowments in the nervous system, and avoiding the risk of the rationalist belief in innate ideas" (178). The stock of instincts that is the result of such inherited endowments transmits to each generation a set of associations between embodied actions that, as a repertoire of inherited habits, come easily and naturally. In thus historicizing the principles of associationism, Spencer nonetheless retained the Lockean contention that stalling the effects of such ease of action to contemplate alternative courses of action was the characteristic feature of the intellectual mind. "Delay in action," for Spencer, Smith thus says, "characterized the rational man" (R. Smith 1992, 149). But this was now a delay effected by neurophysiological mechanisms, albeit still one that was unevenly distributed. The routes taken by the nervous discharges in the brain of the uncultivated man, as Spencer put it, "are less numerous, less involved, less varied in the resistance they offer" than in the cultivated man, with the consequence that "the number of ideas that can follow a given antecedent is smaller, and the degrees of strength with which they can present themselves are fewer," so that "the possibilities of thought are more limited, and the balancing between alternative conclusions less easy" (Spencer quoted in R. Smith 1992, 149).

For Spencer, this capacity of delay was an effect of the will that, rather than taking as a given, he interpreted as the by-product of the processes through which acquired competencies are coded into the body as hereditable instincts that are then transmitted to the next generation as part of a historically accumulating set of aptitudes. It is only the somatic accumulation of the successive experiences of past generations that have come to be coded into the body as a set of compound instincts through the mechanism of organic memory (the term was originally Spencer's) that opens up the space and the time within which the higher faculties of reason and the will might emerge and be exercised. The will, as the final outcome of this process, emerges at a point when the complexity that results from the accumulation of inheritances stalls the force of the automatic mechanisms of habitual repetition. This produces an indeterminacy of action brought about by the relations between inherited motor mechanisms and the will, interpreted as an ideal motor mechanism that, if exerted at such moments of stalled action, becomes actual. It is when this happens that "there is constituted a state of consciousness which, when it finally issues in action, exhibits what we term volition ... and this passing of an ideal motor change into a real one, is that which we distinguish as Will" (H. Spencer 1996, 613). Such antagonistic relations between different mechanical sources of action that open up the possibility for the will to emerge and assert itself are thus, for Spencer, only possible once a certain level of complexity within the makeup of the person has been attained.

Maudsley also interpreted the will as an outcome of the processes of evolution. It is, he says, "the power by which nature developing through man accomplishes the progressive path of its destiny, the nature-made means by which nature is made better" (Maudsley 1884, 190). As the end product of the processes through which environmental influences—natural and social—have been incorporated "by involution in the structure and constitution of his nervous system," man's "well-informed will" constitutes "the initiation of a new step in evolution" (190). Maudsley's conception of this next step is shaped by the complex web he weaves in, on the one hand, rejecting traditional theological conceptions of habit's role on the pathway to grace mediated by a priesthood while, on the other hand, interpreting involution—that is, the storage of evolution's advances in inherited capacities—as the mechanism through which a teleology derived from the dynamics of life and superintended by the evolutionary theorist might be realized. The realization of this "new step in evolution" hinges on whether the will—once it has incorporated the corrective force of inhibition and thus the moment of delay that allows a critical shifting of the desires that would otherwise impel the will to action—might go one step further. This step would consist in an aspiration to free will as "a creation of the imagination which inflames the notion of duty and fortifies the *ought* through the desire that it inspires to realize the ideal" (191). This "path of the moral law in social evolution" is that which confers on the categorical imperative its true authority: "Thou shalt go the right way of development, thou shalt not go the wrong way of degeneration" (191).

A key factor at stake in determining which of these futures might be realized consists in which of the pathways that have been carved into the nervous system by habit's repetitions and those of organic memory might predominate. The accumulation of habits, acquired as consciousness and will break with old habits and initiate new ones that are then performed unconsciously, contributes to a developmental process of "ascending complexity" (13). Maudsley likens this process to "a grand and noble river which, when traced back to its source in a little rill, is seen to have grown by the successive inflow of many similar little streams" (14). A little later in his discussion, this stream is translated into the "chain of causation" that connects individuals to their ancestral past via the mechanisms of organic memory. It is through these mechanisms that the "tricks of manner, of speech, of walk, of handwriting, of gesture and the like" (26) of remote ancestors are acquired as innate capacities in ways that entirely bypass the operations of imitation or consciousness. If habit has the potential to convert these legacies into "energies of organic becoming" (146), it is equally the case that this dynamism can break down so that the tracks that the repetitions of habit have carved in the nervous system become ever more deeply rooted. This occurs when "custom dulls perceptive consciousness, till perception becomes almost or quite automatic; we practice it habitually ... without consciousness of what we are doing, and experience the greatest difficulty in the world to go outside the path of habit" (160).

There is, however, another pathway in which habit is inscribed, one that, neither shaped by a dynamic of becoming nor exhibiting a condition of pure stasis, is governed by a downward dynamic in which the relations between evolution and involution are put into reverse: "All the changes that take place are not ascending steps of evolution, some of them are descending steps of degeneration; not all of them events of a becoming, many of them events of an unbecoming; not all of them the products of doing, many of them the products of an undoing; organisms undergoing degenerative modifications that render them less fit for their purposes, and retrograde organic products being formed that act to produce dissolution" (183). As the opposite of involution, degeneration is a process of *"unkinding*, the undoing of a kind ... a change from a higher to a lower kind, that is to say, from a more complex to a less complex organization" (240). Two paths, then, tending in different directions but conforming to the same logic in which each step along the path makes the next one easier. These paths have their exemplars. "*Some* persons," as Maudsley puts it, "are high on the upward, others low on the downward, path; many are just entering upon the one or the other; but there is no one who is not himself going in the one or the other direction and making the way which he takes easier for others to follow in" (245). And the suspension of the "inhibitive powers of the higher social or moral sort" that accompany each downward step lead to "an ever-increasing mischief as habit makes the way of disorder easier and the return to order harder" (272).

### Desanctifying the conduct of life

The will's "highest quality," Maudsley argues, consists in its inhibitive power "to hold impulses in check" (109). Although interpreting this power as the culmination of a long process of heredity, he looks to the mechanisms of the nervous system for the light they might throw on this "exalted governing function—this capacity, when impulse urges, to act from duty" (109). Invoking the purely physiological mechanism of the reflex arc, he recalls the evidence of experiments in vivisection demonstrating stimulus-response modes of action effected via the nervous system without any intervention of the will or consciousness. This leads Maudsley to posit the existence of two parallel systems, one driven by the "rudiments of volition," effecting "the power to command execution of a purpose," and the second substituting "the path of enlightened prudence or duty in preference to the path of natural proclivity," effecting "the power to stay execution" (112–13). Both are located within and operate by means of the body's structures. However, if the first is grounded in the body's nerve centers mediated by the reflex arc, the second derives its power from the brain's "countless multitude of inter-connected nerve-centers . . . ready to be stirred into action by suitable stimulation to increase, to combine, to restrain, to neutralize, to modify in unknown ways one another's function" (114). He draws on the contemporary *Bradshaw's Railway Guide* to drive his point home. If this tells "the times of starting, the stoppages, the junctions, the destination, and the times of arrival of every train on every line in the country," the brain similarly works through its own and the body's "multitudinous stations, tracks, junctions and branch lines, its quick trains and slow trains of thought" (115). It is in the interactions between these two purely physiological systems that "the ease of performance which we call habit is acquired" (116) as the breaks, disjunctions, and reroutings effected by the brain are translated into new forms of routinized action.

In developing this argument, Maudsley pits it against theological accounts of free will, repeatedly calling into question the grounds on which they have laid a claim to direct conduct along habit's pathways. He identifies his target clearly enough, defining free will as the doctrine that "will is essentially a self-procreating, self-sustaining spiritual entity, which owns no natural cause, obeys not law, and has no sort of affinity with matter" but which yet, as a divine implant in the human, functions as an "immaterial entity in a material world, the events of which it largely determines" (2). While critiquing its theoretical inconsistencies, Maudsley reserves his sharpest criticisms of this doctrine for its lack of any consequential relevance for the tasks of social governance. Although "a cherished dogma of the study . . . it has not imbued the regulations made for the conduct of life" (8). The diversion of "the ill-disposed will from the direction of wrong-doing and to constrain it to take the path of a higher and freer development in well-doing . . . has plainly been the slow effect of the administration of laws upon the conscience of mankind through the ages" (8). The habitual repetitions across generations of the conducts enforced by such laws inscribe a sense of right and wrong as an immediate and instinctive capacity of "well-constituted beings" (9). Interpreting this as "an instance of use-made nature such as is seen everywhere in the transformation of laborious conscious into easy automatic function" (9), Maudsley argues that this is a process that can guide the will along a path of either moral development or moral deterioration.

Which of these will prevail depends on the constitution of the authorities that exercise effective responsibility for the conduct of conduct. Maudsley looks to the combined authority of physiologists and sociologists as the new forms of authority required to guide conduct along a path of evolutionary development impelled by a spiritual force transferred from a deity to nature. The key challenge facing this new disciplinary constellation is that of offsetting the demoralizing effects of the egoistical tendencies of modernity symbolized, at a number of points in Maudsley's discussion, by contrasting the virtues of village life with the demoralizing effects of city environments. The antisocial effects of the egoism prompted by the conditions of city life in one generation prepare the ground for the social disintegration of the next generation. It is the egoistic individual—"the intensely narrow, self-sensitive, suspicious, distrustful, deceitful and self-deceiving individual . . . incapable by nature and habit of genuinely healthy communion either with himself or with his kind" (293)—who is responsible for the degeneracy of his progeny. And it is primarily to sociology that Maudsley looks as the key counter to such tendencies. For it is only sociology that can engage with the higher levels of human complexity that are the product of habit's inscription in the processes through which man accomplishes the progressive path of nature's destiny: "The social organism is not a mere physiological organism; it is that and a great deal more, being essentially of historical significance, and requiring, in order to be understood, the study of antecedent social states; and it will demand in the end a new and more complex conception of organism than anything that physiology alone can furnish" (190). But in no case "is it an inspiration from heaven which giveth the autonomy" to such higher levels of complexity relative to physical, chemical, and physiological laws; "it is always the inspiration that is on earth and is manifested in every pulse of evolution" (190).

Early in his discussion of the reflex arc, Maudsley attributes the responsibility for first introducing the principle of motion into physiology to Maine de Biran. It was, he argues, Maine de Biran's account of the relations between motor adaptations and the senses of touch and sight that established the need for approaches to the ego to take account of its "inseparability from the non-ego" (48). This glosses over the more distinctive role that the relations between speaking and hearing played in Maine de Biran's account of the dynamics of habit. Arguing that the hearing of oneself that usually accompanies the activity of speaking confers the "unique and infinitely precious advantage of making the individual doubly present to himself" (Maine de Biran 1929, 223), he argues that this introduced a form of double consciousness that, prizing apart the chains of "passive habit," opens up the possibility of initiating "active habits." By converting the unthinking repetitions of passive habit into willed repetitions, such active habits give rise to a course of (relatively) free self-development. It was this fusion of contemporary physiological conceptions of habit and earlier Christian conceptions of its role as an aspect of the soul's journey toward grace that laid the foundations for the distinguishing trait of the wayward tradition in habit theory: namely, its conception of habit as having a natural foundation but also giving way to a process of self-formation leading to the acquisition of a "second nature."

It will therefore be useful, before probing the wayward tradition more closely, to look at the role of habit in Christian theology. For this is the root source of habit's conception as part of a pathway of development that is specific to Western intellectual traditions within which it has subsequently been reworked in different ways. Habit's theological conception, however, was always as part of a guided pathway, albeit one along which the "second nature" attained by some was at the price of its denial to others. It is therefore to the light that Foucault's account of the role of habit in the practices of pastoral government throws on these questions that I turn in the next chapter. This will pave the way for the terms in which, in subsequent chapters, I engage with current debates prompted, inter alia, by the rehabilitation of habit proposed by the wayward tradition. It will also provide a context for giving the concept of conduct more sustained attention than I have accorded it so far.

# 4

# Pathways
# to Virtue

TOWARD THE END OF THE FOURTH LECTURE in his *Security, Territory, Population* series, Michel Foucault tells his audience that he had had second thoughts about the title he had chosen for that series, judging a "history of 'governmentality'" a better indication of the issues he had wanted it to address. These, as he summarizes them, concern the respects in which the principles of sovereignty had been partly displaced, and partly inflected in new directions, by the trio of government, population, and economy: that is, by the production of population as a new field of government practices whose form was shaped by political economy as both a distinct science and a set of techniques for intervening in the management of population. In the genealogy of governmentality that he goes on to offer, Foucault focuses initially on the processes through which it emerged "from the archaic model of the Christian pastorate" (Foucault 2007a, 110). In distinguishing pastoral power in terms of its production of a new subject form through the "continuous networks of obedience" (185) that it organized, he argues that this provided "the inner depth and background" (215) of the forms of governmentality that begin to develop in the sixteenth century. And if, as he argues, the trio of government, population, and economy is still with us, the same is true of pastoral government—both as it continues as a specific set of institutions and practices oriented to directing the conduct of Christian communities and also through its provision of an "inner depth and background" for the exercise of modern forms of governmentality.

The concept of conduct constitutes the key hinge through which the practices of pastoral government are carried through into the underpinnings of governmentality. The interactions between the term's two main meanings are key here. These, as Foucault summarizes them, refer to "the activity of conducting" in the sense of leading or directing the actions of others and to "the way in which one conducts oneself," which, in its turn, is affected by how one "lets oneself be conducted" (193). It is, then, how these interactions between being governed, governing others, and governing oneself shaped the Christian pastorate's concern with "the conduct of souls" that constituted its chief bequest to the sixteenth-century emergence of governmentality. Its influence in this regard was identifiable in the intensification of the traditional forms of the spiritual authority of the pastorate occasioned by the struggles between the Reformation and the Counter-Reformation; in the significance placed on questions concerning how one should conduct oneself in the foundational texts of modern philosophy; and in the new significance accorded to the governance of varied forms of public conduct. The new strategies for governing conduct developed for this purpose both redefined the concerns of sovereign power while also becoming progressively more—but never entirely—distinct from the forms of pastoral power they drew on.[1]

So much by way of summarizing the main lines of connection that Foucault attributes to the concept of conduct in mediating the relations between pastoral and governmental forms of power. The distinguishing feature of pastoral power that he identifies for this purpose consisted in the role accorded the pastorate of guiding souls along the road to salvation, a problematic in which habit figured both as that which must be broken with and as that which must be cultivated to secure one's passage along the pathway to virtue. This was a pathway whose course was defined by this tension between habit's dualities. These dualities were not merely definitional; their distribution was profoundly social. The conception of habit as part of a virtuous pathway leading to the acquisition of grace functioned as a selective attribute limited, in its most developed forms, to the higher reaches of the pastorate and those committed to the monastic life. The association of habit with freedom that this engendered was not a freedom of choice, but a freedom associated with a capacity to attain a range of virtues or perfections whose acquisition—particularly spiritual virtues—was unevenly distributed between the pastorate and lay populations and between different levels of the pastorate. The duality of habit thus constituted a lever for acting on habits that was differentiated in its operations depending on its distribution across different sections of the population.

In examining, in this chapter, the role of habit in what Foucault called the "binary structure" (Foucault 2007a, 202) of pastoral government, I prepare the ground for my consideration, in later chapters, of the respects in which this structure has continued to inform key episodes in the subsequent political career of habit. I look first at the significance of the new inflection that Christian thought lent to classical conceptions of habit's dualities by relating these to the concerns associated with theological conceptions of the schismatic structure of the will. I then go on to consider Foucault's discussion of the "economy of merits and faults" (183) through which the pastorate's governance of habits was meant to shepherd souls along the pathway to salvation. This prepares the way for a consideration of how the habit-obedience couplet through which the governance of souls takes place operated in relation to the social divisions composing the binary structure of pastoral government. I conclude the chapter by discussing the role that Foucault accorded communities and mysticism—as two of the late medieval forms of counterconduct directed against the forms of authority exercised by the pastorate—in paving the way for the subsequent refashioning of the techniques of pastoral government in the context of modern forms of governmentality. I do so with a view to identifying how the legacies of such struggles have contributed to the ways in which secularized forms of spiritual authority have been invoked in subsequent contests over the direction of habit's second nature.[2] This constitutes, I shall argue, a legacy of the form of pastoral power that is, as Foucault aptly put it, "doubtless something from which we have still not freed ourselves" (148).

## Habit and the pastoral governance of souls

I have already alluded to the semantic ambiguity of the term *habit*, an ambiguity that derives from the tendency—initially in Christian thought—to merge two usages that were kept distinct in the Aristotelian tradition. Nicolas Faucher and Magali Roques summarize the main issues involved in the distinction Aristotle proposed between the concepts of *consuetudo* and *hexis*—habit as a disabling form of automatic repetition or as an enabling mechanism facilitating the acquisition of new dispositions—that was later carried over into the distinction (never complete) in the theological literature between habit and habitus. Whereas the connotations of the former are deterministic—"a creature of habit is one who is incapable of shedding its usual behaviours"—habitus, although also a product of the repetition of similar acts, differs in the respect that, by placing those acts at our disposal and improving our capacity to perform them, they "are an essential part of being free, in the sense of being capable of performing a broad range of actions" (Faucher and Roques 2018, 19). Habit comprises acts we have no power over; *hexis* or habitus comprises acts that empower—without compelling—us to acquire new capacities. If Christian theology oscillated between these usages, combining or distinguishing them in different permutations, it further complicated matters through the introduction of the will as the locus for desire and voluntary motion—willed acts—aimed at the attainment of the good as determined by the deliberations of the intellect.

The seeds of this conception of personhood are commonly attributed to Saint Augustine of Hippo, who, in introducing the will, also divided it against itself to provide an account of how involuntary chains of servitude could be forged as a result of the will's liability—after the original sin of Adam and Eve—to sinful misdirection. Although the position accorded habit in this account was tied up with its relations to the libido and sexual desire, Augustine also stressed the respects in which the divisions of the will are shaped by a tension between past and present.

> I sighed after [the] freedom [to dedicate all my time to God], but was bound not by an iron imposed by anyone else but by the iron of my own volition. The enemy had a grip on my will and so had made a chain to hold me prisoner. The consequence of a distorted will is passion. By servitude to passion, habit is formed, and habit to which there is no resistance becomes necessity. By these close-knit links, bound one to another—which is why I have called it a chain—an unyielding subjection held me in confinement. The new will, which was beginning to be within me a will to freely serve and enjoy you, God, the only sure source of pleasure, was not yet strong enough to overcome my older will, which had the strength of habit. So my two wills, one old, the other new, one carnal, the other spiritual, were in conflict with one another, and their discord dispersed my psyche. (Augustine quoted in Heiner 2009, 81)[3]

Brady Thomas Heiner, from whom I take this passage from *The Confessions*, cites a further passage from Augustine that attributes habit's negative power to the force of the past—interpreted as the legacy of the Fall—as an "inheritance of our first parents" that has "grown in upon our flesh by a law of nature" (Augustine quoted in Heiner 2009, 81). Peter Brown draws attention to another passage in which the force of habit is linked to that of memory in likening its weight—via a reference to Lazarus lying four days in his tomb—to the dead pull of the past, in which the pleasure of past evils is amplified in being remembered and repeated (Brown 2000, 142). As such, habit was a negative force to be combatted, especially among those sections of the population of the late (fifth-century) Roman imperium in whom its force was believed to be strongest. While registering Augustine's alertness to the corrupting influence of habit among all strata, Brown notes its greater prevalence—both in Augustine's texts and in his performance of his pastoral duties—among the laity relative to the priesthood, and among pagans relative to Christians. Heiner, drawing on Michael Hardt and Antonio Negri's (2000) discussion of the form of sovereign power they attribute to the late Roman Empire, views Augustine's account of habit as the source of a political anthropology that lay at the root of that power in its analogical attribution to the multitude of the intransigent, wayward inertia exercised by the force of habit in the human body. Lacking the capacity for reasoned self-inspection required for self-governance, the predominant force of habit among the multitude required its subjection to both the secular authority of the sovereign and the spiritual authority of the church if its members were to be prized away from the hold of habit and set on the road to salvation.

Daniele Lorenzini (2019), focusing more on Augustine's account of the schismatic structure of the will, places a greater stress on its relations to the development of pastoral power. Unable to trust their will and therefore unable to govern themselves autonomously, the Augustinian subject was obliged to subordinate his or her will to that of another in a relation of ongoing, but supposedly freely chosen, obedience. The role that was accorded habit in relation to the internal divisions of the will contributed to the development of what Foucault regarded as a distinguishing feature of pastoral government: its transformation of those brought under its jurisdiction into governable subjects who, incapable of autonomous self-governance, stand in need of forms of inner direction derived from obedient subjection to the guidance of another. In tracing the development of this ethos through several mutations, Foucault identified how these contributed to the sixteenth-century formation of governmentality as a set of techniques for acting on the actions of others in which aspects of the pastoral governance of souls were translated into ways of shaping the dispositions of individuals and populations.

In introducing his account of these transitions, Foucault notes that, before the sixteenth century, "to govern" meant primarily to "direct, move forward, or even to move forward oneself on a track, a road" (Foucault 2007a, 121). In the initial phases of its development in the Mediterranean East, and especially in its Hebraic forms, the authority invested in the shepherd as the emblematic figure of pastoral government was that of leading his flock "in its movement from one place to another" (125). It was only in its later institutionalized forms in western Europe that the path along which the pastorate directed the souls of men was given a temporal rather than a spatial inflection as the task of pastoral government came to be defined as that of "leading individuals, or at any rate, allowing individuals to advance and progress on the path of salvation" (167–68). The distinctiveness of pastoral power consisted in its bringing this shepherdic role to bear on the whole of humanity rather than a specific group, city, or state; in its claim, as Foucault put it, to effect "the daily government of men in their real life on the grounds of their salvation and on the scale of humanity" (148).

Habit played a crucial connecting role in the "economy of merits and faults" (183) through which pastoral power superintended the passage of souls along the pathway to salvation by means of the constant examination of conscience that this economy enjoined. The direction of souls involved "a permanent intervention in everyday conduct" (154) shaped by a distinctive regime of truth administered and translated into law by the pastor. Simon Oliver interprets habit's role in this regard as contributing to "humanity's motion towards God," which, after the Fall, required "the infusion of grace" in order that we might "move and be moved to our proper end in God" through the progressive acquisition of grace, which, "bestowed salvifically in Christ," is mediated to the congregation by the pastorate through its administration of the sacraments (Oliver 2005, 53). The end toward which particular habits are directed may be good or bad, either leading to or detracting from the realization of man's true nature in God. However, it is the correction and revision of habits by the church through the confession and the forms of training acquired through the repetition of the sacraments that guide the soul along the path toward *beatitude*. This was a pathway leading to the development of an accumulating second nature oriented toward the realization of the form—the movement toward God through volitional self-activity and, thereby, the attainment of grace—that both distinguishes human from animal life and differentiates humans in terms of the levels of grace that they have attained. Oliver refers mainly to Thomas Aquinas in elaborating this account. In his *Disputed Questions on Spiritual Creatures*, Aquinas argues that although the human soul "does not depend on the body but is rather elevated above corporeal matter," the body nonetheless "receives a share in its being, in such a way that there is one being of soul and body, and this is the being of a human." This has the further consequence that the soul cannot achieve "the perfection of its nature except in union with the body" (Aquinas quoted in Stump 2003, 201). The distinctiveness of the Thomist conception of the human soul thus consists, Eleonore Stump argues, in its dual capacity as a "configured configurer" (2003, 200). Directly created by God with, as the result of this divine infusion, its own configuration, the capacity for configuring matter that this confers on the soul is both put to work in the composite that it enters into in its union with the body and is in turn shaped by its interactions with the body in which it is embedded across the course of their shared lifetime.

It is in this context that habit—doubling up as both a set of configured aptitudes and a configuring force—is invoked as a key actor in Aquinas's account of the soul's pathway to virtue. If this interprets habit as a divine infusion, a capacity for the progressive acquisition of grace along the road to salvation, it is habit understood, in its Aristotelian sense, not as *consuetudo* but as habitus or *hexis*. Habit here is directed not by an efficient but by a final cause as it is put into motion by the will—impelled forward on the road to grace—understood as an appetite for goodness determined by the intellect.[4] Its central mechanism, when translated into the techniques of pastoral government, is, Foucault argues, obedience—obedience for obedience's sake, requiring the mortification of the will, as he puts it—but an obedience that takes a particular form, not to "a law or principle of order" in the abstract but as embodied by an exemplary other, to "someone because he is someone" (Foucault 2007a, 175): that is, the pastor who exercises responsibility for "material things and everyday life" as well as spiritual matters. What thus applies to the relationship between the pastor and the congregation under his care is intensified within monastic life through the operation of a series of hierarchical relationships within the monastic community: of monks to abbots, of novices to their masters, and so on.

## Habit-obedience and the binary structure of pastoral government

Viewed in terms of its social articulations, this mechanism—Giorgio Agamben (2013) calls it the habituation-obedience couplet—operated at the intersection of an intricate set of social divisions.[5] These included its role in effecting a hierarchical ordering of positions within the pastorate, and between the pastorate and the upper echelons of the Christian community, distinguishing them in terms of various stages on the pathway toward the acquisition of virtue. This is also a term with different levels of meaning in the Thomist tradition.[6] In one usage, there are multiple virtues associated with the acquisition and development of specific skills. It is, in this sense, the root of the role accorded habit in the development of the virtuosity of the musician, athlete, or chess master, key figures symbolizing the conception of habit as a virtue that results in an increasing ease of action that confers a tutelary authority on the virtuoso. Understood in terms of its relations to spiritual practice, however, virtue refers to the soul's capacity for spiritual perfection and hence a specific kind of freedom.[7] "Virtue is not only compatible with maximum freedom," Robert Miner argues in summarizing Aquinas's position, "but also its necessary condition, since only the virtuous person can consistently and voluntarily choose to perform acts that manifest human excellence" (2013, 82). But this freedom, he continues, has little to do with choosing between different courses of action; it is a freedom for the acquisition of virtue that is only possible for those in whom the power of habit "is perfected or is growing to perfection" (82). The development of this capacity for virtue—understood as a divine infusion in the human—depends on the degree to which it has been cultivated by the subjection of body and soul to the forms of training that are most fully developed in the habitation-obedience couplet of monastic culture. The daily regimens and rituals of monastic life were accorded a particular significance in this regard in view of their capacity to suspend the regular flow of time and permit the development of forms of attention focused on the inner life. The degree of indeterminacy this produces is crucial to Christian conceptions of the transformative development of sensitive appetites and bodily passions in ways that mark out a free—in the sense of self-determined—path to virtue. It is by means of habit, again in its positive sense, that such indeterminacy is translated into powers capable of furthering the soul's capacity for the acquisition of virtue, thereby reconciling the concepts of habit and freedom, efficient and final causality, with each other. It is the acquisition of virtue in this spiritual sense that confers on the pastorate varying degrees of the exemplary authority through which pastoral government is exercised, an authority that was given a distinctive sumptuary form in the moralized clothing of the monk's habit (Scene of Habit 5).

In serving as "both clothing and a way of life" (Agamben 2013, 1), the habit, as the outward sign of a shared habitus, also functioned as a marker of the difference between the monastic community and the varied social orders associated with different secular clothing regimes. The continuing currency of this moralized clothing was later contrasted to the etymological connection between *custom* and *costume* as the prescribed clothing of the common people. In commenting on this distinction, Miner notes the respects in which medieval theological traditions typically distinguished the routine forms of training associated with custom as a type of *consuetudo* applicable to pagans, heretics, and layfolk—and specifically to the forms of training linked to particular secular occupations—from the association of habit, as *hexis*, with the cultivation of Christian grace. In asking whether and how far this distinction applied to Aquinas, Miner argues that it did, but in a particular way. What

---

*Scene of Habit 5—The Monk's Habit and the Monastic Habitus*

In commenting on Jean Cassian's fifth-century text *On the Habit of Monks*, Giorgio Agamben highlights Cassian's concern with monks' clothing as a central component of the communal habitation that constituted the foundation of monasticism. He sees this text as a significant moment in the processes through which—while remaining distinct—the concepts of habit, as an item of clothing, and of habitus, as a way of life, were progressively fused as the monk's habit came to be viewed as "a necessary part of the 'way to conduct oneself.'" This reflected a history through which the items of monks' clothes had "been submitted to a process of moralization that makes each of them the symbol or allegory of a virtuous way of life." Short sleeves, for example, signified a monastic severance from worldly deeds and concerns; sandals stood for the feet of the soul, always ready for spiritual pursuit; and the leather belt symbolized the monk's recruitment as a soldier of Christ. (Agamben 2013, 12–14)

---

custom lacked compared with habit was a capacity for the redirection of conduct brought about by the reflective redirection of the will that was made possible by moments of awareness. This capacity was brought to bear on the sensitive appetites and bodily passions—ordered in ways limited to the performance of determinate acts—through the mediation of the indeterminacy that characterizes the "sensitive apprehensive powers" of the imagination, memory, and cognition. Habits that have become unduly repetitive—which have a hold on conduct rather than being held—were, for Aquinas, "stubbornly held customs that prevent the self from acquiring genuine *habitus* which confer the freedom to act in ways that are noble and excellent" (Miner 2013, 84).

Medieval Christianity was thus, Foucault argues, characterized by a "binary structure within the pastoral field, distinguishing the clergy from the laity" (Foucault 2007a, 202) in terms of both their civic rights and obligations and the spiritual capacities accorded them. We get a further sense of the historical specificity and social articulations of these different forms of training (custom and habit) from Thomas Piketty's remarks regarding the distinctiveness of the Catholic Church relative to other world religions in the role it played in the "trifunctional inequalities" that characterized medieval Europe: that is, the divisions between the military leadership of the landed aristocracy, the spiritual direction provided by the clergy, and the range of productive functions provided by the third estate comprising peasants, artisans, and merchants. With its clergy forming between 3 and 4 percent of the population (Piketty 2020, 157) and owning between 25 and 35 percent of all property (91), the church faced a unique difficulty among world religions in the respect that the enforcement of celibacy meant that its priesthood could not reproduce itself as a hereditary class.[8] This lent an exceptional importance to the cultivation of a socially distinctive ethos via the enlistment and training of new recruits by means of the habit-obedience couplet.

Although not what he had in mind, the role played by habit in the organization of inequalities is one of the aspects of pastoral government from which, as Foucault put it, "we have still not freed ourselves" (2007a, 148). Its continuing influence, albeit subject to a disciplinary and biopolitical mutation, was evident in the racially schismatic functioning of the habit-obedience couplet that was put into effect, in the mid-twentieth century, by the Benedictine monastic community of New Norcia in Western Australia. And its consequences were tellingly testified to by members of the "stolen generation" of Indigenous Australians who were forcibly removed from their families, purportedly in order to be brought up under the civilizing influence of the monastic community in the orphanage it administered. Interviewed as a part of the television documentary *The Habits of New Norcia*, their testimony highlighted the dual operations of habit as part of a racialized system of exploitation and dispossession.[9] On the one hand, the role of habit in the cultivation of an elite and white spirituality was pointedly foregrounded by scenes from the tourist itinerary of New Norcia focused on the routines of monastic life committed to both the cultivation of New Norcia's agricultural estate—initially, of course, Aboriginal land—and the acquisition of spiritual virtues in the community's abbey, cloisters, and library. On the other hand, the testimony of the Indigenous witnesses revealed the dependency of this regime of habit on the quite different forms of its disciplinary deployment in the daily routines of the orphanage whose barred windows—prior to their removal after the orphanage's closure in 1973—were the outward sign of its penal operations: a daily regime of discipline and punishment oriented toward the training of a source of unfree labor that both worked the monastery's agricultural estate and the land and households of neighboring settler landowners.

## Counterconducts: Contesting the superintendence of habit's pathways

At the outset of *Security, Territory, Population*, Foucault argues that the governing problematics of sovereignty and security share with discipline the characteristic of being a "mode of individualization of multiplicities"—that is, of acting on particular prisoners, soldiers, pupils, and so on only insofar as their conduct needs to be ordered and managed as a means of governing the multiplicities they belong to—rather than constructing "an edifice of individuals who are worked on as, first of all, individuals" (Foucault 2007a, 12). The examination of conscience governed by the economy of merits and faults within the operations of pastoral power, by contrast, works through a highly specific mechanism of individualization. Not one that celebrates a triumphal egoism of the individual or confers a capacity for self-mastery on the individual, but rather one that—although differing in the degree of its application across the binary structure of the pastoral field—works through superintended forms of individual self-examination that ensure each and every individual's subordination to the regime of truth mediated by the pastorate. It was this form of individualization that prepared the ground for the subsequent development of the forms of self-examination, guided by particular regimes of truth, that subtended the distinctive form of the subject required, cultivated, and pointed in different directions by governmental power.

A crucial step in this transition consisted in the ways in which the various forms of counterconduct that were developed in the late medieval period targeted and reworked the "systems of salvation, obedience and truth" (Foucault 2007a, 204) composed by the habit-obedience couplet. Precisely by challenging and disrupting them, these effected a wider dispersion of the forms of spiritual authority monopolized by the pastorate. In doing so, they prepared the way for their subsequent incorporation into the techniques for the "conduct of conduct" that signaled the transition from the "economy of souls to the government of men and population" (227). In probing what he variously refers to as revolts or insurrections of conduct, Foucault calls attention to his reasons for wanting to retain the concept of conduct in view of the range of ambiguities that it registers. In some cases, such insurrections aimed to make it possible for individuals to conduct themselves free from the direction of others; in others, they critiqued existing forms of pastoral power in order to reinstate them in other guises: "wanting to be conducted differently, by other leaders (*conducteurs*) and other shepherds, towards other objectives and forms of salvation, and through other procedures and methods" (194–95).

The forms of insurrection associated with the religious communities that shaped the development of Protestantism thus took issue with the binary structure of pastoral power, undermining the "priest-laity dimorphism" (210), through communal forms of challenge to the role of priestly forms of authority: the election of pastors, the translation of the Bible into common vernaculars. Protestant disputes with the institutionalized forms of the confession administered by the pastorate that were so crucial to the economy of faults and merits of the Catholic Church were important here. However, while drawing on and enunciating the forms of counterconduct associated with self-directed forms of interior inspection and self-confession through which individuals operated their own economies of merits and faults, this should not detract from the respects in which, as Johannes Wolf puts it, such disputes took place "*within* the depth model licensed by pastoral power" (2017, 222). In the more radical sects, the role of pastor as guide on the path to salvation was distributed across the whole community in parallel with the application of egalitarian principles to other areas of life articulating a commitment to an ethos of the common. In discussing the role of mysticism as another instance of the "revolts of conduct" (Foucault 2007a, 196), Foucault stresses the respects in which it aimed to short-circuit the highly mediated forms of priestly authority by substituting the directness of the forms of intuition and illumination produced by embodied spiritual exercises as the basis for the forms of counterconduct they authorized. These undermined the authority of the pastor based on a "structure of teaching and the passing on of truth from someone who knows it to someone to whom it is taught" (212) to the more enigmatic, nondirective forms of guidance offered by the mystic. This involves an interpretation of mysticism as an alternative form of authority but one that, in the forms of guidance it offered—opening up the possibility of direct communion between the soul and God rather than proceeding through the mediation of a pastor—was still partly defined by that which it was pitched against.

The significance of the continuities between pastoral and governmental power, and the counterconducts they generate, has been usefully highlighted by Arnold Davidson (2011).[10] There are differences, of course: the forms of counterconduct developed in critique of specific governmental programs seek to limit or redirect the forms of authority exercised over the conduct of conduct by political rather than religious institutions. In both cases, however, Foucault stresses that the logic of counterconducts goes beyond purely negative acts of disobedience or resistance to propose a refashioning of the forms of power they are pitched against but always, so to speak, from an insider relationship rather than one of a pure exteriority. Counterconducts, that is to say, draw on the elements of the specific governmental programs they oppose to propose alternative means of acting on conduct by structuring the possible fields of action of others. In refusing particular ways of being conducted—of being governed in such-and-such a fashion—the issue at stake for counterconducts is that of developing new forms for the conduct of conduct to be exercised under newly constituted regimes of authority.[11] Davidson also draws attention to a number of texts in which Foucault detaches the language of freedom from its currency in emancipatory discourses, interpreting it instead as "part of the semantic field of counter-conduct" (2011, 30). Foucault's purpose in doing so was to identify the production of a zone of freedom in which conduct was detached from the more explicitly directive forms of its governance to be inscribed in more hands-off forms of direction that operated through the induction of individuals and populations into techniques of self-governance.

This last consideration has a significant bearing on the role assigned to freedom in the versions of habit's pathways proposed by the wayward tradition that I turn to in the following chapters. At the same time, however, there is another aspect of Davidson's discussion that I shall part company with. It is that expressed in his argument that "when a regime of scientific veridiction provides the framework of intelligibility for conduct," the concept loses "its ethical and political dimensions" in "becoming the object of scientific explanation" (36). This is far from being true of how questions of habit and conduct have been worked through in the debates that have accompanied the development of the life sciences. We have already seen, in the discussion of Henry Maudsley's work at the end of the previous chapter, how the authority of those and other sciences was invoked in an explicit ethical and political critique of, and as an alternative to, the earlier and ongoing power of the pastorate in the conduct of conduct. And, as we shall see in chapter 7, the same was true of John Dewey. I shall, then, while shifting my attention from "habit then" to "habit now," continue to develop my excavations of the habit archive in articulating their relevance to current concerns. I do so in the next chapter by charting the influence exerted on contemporary debates by the ordering of the relations between scientific, pastoral, and mystical forms of authority that characterized Henri Bergson's conception of habit's pathways.

# 5

# Unfolding
Pathways

HABIT, FREEDOM, BECOMING

THE "EXTRAORDINARY BLESSEDNESS OF HABIT" for Bruno Latour's hiker, it will be recalled, is that, without it, "we would constantly hesitate as to the path we should take" (Latour 2013, 266–67). Clare Carlisle, by contrast, sees moments of hesitation along habit's pathways as crucial to the dialectic of receptivity and resistance that she attributes to the dynamic of both ordinary habit and spiritual practice. The resistance to the routines of ordinary habit that is generated by moments that interrupt or stall its automatisms cultivates an awareness that "has the power to *unconceal* habits" (Carlisle 2006, 33). This opens up the possibility of turning habit against itself, transforming the "threefold process of action, repetition and formation" (33) from a mechanism of bondage into a force for liberation, for transcending the material determinations that condition us. This *"receptivity to the good,"* exemplified by spiritual practice, is facilitated by ritualized forms of interruption—prayer, meditation, the Eucharist, yoga postures—that take us "along the path of attentiveness, from a familiar activity to an experience at once mysterious and revelatory, poetic and down to earth" (Carlisle 2014, 133–34).

For Elizabeth Grosz, the past trajectories of habit's pathways produce "the resources for multiple futures, for open pathways, for indeterminable consequences, as well as for those regularities and norms that currently prevail" (2004, 253). They do so through the moments of hesitation that interrupt them, "nicks in time" in which the force of habit is both suspended and renewed, disconnected from its previous trajectories to embark on new pathways whose direction unfolds only as they are opened up. Like Carlisle, Grosz aligns her assessment of habit's liberating potential with what she calls the "wayward tradition"—leading from Maine de Biran through Félix Ravaisson and thence, via Henri Bergson, to Gilles Deleuze—in which habit is not "that which reduces the human to the order of the mechanical . . . but rather a fundamentally creative capacity . . . an anchor, the rock to which the possibilities of personal identity and freedom are tethered, the condition under which learning is possible, the creation of a direction, a 'second nature,' an identity" (Grosz 2013, 219).

This conception of an interrupted pathway has played a significant, albeit varied, role in post-Deleuzian conceptions of the duality of habit as a form of repetition that, just as it might become locked in on itself, might also generate dynamic propensities that lead it along the emerging course of unfolding pathways. The relations between habit, interruption, and freedom that are in play here depend on the logic of indetermination, through which the force of external determinations of conduct is temporarily suspended. The role accorded this logic in the wayward tradition has involved a revival of interest in earlier theological conceptions of habit as a resource for the critique of two related tendencies: first, of the Kantian condemnation of habit as mere mechanism, posing habit and the pursuit of freedom as necessary contraries (Scene of Habit 2); and second, as my main concern here, of the increasing association of habit, since the nineteenth century, with what Michel Foucault describes as the normalizing force of "impulses, drives, tendencies, inclinations, and automatisms" (Foucault 2003a, 131), which make habit increasingly liable to the superintendence of the biological, psychological, and medical sciences. Ravaisson's work, as Carlisle puts it, drew on a range of sources that combined to "subvert the project of a modern science" (Carlisle 2013b, 44).

The most critical influence on Ravaisson in this regard was that of Maine de Biran, who, in his 1802 essay *The Influence of Habit on the Faculty of Thinking* (Maine de Biran 1929), disconnected habit from its Lockean conception as an attribute of the association of ideas effected by a mind turned in upon itself. He did so by interpreting it rather as the product of the willed motor activity of a body in motion in a material world, inscribing its dynamics in the relations between the sensations arising from the faculty of feeling and the perceptions arising from the experience of moving.[1] At the same time, however, he qualified this physiological materialism with an account of how the force of purely passive forms of habit might be displaced by more active forms in a process of perfectibility that echoed Christian conceptions of grace in a synthesis that Jerrold Seigel has aptly characterized as "spiritualist positivism" (2005, 251). Grosz (2013), in recounting the influence of both Maine de Biran and Ravaisson on Bergson, inscribes the wayward tradition in a similar place, setting up an opposition between those approaches to habit that operate as a way of connecting with and governing behavior and those that open it up as a road toward openness, difference, and (relative) freedom. She presents this opposition in disciplinary terms. The medical and social sciences concern themselves with habits as parts of us that can be manipulated in order to meet social goals. Philosophy is different. Rather than relating to habits as a conduit for the transformation of behavior, it aims—in a Deleuzian spirit—to create concepts that will enlarge habit's capacity as a dynamic bridge between the organic and inorganic worlds that is generative of spontaneous and undirected processes of becoming.

My main argument in this chapter is that the terms of debate proposed by the wayward tradition are ones in which philosophy opposes its own forms of authority and modes of intervening in the governance of conduct to those of other disciplines. What is at issue in such debates is precisely a struggle over the forms of authority that are to be accorded pride of place in how habit's second nature is conceived and engaged with. The wayward tradition has constructed habit as a part of practices of "guided freedom" that depend on the exercise of particular forms of spiritual authority that, among other things, constitute a reworking of the power of the pastorate in the governance of conduct.[2]

In bringing these considerations to bear on the wayward tradition, I organize my discussion initially around the work of Bergson as the key point of connection between the earlier representatives of this tradition and its revival in post-Deleuzian theory. If, as Foucault argues, mysticism was one of the counterconducts directed against the forms of authority represented by the pastorate, the position that Bergson accords habit on the path of life revives the authority of the mystic as a counter to those tendencies in physiology and psychology that he took issue with. In developing this argument, I draw on Walter Benjamin's criticisms of Bergson, whom he regarded as a metaphysician who abstracted the aspects of human conduct he engaged with from both historical time and the influence of technological forces.

I then look at Grosz's account of the role played by "the nick of time" that she attributes to Charles Darwin's account of evolution as one that opens up the possibility of, and proceeds via, mechanisms of differentiation that she attaches to a gendered politics of becoming. I am, however, less concerned with the specifically gendered aspects of her account than with the respects in which her reading of the relations between habit and freedom through a Bergsonian lens gives rise to similar difficulties. At root, these concern the abstraction of questions concerning the politics of repetition from the institutions and apparatuses in which its diverse forms are enacted and superintended. In developing this argument, I take issue with Grosz's reading of Darwin. Reviewing his discussion of the relations between habit and the instincts, and its implications for his account of the relations between animal and human life, I question Grosz's reading of the position that Darwin's work occupied within the politics of the late Victorian period. In concluding, I take further issue with Grosz's failure to adequately consider the implications of the politics of gapped time that are central to her account of the relations between habit, repetition, and freedom.

## Habit, memory, becoming:
## Indeterminacy and the interval

In discussing the relationship between variation and heredity in *Creative Evolution*, Bergson argues that the fact that the son of a fencing master might become a good fencer more quickly than his father is no justification for assuming that "the habit of the parent has been transmitted to the child" (1998, 79). Why? Because the natural dispositions transmitted from "the plasma engendering the father to the plasma engendering the son, may have grown on the way by the effect of the primitive impetus, and thus assured to the son a greater suppleness than the father had, without troubling, so to speak, about what the father did" (79–80). Drawing on the work of August Weismann, which had severed the connection between the soma and the germ plasm on which the logic of the inheritance of acquired characteristics depended, Bergson thus registers his objection to the currency of the blacksmith's arm on which the tradition of organic memory drew and which, as we saw in chapter 2, informed the work of Herbert Spencer and Edward Drinker Cope, both of whom Bergson groups alongside Jean-Baptiste Lamarck as the objects of his criticism.[3] In place of the cumulative inheritance of character, the dynamic of the "primitive impetus" that he refers to is that of "the hereditability of *deviation*" (83)—a capacity for the acquisition of a new character that would deviate from its previous forms.

It is this impetus, in propelling the dynamic evolution of life, that shapes life's course. This does not take the form of a plan to be realized or of a series of adaptations to accidental circumstances but is rather "found solely in the impetus that pushes it along the road of time," its harmony lying "not in front, but behind" (103). This was by way of clarifying a version of the pathway metaphor that Bergson had used a little earlier in both likening the movement of evolution to, while distinguishing it from, that of a road that leads to a town. Whereas such a road is obliged to follow the ups and downs and other contours of the terrain, such "accidents of the ground," considered from the perspective of the road as a whole, are impediments to the realization of its goal: "for the road aims simply at the town and would fain be a straight line" (102). And so it is with the founding impetus that propels the evolution of life, with the difference "that evolution does not mark out a solitary route, that it takes directions without aiming at ends, and that it remains inventive even in its adaptations" (103). It is the force of this push, there from the start of life and leading to "higher and higher destinies" (103), that is missed by mechanistic accounts dealing solely with the "accidents of the ground" constituted by adaptations of particular forms of life to changing environments. But this progression of life is not guaranteed. Its forward movement along the path of evolution is accompanied by moments of "marking time" or of "turning back," a "crowd of minor paths in which . . . deviations, arrests, and set-backs, are multiplied" (104).

A little later in his text, Bergson registers his departure from the role accorded habit in the organic memory tradition of transmitting modified instincts as a cumulative transgenerational inheritance. Where the mechanical performance of habitual actions is undertaken unconsciously or automatically, this is owing to the sheer force of the act in question holding in check its representation in consciousness. "*Representation*," as he puts it, "*is stopped up by action*" (144). Where consciousness does intervene, it introduces a moment of hesitation around the possible actions that might be embarked upon. He accordingly concludes that "*the consciousness of a living being may be defined as an arithmetical difference between potential and real activity. It measures the interval between representation and action*" (145). He returns to this theme when discussing how the creative energy that is bestowed by the impetus of life results in an endless expenditure of effort through which forms of life, in engaging with matter, seek to transfigure the cause-and-effect logic of its spatial determinations into "flexible channels, changeable in shape, at the end of which it [life] will accomplish infinitely varied kinds of work" (254). Life canalizes energy so that, in flowing across time, it interrupts the chain of inheritance by introducing into matter "the largest possible amount of indetermination and liberty" (251). This foundational impetus of life is a divine infusion of vital energy through which life, in making/unmaking/remaking the forms it has created through its dynamic engagements with matter, carves out new directions for itself. "God thus defined," as Bergson puts it, "has nothing of the already made; He is unceasing life, action, freedom" (248).[4]

In asking what the great guide of life might be, Bergson disqualifies intelligence from performing this role. For intelligence interprets life from the outside, converting its dynamism into a set of spatially configured causal relations compatible with the sciences' construction of matter. It is rather intuition, understood as "instinct that has become disinterested, self-conscious, capable of reflecting upon its object and of enlarging it indefinitely" (176), that he looks to. But this power of intuition needs to be guided by philosophy: not philosophy understood as a holistic and reasoned vision of the cosmos, but philosophy as a spiritual practice that dissolves the abstractions of intelligence to reimmerse life in, and guide it along, the flows of energy conferred by the "beneficent fluid" of life (191). In developing this argument, Bergson draws on another metaphor of habit's pathways in likening the limitations of human intelligence to those of a person who, harnessed "like yoked oxen, to a heavy task," registers only the forces, "the play of our muscles and joints, the weight of the plough and the resistance of the soil," that are relevant to "the furrow that is being ploughed" (191). It is only when the force of intuition, guided by philosophy, prompts action to "make the leap," to "take things by storm," that the circle that binds habit to the repetition of the same can be broken as life is impelled on a new course of action. It is thus philosophy, in guiding life as it leaps across the moments of indetermination, that superintends the role of freedom in mediating the relations between the continuity and the discontinuity of life, between the known and the unknown, between the already made and what is in the process of being made.[5]

In his study of Bergson, Deleuze dwells on the significance that Bergson imputes to the cerebral interval between "received and executed movement," which, stalling the force of any determinate connection between them, introduces a moment of hesitation or "choice" in which volition is possible (Deleuze 1991a, 52). The distinctiveness of Bergson's position on this matter becomes clearer when contrasted with how the development of the will was accounted for in the organic memory tradition as represented by Théodule Ribot.[6] Ribot's scholarly mission, as Laura Otis summarizes it, was to rescue memory and, alongside memory, the concepts of habit, will, instinct, and attention, "from the territory of metaphysicians." He sought to do so by incorporating them into "the new discourse of biology and physiological psychology" and thus disconnecting them from the "artificial mysticism" that interpreted them as properties of the soul rather than as relations of "work, force, energy, and particle motion" (Otis 1994, 15–16).

Like Spencer, Ribot viewed the action of habit as a key mechanism in the evolution of the will. In doing so, he combined naturalistic and social principles of explanation in the significance he accorded to the interruptions of habit effected by those moments of indetermination that allowed individuals to develop new aptitudes by curbing the force of inherited reflexes. Interpreting this stock of inherited reflexes as "the materials out of which the will is to be built up" (4), Ribot argues that this requires that there must also be an interval in which this set of automated responses is brought under the influence of an alternative force that loosens the hold of inherited reflexes to initiate a process of free self-formation. He accounts for the emergence of such an interval as an outcome of the two routes through which external excitations divide themselves on arrival in the spinal cord, traveling to the reflex center by the traverse route (the longer way) and to the brain via the shorter, longitudinal and ascending route. The interval this produces means that the "suspensive action of the brain has time to take place and to moderate the reflexes" (57). Ribot inserts into the interval produced by this delay the social mechanisms of "education, habit, and reflexion" (4), which intervene between the reflexes and the development of the will and the intellect to inhibit and modify the immediacy of action that would result if the inherited repertoire of reflexes held undisputed sway. It is, then, the delay caused by the different routes through which external stimuli reach the body's neural and reflex centers that produces the interval within which habit can enter into and become a consequential part of the sociophysiological processes through which "character" is progressively shaped and formed.[7] And it is through habit, not against it, that the evolutionary and physiological history of the body is connected to the social and cultural institutions through which will and consciousness are given a specific form and enacted.

Ribot's antimetaphysical bent made him, alongside Spencer and Maudsley, a significant point of engagement for Bergson in his concern to read the dynamics earlier attributed to the soul back into an account of life in which "work, force, energy, and particle motion" had their place, but one that was ultimately trumped by the spiritual force of life's creativity. Félix Ravaisson's work proved a key resource for Bergson, who praised it for the prospect it opened up for thinking about habit not just externally, as mere mechanism—"a series of movements which determine one another . . . that part of us which is inserted into nature and which coincides with nature"—but from within where "our inner experience shows us in habit an activity which has passed, by imperceptible degrees, from consciousness to unconsciousness and from will to automatism," thus demonstrating that "mechanism is not sufficient to itself: it is, so to speak, only the fossilized residue of a spiritual activity" (Bergson 1946, 275).[8] What we might call Bergson's "geology of the soul" thus built on Ravaisson's understanding of habit as the linchpin of a mechanism of change that, by consolidating through repetition behaviors that are contracted via contact with the environment, prepares the organism for future change. Habit equips the body for a "change which either is no longer or is not yet; it remains for a possible change" and "is not, therefore, merely a state, but a disposition, a virtue" (Ravaisson 2008, 25). New habits that are originally induced as responses to changes in the external environment prepare the way, through repetition, for further changes that the living being brings on itself, a capacity that comes to be proper to and constitutive of it. Habit thus generates a capacity for a certain degree of self-directed freedom. No longer the purely mechanical effect of an external impulse, habit is a capacity that inclines the body to the end the will proposes: it is "a *law of the limbs*" that is, at the same time, "a *law of grace*," the "final cause" that "increasingly predominates over efficient causality and which absorbs the latter into itself" (57).

It was in thus connecting "an ontology of habit" to "a theology of grace" (Carlisle 2013a, 167) that Ravaisson contributed to the reinstallation of habit as a virtuous practice whose productivity both reaches back into the nature from which it originally derives while also extending into the limitless future it generates. It derives its positive force from its dynamic mediation and refutation of a series of opposites linked to its fusion of the law of the limbs and that of grace. In mediating the relations between will and instinct, habit operates as a middle term—but always a moving middle term—between will and nature. Transforming voluntary movements into instincts and instincts into voluntary motions, habit effects a "dynamic *fluxion* from Will to Nature" (Ravaisson 2008, 59). If it is this fluxion that accounts for habit's conception as an acquired or second nature, it has its ultimate ground in nature understood as the generative force—a "*naturing* nature"—of which habit is both "the product and successive revelation" (59). Returning to his conception of the relations between habit and virtue as consisting in the pursuit of the good, which, although initially a wearisome burden, becomes "attractive and a pleasure" through repetition, drawing near to "the holiness of innocence" (69), Ravaisson connects this to the theme of grace, citing Augustine's conception of nature as "prevenient grace" that derives its power from the "God within us" (71).[9] Whereas, in the organic memory tradition, the will is given a neurophysiological location, Ravaisson's interpretation of the mediating role of habit locates it as part of processes of change in which freedom is derived from a primary nature and imported back into a second nature along a pathway that leads to the attainment of grace, a concept that Ravaisson leaves hovering between its spiritual associations and its sense of an accumulating ease of action, a virtuosity.[10]

While Bergson draws on these aspects of Ravaisson's work, there are also significant differences regarding the particularities of their interpretations of habit. The dynamism that Ravaisson attributes to habit is sui generis. There are, as we have seen, several versions of the mechanisms through which habit, by virtue of the very familiarity that its repetitions produce, is attributed a capacity to generate a momentum that leads beyond itself. Ravaisson's version of this logic in his "double law of habit" is distinctive. Arguing that the impressions external objects make on the organism "lose their force the more frequently they are produced," he interprets this effect of repetition as signaling the increasing independence of actions from "the material alteration of the organism" (37). This in turn indicates the operation of a center within the organism that is capable of regulating "by itself and in its own way ... the less and less immediate and necessary relation of the reaction that it produces with the action that it has suffered" (37). It is, Ravaisson argues, the principle of the soul that introduces into the widening gap between the action it has suffered and the action it produces the "reign of knowledge, of foresight ... and thus the first light of Freedom" (37).

For Bergson, by contrast, it is memory that introduces a dynamism into what would otherwise be habit's stasis. The key to this account is the distinction he proposes between habit-memory and memory proper: between, that is, the memory stored up in the mechanical routines that are coded into the body through repetition, and the memory that works through the mechanism of consciousness and representation and is thus singular to the particular moment in which it is enacted. "Habit, rather than memory," he says of the first, "it acts our past experience but does not call up its image." The other, he continues, "is the true memory": "Co-extensive with consciousness, it retains and ranges alongside of each other all our states in the order in which they occur, leaving to each fact its place and consequently marking its date, truly moving in the past and not, like the first, in an ever renewed present" (Bergson 2004, 195). Bergson clarifies the difference between this position and the logic of organic memory—the view that "the body preserves memories in the mechanical form of cerebral deposits" (231)—by insisting that the only past that is real for us is that which is selectively illuminated by "the fundamental law of life, which is a law of action" that animates memory proper (194).

While undoubtedly significant, these differences should not, Mark Sinclair (2018) argues, obscure the respects in which Ravaisson's account of habit prepared the way for the conception of time as duration—*la durée*—that became the signature concept of Bergsonian philosophy. The conception of time as a fusion of past, present, and future; of the present as a moment in which the past is no more over than the future is not yet, but in which the past is synthesized with the present in being tilted in the living being's orientation toward the future: if this is worked through in Ravaisson's conception of habit as marking a change that either is no longer or is not yet but a possible change to come, it is worked through for Bergson via how memory proper cuts into habit-memory. While in both cases time as duration is substituted for clock time, there are significant differences with regard to how habit's pathways are conceived in relation to processes of becoming: as constituting and marking such processes in the case of Ravaisson and, in Bergson's case, as a pathway that must be interrupted by the force of memory. Bergson's construal of the relations between habit-memory and memory proper both grounds personhood in matter and the chains of chemical, physiological, and neurophysiological causation and, at the same time, frees it from such chains by virtue of the ways in which memory proper pauses time, thereby enabling singular forms of free and conscious agency to emerge and be asserted.

This imagery of the chain also informs Bergson's account of the positions that different species occupy on the pathway of life, of the differences in kind that distinguish man's position on this pathway from that of other animals, and of the varying degrees to which it has been traveled by average men and spiritual leaders. It is the connections between consciousness, the power of choice between different possible courses of action that this confers, and the capacity for invention and freedom to which this gives rise that mark the stages along this pathway. The invention evident in animal life is never anything "but a variation on the theme of routine," escaping automatism "only for an instant, for just the time to create a new automatism," and thus "by pulling at its chain . . . succeeds only in stretching it." With man, by contrast, "consciousness breaks the chain" (Bergson 1998, 264). Bergson attributes this to the interactions between three forces: first, the superiority of man's brain, which, by opposing the new habits acquired through the operation of memory proper to the sedimented ones of habit-memory, allows him to divide automatism against itself and thus to rule it; second, the role of language as the immaterial storehouse of consciousness; and third, social life, which, in storing and preserving effort as language preserves thought, provides an initial stimulation that "prevents the average man from slumbering and drives the superior man to mount higher still" (265). But the achievements that are registered in the development of the brain, language, and society do not signal man's place as the telos of evolution; they rather register the force of life as a "current sent through matter, drawing from it what it can" (265) without any sense of an end or direction.

It is in this sense that man is the "ground of evolution" rather than its telos, the continuation of life's vital impulse, which, when translated into consciousness, pushes him along life's path as he leaves other forms of life behind. But for Bergson the pressing practical question in the present is that consciousness has come to a new crossroads, divided between the route mapped out by intelligence (the cause-and-effect reasoning of science)—a route limited to the movement of matter—and that mapped out by intuition, which goes in "the very direction of life" (267). Fearing that the light that the lamp of intuition throws on the possible future paths of life is close to being extinguished by the dominance of science, Bergson calls on philosophy to rekindle the force of intuition. To do this, he argues, it needs to jettison those forms of spiritualism that have suspended the life of spirit "as high as possible above the earth" and instead anchor "the life of spirit to that of the body" (268). But this is, at the same time, a force that dissolves the particularity of the individual souls that result from such fusions. As the emanations of life's creative force, such souls are "nothing else than the little rills into which the great river of life divides itself, flowing through the body of humanity" (270). The latter constitutes the bed across which the river of life must flow, adapting itself to "its winding course" (270) but, at the same time, like the road into town, overriding and overdetermining its direction at every turn.

## Philosophy's pastorate:
## Spiritual guides along life's path

In his study of Bergson, Keith Ansell-Pearson (2018) notes the debt that Pierre Hadot acknowledges to Bergson for his own interpretation of philosophy as "a way of life," a distinctive form of spiritual practice through which, in varying forms, from classical philosophy through Christian theology to the contemporary philosophical trends in which Hadot placed his own work, philosophers have sought to mark and exemplify a path for others to follow. In discussing the distinguishing features of such practice, Hadot argues that, like those who respond to the monastic calling, the philosopher lives in an intermediate state, torn between the habitual and the everyday on the one hand and the domain of consciousness and lucidity on the other. It is a way of life committed to exemplifying the means by which others might turn themselves away from their habitual ways of life to embrace a world "radically metamorphosed into a cosmic-'physical' perspective" (Hadot 1995, 104).

It was in casting philosophy as the interpreter of the guiding light of intuition that Bergson proposed a new role for philosophy as instantiating and exercising a reworked form of pastoral authority in order to guide our free self-development as beings-in-time along life's path. As such, this authority was most clearly embodied in the mystic. This is the theme that Deleuze accentuates in concluding his study of Bergson, where—with *The Two Sources of Morality and Religion* (Bergson 1935) primarily in view—he identifies two different forms of action that take place in the cerebral interval. In the first of these, ordinary memory, on descending into this interval, actualizes useful recollections, thereby nurturing the development of intelligence as the "organ of domination and utilization of matter" (Deleuze 1991a, 108). If it is this that enables humans to form societies, these are just as closed as those of animal species; man "goes round in circles in his societies much as the species do in theirs," lacking the "exceptional opening" that would yield "the power of going beyond his 'plane' (*plan*) and his condition" (109). It is, then, only the operation of "*another intercerebral interval* between intelligence itself and society" that opens up the possibility that man might, with a leap, break the circle of closed societies, a possibility that is dependent on the intervention of emotion—understood as cosmic memory made actual in the human power of creation—into this interval. It is the operation of this force, through which intelligence is converted into intuition, that opens up the prospect of liberation through which man might emerge as a creator. But this is a possibility, Deleuze cautions, that is only available to "privileged souls": to philosophers to a certain degree, but more especially to artists and mystics, the locus of a creative power that passes from soul to soul through "the intermediary of disciples or spectators or hearers" (111).

There are, then, parallels between the role accorded habit in the techniques of pastoral government and the role Bergson assigns to the spiritual exercises of what might be called "philosophy's pastorate." In singing the praises of the mystic, one of the figures of Foucault's counterconducts, Bergson subscribes to a form of counterconduct directed against the authority of science rather than that of an established church. The authority to which philosophy thus lays claim seeks, rather than directing conduct by disciplinary rules and proscriptions, to guide it along paths that others might then freely choose to follow and, in so doing, to initiate creative deviations. This is a form of authority that clears a space for its own operations by discrediting its competitors. In the case of Bergson's relations to the organic memory tradition, this struggle was essentially a struggle over the kinds of opportunities the gap or interval associated with moments of indetermination presented for guiding conduct, and the means by which this might be effected.

It is partly on these grounds that Walter Benjamin (1970) calls Bergson to task in his essay on Charles Baudelaire. In a forensic analysis of this critique, Claire Blencowe (2008) highlights the light it throws on the limitations of Bergson's account of the relations between habit and the two forms of memory he invokes. Benjamin opens up these questions indirectly via his discussion of the play between the two forms of memory—*mémoire voluntaire* and *mémoire involuntaire*, the equivalent, Blencowe notes, of Bergson's intellect and intuition—that informs the "Spleen et idéal" cycle of Baudelaire's *Les fleurs du mal* (Blencowe 2008, 147). In focusing on the opposition that informs this cycle between the ideal as the "power of remembrance" and the role of scent as "the inaccessible refuge of the *mémoire involuntaire*," Benjamin (1970, 185–86) identifies the role accorded scent in this regard as that of constructing a time outside history. Casting Bergson in the role of a metaphysician who "suppresses death" (187) in his conception of the endless flow of life constituting *la durée*, Benjamin interprets this as a transcendental force that is effectively isolated from history. In doing so, he draws on an essay, first published in 1934, in which Max Horkheimer argues that Bergson, in "making up a story about a divine current of experience as absolute being," had simply reverted to an "outmoded pantheistic metaphysics" that entailed the denial of historical time (Horkheimer 2005, 13).

This fed into Benjamin's more pointed criticism of Bergson's account of the relations between habit-memory, memory proper, the intellect, and intu-ition as one that interpreted these as ahistorical invariants. He stresses, as a counter to this, the need to take account of the ways in which varied mate-rial technologies operate on the "human sensorium" (Benjamin 1970, 177) to subject its components to varied kinds of training that periodically reconfig-ure the relations between them and the kinds of power they are able to exercise. The role Benjamin attributes to contemporary technologies of reproduction thus undermines the spiritual force, the aura, that Bergson attributed to intuition, to art, or to the *mémoire involuntaire* as though these were gener-ally accessible to human comprehension independently of the action of such technological mediations. The reproducibility of the work of art, as Benjamin puts it in his essay "The Work of Art in the Age of Mechanical Reproduction," detaches art from the cultic forms of appreciation arising from its earlier de-pendence on ritual. In doing so, it shatters the illusion of art's autonomy. Art's effects, as he puts it, can henceforth no longer be deduced from a "theology of art" (226) but must rather take account of the ways in which its relations to its consumers are socially, institutionally, and technologically mediated. It is from this perspective that Benjamin engages explicitly with Bergson's *Matter and Memory*, taking it to task on two grounds: his assessment that only a poet could fully and adequately experience *la durée* as Bergson inter-prets it; and his presentation of the relations between the two memories and habit as if "turning to the contemplative actualization of the stream of life is a matter of free choice" (159–60). In questioning this, and thereby questioning also the automatism that Bergson attributes to those who remain in the grip of habit-memory ("his fictitious characters who have completely liquidated their memories," 180), Benjamin draws on Karl Marx's account of the role of the technologies of machinofacture. He does so in order to argue against the generalized attribution of automatism to the crowd that characterized the fin de siècle literary and intellectual culture on which Bergson drew, localizing it, instead, as a specific form of degradation of the unskilled worker subjected to the "drill of the machines" (178).

The limitation that is at issue here applies more generally to the accounts of the duality of habit that characterize the nineteenth-century theorists who have been recruited into the wayward tradition. This is a duality that is attributed to what are presented as invariant internal dynamics of personhood that are activated to varying degrees according to the differential distribution of the capacity to register and respond to the possibility of moving from the grip of necessity to the realm of freedom that is presented by the moments of indetermination associated with the cerebral interval. Benjamin's critique of Bergson resonates with the perspective I am advocating, which, rather than interpreting habit's duality as an opposition between automatism and free acts, views it as an aspect of the operation of different technologies, machineries, and apparatuses through which repetition is brought under the direction of different authorities with markedly different consequences for different social groups. The duality of habit, in sum, arises out of the different forms of power that are brought to bear on the production, organization, and governance of different institutionalized forms of repetition and their social distribution. Rather than there being some invariant mechanism of transition between the two, the possibility of habit as an accumulating second nature on the part of some groups depends on its suppression among others. Its liberatory potential for some is predicated on its denial to others.

It is to a further elaboration of this perspective that I now turn in exploring how Grosz brings a Bergsonian perspective to bear on her account of how relations of difference, becoming, and freedom are produced by the "nicks in time" that fracture the dynamics of evolution.

## Habit and the fringe of freedom

The fusion of Lamarck and Darwin that shaped the work of Spencer and others in the late Victorian period was not the only or, indeed, the most authoritative post-Darwinian interpretation of Darwin's work. And Darwin himself, while occasionally using formulations that resonated with Lamarck's account of the inheritance of acquired characteristics, was inclined, for the most part, to discount such views. This was the guiding motif of the chapter on instinct in *The Origin of Species*. While acknowledging that there are significant points of resemblance between habit and instinct, these relate, Darwin argues, not to their origins or to any regular order of connection between them, but to the "frame of mind" (Darwin 1968, 235) under which the actions they reference are performed: that is, largely unconsciously. Habits that are acquired and combined with one another at particular moments in time are connected to particular states of the body, and "once acquired, they often remain constant throughout life" (235). But it would, Darwin goes on to say, be a "most serious error to suppose that the greater number of instincts have been acquired by habit in one generation, and then transmitted by inheritance to succeeding generations" (235). Instincts might accumulate within species across generations, but this is the result of the accidental variations effected by the mechanisms of natural selection to which, if there be such, any effects of habit are "of quite subordinate importance" (236). The main exception he allows concerns the relations between natural instincts and domestic instincts in conditions of artificial selection. The curious mingling of instincts, habits, and dispositions in such circumstances gives rise to a range of outcomes, mostly ones in which natural instincts are lost and domestic instincts acquired and passed on to the next generation through the combined action of habit and artificial selection.

But not, he insists, in a state of nature, a point he drives home explicitly against Lamarck in his discussion of the problem posed by the existence of caste-like differences among neutered or sterile females in insect communities. He explains how, in the case of worker ants, this might have come about through a method of selection operating at a transindividual level that prevented any cross-fertilization of the worker ants. For the blending of the instincts of differentiated castes to which such cross-fertilization would give rise would be antithetical to the communal benefits derived from the differentiated instincts and associated skills of worker ants. The case is instructive, Darwin concludes, since such caste-like variations testify to a modification of structure having been brought about "without exercise or habit having come into play" since "no amount of exercise, or habit, or volition, in the utterly sterile members of a community could possibly have affected the structure or instincts of the fertile members, which alone leave descendants" (262).

At the start of the chapter, Darwin is careful not to draw a dividing line between humans and the rest of nature. "A little dose . . . of judgement or reason," as he puts it, "often comes into play even in animals very low in the scale of nature" (234). This is a theme he turns to in his later study of the habits of worms, where he is at pains to stress how far "animals so low in the scale of organization" acted consciously "and how much mental power they displayed" (Darwin 1881, 3; Scene of Habit 6).

This insistence on the continuities between animal and human life played an important role in the contribution made to late Victorian liberalism by two of Darwin's most influential interpreters: Thomas Huxley and George John Romanes. Both of these rejected the inheritance of acquired characteristics of the organic memory tradition while also, in their subscription to the

Darwin goes to some length to emphasize how far the expectation that all he would find among worms were constant habits shaped by instinctive reflex actions was constantly confounded. "When a worm is suddenly illuminated and dashes like a rabbit into its burrow...," he tells us, "we are at first led to look at the action as a reflex one" exercised "independently of the will or consciousness of the animal, as if it were an automaton" (Darwin 1881, 23–24). But recalling the different reactions of worms in a variety of different circumstances, he rules this option out. Just as he rules out the option that worms are incapable of focusing their attention on specific objects by disregarding the impressions of other objects, concluding that their capacity for "attention implies the presence of a mind" (24). He is most surprised, however, by the aptitudes exhibited by worms in the manner in which they plug up the mouths of their burrows. The varied objects they use for this purpose, and how they adjust the ways in which they drag different objects to their burrows to take account of their specific properties, lead Darwin to conclude that their habits incorporate intelligent adjudication of the experience of trial and error.

motto that "nature makes no jumps," connecting evolution to gradualist conceptions of social change that were entirely at odds with the saltational logic of Bergson's interpretation of evolution.[11] For while stressing the respects in which all forms of life are shaped by their interactions with natural environments, Bergson also proposed a number of distinctions between them. He thus distinguished the mainly static role of torpor in mediating the relations that vegetative forms of life have with their environments from the more dynamic role played by the variable species instincts of different forms of animal life arising from the more active and varied relations to environments effected by animals' capacity for locomotion. And he distinguished both from the role of intelligence as more markedly associated with the mediation of human-environment relations, interpreting this as a difference of a qualitative kind. The difference between the human brain and all other brains, Bergson says, "is not a difference of degree, but of kind" (1998, 263). And as we have seen, his interpretation of life's path is not that of a smooth progressive development but one of leaps and bounds fueled by the explosive energy of life, which limits and qualifies the role of intelligence.

Grosz registers her distance from these aspects of Bergson's work. In stressing the value that Darwin placed on the similarities between human and animal life in *The Descent of Man* (Darwin 1981), she also distances herself from the phallic imagery of the metaphors of explosion and the discharge of energy that Bergson uses to characterize the moments of discontinuity that mark time's passage. What she retains from Bergson in her reading of Darwin's account of natural selection is a conception of the founding impetus of life giving rise to a multiplicity of divergent pathways through moments and mechanisms of interruption that, rather than taking the form of explosions, she characterizes as nicks or cuts in time in which life—natural, social, and cultural—diversifies itself through a series of sideways moves.[12] What evolves in Darwin's conception, she argues, are not "individuals or even species, which are forms of relative fixity, but oscillations of difference (which underlie and make possible individuals and species) that can consolidate themselves, more or less temporarily, into cohesive groupings only to disperse and disappear or else reappear in other terms at different times" (Grosz 2004, 24). The three basic principles of Darwin's thought—an abundance of variation, the long-term magnification of such variation effected by mechanisms of reproduction, and the selection of differential fitness from among competing individuals, varieties, and species—account for the dynamic "transformability of living systems . . . the impulse toward a future that is unknown in and uncontained by the present and its history" (32).

Natural selection, in sum, does not "simply limit life, cull it, remove its unsuccessful variations"; it also incites the living to "differentiate themselves by what they will become" (64). Its consequences in this regard are both complicated and enhanced by the mechanisms of sexual selection. While according these a number of contradictory effects, Grosz's central interest is with how the role played by aesthetic criteria in the processes of sexual selection "deviates natural selection through the expression of the will, or desire, or pleasure of individuals" (75). This is the result of the choice of sexual partners being based on the aesthetic value attributed to specific differences that are further magnified through the adoption of distinct cultural strategies of sexual allurement. This gives rise to two paths that, just as they are destined to become irreducibly different from each other—paths, in effect, leading to the development of not one but two gendered "second natures"—also generate their own internal differentiations and, in a further extension of the argument, constitute the force underlying processes of racial differentiation. In producing and exaggerating differences that do not confer any evolutionary advantage, sexual selection confirms "the ineliminable variation of sexual difference, and its productive inventiveness for future forms of life" (68). Sexual difference, in a later formulation, is "the very machinery, the engine, of living difference, the mechanism of variation, the generator of the new"; without it there would only be "the endless structural (bacterial or microbial) reproduction of the same" (Grosz 2011, 101). In thus drawing on the primacy that Luce Irigaray accords to sexual difference, Grosz also endorses Irigaray's work for providing a nonessentialist basis for a feminist politics of difference that opens up affirmative possibilities beyond those generated by feminist egalitarianisms that, in seeking an equivalence between women's and men's life chances, are "necessarily rooted in sexual indifference" (Grosz 2011, 71). No matter whether directed to the relations between the sexes, races, or classes, since egalitarianism "entails a neutral measure for the attainment of equality," it is antagonistic to "the project of the specification of difference" (148).

It is through the lens provided by her reading of the relations between natural and sexual selection, alongside her reading of Bergson and Friedrich Nietzsche's conception of the untimely, that Grosz engages with the political implications of those moments that, in dislocating the flow of time, generate unexpected possibilities within open-ended processes of becoming. She does so from the perspective of the contribution that such a conception of the inherent unpredictability and nonteleological structure of time might make to feminist and antiracist political struggles, which, "directed to bringing into existence futures that dislocate themselves from the dominant tendencies and forces of the present[,] ... are about inducing the untimely" (Grosz 2004, 14). It is only the possibilities opened up by such nicks, cuts, or ruptures in time that generate the prospect of a politics of freedom. The concept of freedom that informs this position is not that of a *freedom from*—from the arbitrary constraints and limitations of a masculine social order, a goal that Grosz associates with egalitarian feminisms—but that of a *freedom to*, a capacity for free acts. While this capacity assumes a distinctive gendered form through its association with the autonomy that arises from irreducible sexual difference, it is a potential that arises from the more general dynamics of the relations between life and matter. Freedom, as a capacity for free acts arising in moments of indeterminacy, "is not the transcendent property of the human, but the immanent and sometimes latent capacity of life in all its complexity" (Grosz

2011, 68). There is, for all forms of life, whether regulated solely by instinct or by gradations of intelligence, "a 'fringe' for freedom, a zone of indetermination that elevates it above mere automated response to given stimuli" (69).

Habit functions as a key operator in this account of freedom in the role it is assigned on both sides of the creative opportunities presented by such moments of indetermination and within them. In glossing, and endorsing, Bergson's account of habit, Grosz interprets the orderly repetitions of habit as producing forms of stability that do not, like instincts, anchor living beings to their environment but rather, by allowing some actions to be performed automatically, release the energy "to create, to produce anew, to live artistically" (2013, 225). It is, for all bodies in motion, via the unhinging of the automatism produced by the delay or gap between stimulus and response that is generated by the sensations of pain or pleasure and, additionally for humans, through the relations between habit-memory and memory proper, that new habits are generated as "*forms of desire*" that are generative of putatively free acts. But such acts are extremely rare and exceptional. If habit is a taken-for-granted substratum that makes possible acts of creative freedom, it is also what deprives acts of their freedom if they become unduly bound to it. For Grosz, endorsing Bergson's position, it is the creativity derived from free acts that generates new habits that will, in due course, become routinized and thus stifle our capacity for freedom unless this constantly asserts itself against habit's tendency toward dogged automatism (Grosz 2011, 70). Habit as a platform for freedom; as the means by which the desire for freedom is temporarily realized; and as freedom's antithesis: it is through habit's shifting operations in these regards that the virtualities latent in forms of life are released, set forth along the pathways of their divergent actualizations, and potentially curbed. But it is in those moments when, freed from those forms of authority that would direct it toward particular forms of conduct committed to the realization of particular social goals, that habit, operating "on the border between the absolutely constrained and the radically free, transforms the constrained into degrees of freedom, degrees of openness" (Grosz 2013, 233).

### The distribution of freedom's pathways

In reflecting on how she brings together perspectives drawn from Darwin and Irigaray to articulate a feminist politics based on the primacy of sexual difference rather than on egalitarian aspirations, Grosz acknowledges that the significance she attributes to oscillations of difference in producing the "nicks in time" that generate possibilities for freedom runs counter to what she interprets as Darwin's own commitment to egalitarian principles. She derives this from his tendency to consider all sexes, races, and classes as "fundamentally equal, as governed by degrees rather than by any unsurmountable gap" (Grosz 2011, 157). I have some doubts about this interpretation. For while Darwin's opposition to conceptions of fundamental divisions between either races or sexes did derive from his subscription to the doctrine that "nature makes no jumps," the contemporary political implications of this doctrine were far from egalitarian. In offering an account of the relations between the natural and social orders, it had, by the mid-nineteenth century, already had a long and somewhat varied political career (Bynum 1974). Its predominant associations thereafter, however, were with a progressive liberalism in which the principles of evolutionary gradualism ("nature makes no jumps") served to legitimate existing social inequalities by subjecting their reduction or removal to a logic of deferment. The laws of evolution, as Darwin put it, "baffle the idea of revolution" (Darwin quoted in Desmond and Moore 1992, 294).

The account that Grosz offers, following Irigaray, of the primacy of sexual difference has also been a subject of extended debate prompted by alternative feminist accounts of the performativity of gender differences, notably in Judith Butler's (1999) work, and the queering of binary sexual distinctions in transgender debates. These, and related questions concerning the apparent prioritizing of gender over racial politics, are ones that Grosz has addressed in some detail and in an open-ended way that acknowledges that many of the issues in question remain unresolved.[13] My own position, however, aligns more closely with that of Butler, who, in taking issue with Irigaray's "efforts to derive a specific feminine sexuality from a specific female anatomy," sides with Foucault in arguing that "the postulation of a normative sexuality that is 'before,' 'outside,' or 'beyond' power is a cultural impossibility" (Butler 1999, 39–40). I am also in agreement with Butler's argument, in relating this position to questions of habit, that the politics of sexualities do not hinge on stopping the power of repetition but on disconnecting that power from the heterosexual and phallogocentric forms of its exercise to harness its force to different ends.[14]

While it is important to note these debates, they go beyond the more specific issues prompted by Grosz's account of habit. This has had a significant impact on feminist engagements with the affective aspects of habit practices. Simone Fullager (2021) thus draws on the significance that Grosz attributes to the role of "nicks in time" within the dynamics of habit change in discussing how women's walking practices often afford an interval in which the normative force of gendered habits can be potentially disrupted.[15] In doing so she brings together two senses of the concept of the interval: its spatial conception as the "intervals and inbetween spaces—the parks, walkways, paths and public spaces that are neither home or work"; and the temporal register of such intervals in opening "possibilities for different gendered logics and ways of thinking-feeling to be enacted" (Fullager 2021, 191). Fullager is equally clear, however, that the realization of such possibilities depends on the discursive and institutional forces that are in contention regarding how the affective registers of walking are organized and experienced. In reporting the findings of her research into the different forms of walking engaged in by women suffering from depression, she distinguishes two therapeutic regimes in which walking might be prescribed to different effect: those that aspire to "open up an interval for becoming other than depressed" (191) and what she calls "regulatory walking habits," which, as a prescribed form of exercise for recovery from depression, instrumentalize walking as "a dutiful exercise within the normative milieu of family life" (192). In such cases the requirement of readjusting to the demands of home accompanies the walker while en route and reasserts itself in reterritorializing the self once the walker returns home.

Difficulties arise, however, when the level of analysis shifts from such specific habit practices to the more general aspects of Grosz's account of the relations between habit and freedom. I have already outlined my reasons for doubting Grosz's contention that the wayward tradition differs from the accounts of habit offered by other disciplines in eschewing a concern with ordering or regulating habits in the interest of facilitating the realization of freedom. There are certainly significant differences between the forms of spiritual, aesthetic, and intellectual authority endorsed by Ravaisson, Bergson, and Deleuze and those associated with other disciplines. But that specific forms of authority are nonetheless in play as freedom's guides is clear. There is, however, a further issue regarding who might be susceptible to being led along habit's pathways by such authorities. The central motto of the wayward tradition—we are habits, nothing but habits, the habit of acquiring habits—suggests a degree of indifference to the consequences of the socially variable ways in which this mechanism might operate owing to the different degrees to which the dynamic potential arising from the logic of indetermination might be actualized across different conditions of social life.

There is consequently little recognition of the ways in which such conditions might impose severe limits on the general account of the relations between habit and freedom that Grosz offers. In illustrating her position, she cites an example from Bergson regarding the relations between the experience of being wakened by the early-morning alarm clock and the "habitual routines of each working day." It is, she argues, only because we perform the "chain of reactions" that the alarm occasions automatically—getting out of bed, putting on slippers, and so on—that we are enabled to "elaborate relatively free acts" (Grosz 2013, 226). But this depends on, so to speak, for whom the alarm rings. For its functioning varies much in the same way as the blacksmith's arm does for Sara Ahmed in standing for "not only how a workload is eased *but how a workload is acquired*" (Ahmed 2019, 90). Recalling Friedrich Engels's invocation of the "despotic bell" that enslaves the laborer by calling him from his bed, breakfast, and dinner (Engels quoted in Marx 1970, 424), the routines set in motion by the morning alarm may just as well—and, indeed, manifestly do—prepare many for their subjection to the enforced repetitions of administered workloads. They may also have disciplinary effects beyond that. E. P. Thompson cites an eighteenth-century member of the clergy for whom "the necessity of early rising" enjoined by the rhythms of factory life brought added benefits since it would, in also necessitating "going to Bed betime . . . prevent the Danger of Midnight revels" (1991, 387).

The more general issues at stake here concern the validity of the classical philosophical distinction between "freedom from" and "freedom to" and the place accorded habit in relation to this distinction. Grosz accepts that these two freedoms are connected in the sense that "freedom to" requires the absence of constraints of the kind associated with slavery and prison camps. "It is," she writes, "perfectly obvious that a freedom to create, to make, or to produce is a luxury that can be attained only with a certain level of the absence of constraint" (Grosz 2010, 153). However, she sees the political limitation of questions concerning "freedom from" as that of failing to provide "any positive direction for action in the future" (141). By contrast, the conception of "freedom to" that she derives from Bergson is integrally connected to a conception of the dynamic discontinuity of the subject that arises from a self-transformative capacity generated by the relations between the agency of life and that of matter. Free acts arising from the capacity of the subject to be "always and imperceptibly becoming other than what it once was" are those "which transform us, which we can incorporate into our becomings in the very process of their changing us" (146). As such, free acts operate independently of any pathways that might chart a course between "freedom from" and "freedom to." Since free acts transform us, they also transform the becoming that we are, with the result that no path can be constructed until after such acts have been completed. Paths exist "only in reconstruction and not in actuality" (147).

When habit is brought back into the picture, however, Grosz's pathways describe a different trajectory, one in which free acts acquire their distinctiveness through their movement away from the curtailing and limiting effects of the regimes of habit that they break with. The autonomy of the living being that such acts assert, she argues, can only function against, and as the vis-à-vis of, "a background of routinized or habitual activity" (148). Derived as an immanent property of the relations that living beings have with the material world, the capacity for such acts arises from the "'fringe' of freedom" generated by the "zone of indetermination" that elevates different forms of life, albeit to varying degrees, "above mere automated response to given stimuli" (149). If the dynamism that life derives from this indeterminacy is returned with interest to the nonliving material world through life's interactions with it, the seeds of life's dynamism have their roots in the inner recesses of indeterminacy that are lodged in the vibratory constitution of matter. If at one level matter is a source of the regularity, predictability, and determination that shape and make possible habitual actions, it is also the ultimate source of the indetermination through which its own dynamic potentiality is extended.

However, while the final direction and outcome of the courses of action arising from this tension are not determinable in advance, the trajectories of the unfolding pathways that compose the course of particular becomings are initially constituted by the break they make with the conditions from which they set off. And such breaks, in the case of particular regimes of habit, are, contrary to Grosz's contentions, usually marked by attempts to weaken or sever the bonds that tether the possibilities associated with particular distributions of the capacity for the "freedom to" initiate new courses of action relative to the "freedom from" the limiting constraints that arise from the unequal power relations between different groups. It is precisely the struggle to weaken or break the hold of such differential articulations of the relations between these different freedoms that gives an initial impetus and direction to political programs of subordinate groups directed at securing a greater degree of freedom from the restrictive effects of particular habit regimes.

### The social and material determinants of gapped time

These difficulties point to a further difficulty associated with the wayward tradition more generally concerning the forms of materialism that it lays claim to. These largely pertain to the dynamic relations between life and matter that arise from, in Bergson's terms, the founding impetus of life and how this propels the dynamic through which forms of life differ and diversify. There is, however, no equivalent significance accorded to the effects on human capacities and conduct of the specific forms of agency exercised by those forms of socially organized matter instanced by particular social and cultural apparatuses. This was, as we have seen, one of the grounds on which Benjamin called Bergson to task for his abstraction of the aesthetic from the effects of the place of art in the age of mechanical reproduction and his account of habit memory. Ruth Leys (2011) takes a similar tack in her assessment of a limitation of the turn to affect in post-Deleuzian theory more generally. The significance accorded affects as autonomic processes that take place beneath the threshold of consciousness, she argues, has unduly diverted attention from the role of discursive and institutional forces in shaping affects and their role in relation to conduct.[16] It's worth adding to this the doubt that historical accounts of the highly variable effects of different technologies of memory, and the varied practices of remembering that they engender, throws on the simple polarity that Bergson posits between habit-memory and memory proper. It does, indeed, beggar belief that such a polarity should continue to recruit any credence given the light that recent developments in the fields of museum and heritage studies have thrown on the marked variability, both within and across cultures and historically, of the institutional and discursive forces shaping memory practices.[17]

What is missing, then, is any working through of the respects in which the alleged autonomy of "freedom to" from "freedom from" questions might vary across economic and political systems as well as across relations of race, class, and gender as a consequence of the operation of distinctive technologies of power through which relatively high degrees of "freedom to" relative to "freedom from" for some are the effect of the imposition of an inverse set of such relations on others. These are questions that a general account of the mutual interactions of the indeterminacy of life and matter in directionless processes of becoming connects with only obliquely, if at all. They are also ones in which the shifting ratios between "freedom to" and "freedom from" across social positions have no more to do with habit's double-dealing relations between freedom and automaticity than with a supposed dialectic between two different forms of memory.

There is a more pointed set of contemporary concerns at issue here. There is now a substantial literature focused on the new forms of material agency exercised by digital media suggesting that new processes of habit formation are in play that suspend the logic of "we are habits, nothing but habits, the habit of acquiring habits" by displacing habit's pathways from humans to the operations of digital infrastructures. One suggestion along these lines is that the "habit of acquiring habits" is now most significantly exercised via the routine acquisition of our habits in the form of digital data and their permutation in increasing and unexpected correlations. It is this, it is argued, that provides a lever for the direction of our conduct in ways that bypass our awareness, giving rise to new dynamics of the self, including ones that suspend its operations. Wendy Chun, in elaborating this perspective, suggests that it presents a challenge to Grosz's account of the role of gapped time in the mechanisms of habit change. While endorsing the connections that Grosz and, indeed, the wayward tradition generally propose between the forms of reflection and the free acts to which they might give rise that are made possible by the forms of undecidability associated with moments of gapped time, Chun argues that the operations of new media tend to close down such possibilities precisely through their routinization of gapped time. If new media are driven by the logic of acting on our practices and desires as consumers by establishing endlessly differentiating sets of correlations between our habits, they are also driven by the market-driven need to constantly interrupt those correlations in order to establish new ones by means of artificially generated crises. Proposing the formula Habit + Crisis = Update as a summary of the "twinning of habits and crisis that structure networked time" (Chun 2016, loc. 217), Chun argues that this represents a powerful tendency to deprive habit of any dynamic potential it might once have had by "making the present a series of updates in which we race to stay close to the same" (loc. 218).

This is a line of argument I consider more fully in my final chapter. I introduce it now, however, as it connects with a significant criticism that has been directed at the wayward tradition by one of its most influential advocates. I refer to Catherine Malabou, who has recently drawn on the literature relating to machinic forms of artificial intelligence to critique the use she had made of Bergson in her earlier accounts of the liberating potential of the explosive plasticity that she attributed to the interruptions of habit's pathways produced by neural synapses (Malabou 2008). It is to these accounts, and their subsequent revision, that I turn in the following chapter.

# 6

# Exploded
# Pathways

"IN THE USUAL ORDER OF THINGS, lives run their course like rivers" (Malabou 2012, 1). In this, the opening sentence of *Ontology of the Accident*, Catherine Malabou alludes to those conceptions of habit's pathways that have been analogized with reference to waterways. We have already seen examples of this, in our discussion in chapter 2, of the role played by such conceptions in George Eliot's *The Mill on the Floss*. It was, however, William James who most influentially interpreted habit's pathways as akin to the courses carved by rivers. In doing so he drew on the formulations of the French psychologist Léon Dumont: "Water, in flowing, hollows out for itself a channel, which grows broader and deeper; and, after having ceased to flow, it resumes, when it flows again, the path traced by itself before. Just so, the impressions of outer objects fashion for themselves in the nervous system more and more appropriate paths, and these vital phenomena recur under similar excitements from without, when they have been interrupted a certain time" (Dumont quoted in James [1890] 2007, 106). James's endorsement of such conceptions reflected his subscription to the accounts of automatic action that had been developed in the earlier history of the reflex arc. However, he also qualified the role accorded the nervous system in such accounts in attributing a potential for plasticity—for, as David Leary puts it, "the establishment of new or altered neural pathways through which electrophysiological currents pass on their way from sensory input to motor output" (2013, 190)—to the operations of the brain's central hemispheres. Viewed as the legacy of evolutionary advancements differentiating humans from animals, this capacity for plasticity was central to James's account of the dynamics of habit. Should the regular flow of electrophysiological currents along the neural pathways inscribed by the repetitions of earlier habits be inhibited by the operations of the cerebral hemispheres, such currents will then forge new pathways, providing the routes for new courses of action across the relations between neural pathways and the body's nervous and muscular systems. In becoming, in their turn, easy and habituated through unconscious repetition, the motions that are enacted across such pathways provide the basis for the cumulative development of new capacities.

For Malabou, by contrast, interruptions of habit's pathways are to be celebrated because of the ruptural possibilities they present. Rivers sometimes, she argues, "jump their bed, without geological cause, without any subterranean pathway to explain the spate of flood," their "suddenly deviant, 'deviating form' representing instead an 'explosive plasticity'" (Malabou 2012, 3). This allusion to habit's pathways recurs at a number of points in her *Ontology of the Accident*, but only to disrupt the assumption of the accumulating continuities usually attributed to such pathways in favor of a ruptural plasticity that knows no end. She delights, in her discussion of Marguerite Duras's *The Lover*, in undermining the association between repetition, habit, and involuntary addiction. "All of a sudden, habitually. A habit from the first time" (60) is how she interprets Duras's statement that she became an alcoholic not bit by bit but all at once—"as soon as I started to drink"—thereby bringing it into collision with the more regular accumulating repetitions attributed to habit's degenerative pathways. A similar perspective informs her discussion of what she calls "accidental aging" (49) as something that can happen at any time, the result of a moment of rupture that establishes old age as "an existential break—not a continuity" (42). And it recurs again in her account of Marcel Proust's celebration of the "plastic ambiguity" of time. There is "progression, evolution, inflection, repetition" but also "the infinitely rapid, the bump, the accident," which "introduce into the thickness of succession the undatable bifurcation of destruction, sharp as a claw, unpredictable, throbbing, magnificent" (54).

It is not just James's conception of habit's neural pathways that Malabou wishes to trouble in these remarks. It is rather all accounts that give the cumulative acquisition of habits a neurobiological anchorage in the brain's pathways that she has in mind. In her *What Should We Do with Our Brain?* (2008), Malabou draws on her earlier account of the role of habit in G. W. F. Hegel's philosophy (Malabou 2005), and on recent developments in the neurosciences, to present habit's pathways as being constantly blown up by the explosive properties that she interprets as defining current conceptions of neural processes: "Cerebral space is constituted by cuts, by voids, by gaps, and this prevents our taking it to be an integrative totality. In effect, neuronal tissue is discontinuous.... Between two neurons, there is thus a caesura, and the synapse itself is 'gapped.' ... Because of this, the interval or the cut plays a decisive role in cerebral organization" (Malabou 2008, 36).

Malabou is not the first to introduce gaps and intervals into the discussion of habit. To the contrary, as we have seen, such conceptions have often been invoked in accounts that accord some individuals, but not others, a capacity to pause and reflect on habits that have become unduly fixed as a prelude to restoring a self-willed progressive dynamic to habit's pathways. Her account is, however, distinctive in drawing on Gilles Deleuze's account of neural indetermination to elaborate the scope it offers for aesthetic practices to lend an explosive plasticity to habit's pathways. It is also distinctive in the manner in which it mobilizes this interpretation of the politics of "the gap" against its manipulation by the various forms of "managed mindfulness" that have been developed by a range of governmental programs premised on quite different interpretations of the neurosciences. I therefore look at some examples of these programs first, and the counters to them proposed by sociological programs of governing habit by cultivating a capacity for "reflexive flexibility," as a means of identifying the targets that Malabou has in view in her own conceptions of the politics of "the gap." I then come back to look at Malabou's conception of habit's "explosive plasticity" in more detail before identifying what strike me as its central weaknesses.

These coincide, in some respects, with the criticisms that Malabou has subsequently made of *What Should We Do with Our Brain?*, which, in her later *Morphing Intelligence*, she frankly assesses as "wrong-headed" and needing "revising, if not a complete rewrite" (Malabou 2019, 82–83). The rewrite she proposes has, however, a broader cast as, in reappraising the "wayward tradition," she distances herself from some of its characteristics, seeking instead an anchorage for the new position she proposes in an amalgam of perspectives culled from the work of Pierre Bourdieu, Jean Piaget, and John Dewey. This underwrites a new conception of habit's contribution to the "critical task" of rediscovering "the pathway for interrupting automaticity so as to better emancipate automatisms" (133). If this conception of an "automaticity interruptus" differs in some respects from the conception of a "habitus interruptus" that characterizes her earlier account of the relations between habit and neural plasticity, it nonetheless retains a similar structure in failing to take adequate account of the ways in which the dynamics of mind-body-environment relations vary in accordance with the classed, raced, and gendered aspects of social position. In pursuing these arguments in the second half of the chapter, I place them in the context of an alternative assessment of current debates concerning the relations between artificial intelligence (AI) and habit. I also engage critically with her reading of Bourdieu's work to question the role that she accords aesthetic practices as a counter to habit's potentially sclerotic effects.

## Governing through plasticity

There is not space here to do more than skim the surface of what is now a burgeoning literature exploring how the neurosciences have reshaped our conceptions of personhood in ways that have opened up the governance of conduct to the interventions of a host of new authorities and technologies of behavior management (Brenninkmeijer 2010).[1] I shall instead take Nikolas Rose and Joelle Abi-Rached's (2013) account of the relationships between the neurosciences and the development of what they call the "neurobiological complex" as my point of entry into these questions. This complex consists of those apparatuses in which perspectives culled from the neurosciences interface with programs of governance and self-governance, taking over many areas of "managing the mind"—and thence persons and social relations—that had previously been the domain of the psy disciplines. The neurosciences' understanding of neural plasticity as continuing across the life course has given rise to new forms of intervention into the management of personhood by posing the question of how "to govern, these processes of shaping and reshaping our plastic brains" (Rose and Abi-Rached 2013, 12). It is not the concept of the brain's plasticity that is new here. This informed late nineteenth-century neurophysiological conceptions of the brain that, in turn, informed James's influential conception of habit, summed up in his proposition that "*the phenomena of habit in living beings are due to the plasticity of the organic material of which their bodies are composed*," where plasticity is defined as "the possession of a structure weak enough to yield to an influence, but strong enough not to yield all at once" (James [1890] 2007, 105). But this was a limited plasticity that, as we saw in chapter 2, was due to end by the age of thirty when, as James put it, "the character has set like plaster, and will never soften again" (120), as habit loses its earlier developmental potential in coming, instead, to operate as a conservative mechanism that binds us and limits our horizons to the occupations for which we have been trained.

The key discovery of the neurosciences—a largely post-1960s disciplinary cluster whose distinctiveness is that of anatomizing the human brain "at the molecular level" (Rose and Abi-Rached 2013, 9)—is that of the ongoing mutability of the brain across the life course. This conception of a plasticity without fixed limits locates "neural processes firmly in the dimensions of time, development and transactions within a milieu" (23), thus opening up the brain to dynamic historicities at the biographical, societal, and cultural levels. The brain's plasticity has also been given a greater latitude in being freed from the restrictions placed on it by earlier conceptions of its conditioning as being effected solely through the sensorial mediation of its relations to external environments. Felicity Callard and Daniel Margulies (2011) thus emphasize the respects in which the neurosciences have extended early twentieth-century critiques of the limits that James placed on the brain's plasticity by attending to the more mobile plasticities produced by the internal dynamism of neural processes. James conceived the brain and the spinal cord as "bony boxes" shut off from the mechanical pressures to which other bodily organs were subject. Their plasticity derived from the impressions made on them by the channels produced by "the infinitely attenuated currents that pour in" to them "through the blood, on the one hand, and through the sensory nerve-roots, on the other" (James [1890] 2007, 107). By contrast, current conceptions of the brain as being always active irrespective of the degree to which it is exposed to environmental stimulus have brought attention to bear on the rhythms of its intrinsic dynamics.

The implications of such conceptions of the brain's enhanced plasticity for our understanding of habit, and how it might operate as a mechanism for shaping and governing thought and behavior, have been many and varied. One response, Rose and Abi-Rached (2013) argue, has been to open up the brain to various forms of "managed mindfulness" in which nonconscious processes are brought to the fore in programs of neurological reflexivity through which we re-form our habits by acting on ourselves through our brains under the guidance of new forms of neurological and quasi-neurological expertise. A good many of these programs depend on quite mechanical interpretations of the neurosciences that merely rehearse the formulations of the earlier forms of cognitive neurobiology that the neurosciences have called into question. Charles Duhigg, distilling a formula for regulating habits from a survey of the neurosciences, thus identifies what he calls the "habit loop," consisting of a set of relations between behavioral cues, routines, and rewards that, through repetition, become automatic (Duhigg 2012, 19). The lever that this provides for the management of habits, Duhigg argues, consists in the relationship between cues and rewards: keep these as they are but insert a new set of routines connecting them and habits can be changed without disrupting the continued operation of the habit loop.

Richard Thaler and Cass Sunstein take a different tack in advocating the organization and manipulation of "choice architectures" on the part of experts to "nudge" people into making lifestyle changes via unconscious adaptations of their daily routines, choices that—in a somewhat optimistic leap of faith—they will subsequently recognize as having been in their best interests. The chief lesson of the neurosciences, they argue, is that of having demonstrated a distinction between two different thought-action systems (Thaler and Sunstein 2008, 22): the automatic system (uncontrolled, effortless, associative, fast, unconscious, skilled), associated with the oldest parts of the brain, and the more recently developed reflective system (controlled, effortful, deductive, slow, self-aware, rule-following). The tactics of "nudge," while not disputing the efficacy of the reflective system, leave it—as Thaler and Sunstein put it—to the few Mr. Spocks among us to cultivate in order to focus on the automatic system as the best way of transforming the more numerous Homer Simpsons in their own best interests (24). The tactics of nudge have had considerable influence. Thaler was an adviser to the United Kingdom's Behavioural Insights Team in establishing a "nudge unit" in David Cameron's Office of Cabinet, and that team in turn advised the Liberal government in New South Wales on its plans to establish a similar unit.[2] At the same time, the concept of nudge has been widely criticized as paternalistic, illiberal, technocratic, and antidemocratic; it "treats people like consumers rather than citizens," as one critic has put it, "presenting them with only the information required to lead an individual to a pre-defined conclusion" (Evans 2012).

### Reflexive flexibility and self-governance

These are among the grounds on which the Social Brain project took issue with nudge and similar programs in seeking to connect new conceptions of neural plasticity to liberal strategies of governing by working through the freedom and autonomy that they produce as a space for the self-action of the governed. Run by the Royal Society for the Encouragement of Arts, Manufacture and Commerce, its primary contention was that the neurosciences demonstrate not a polarity between the automatic and the reflective systems but the capacity of the latter to pause the effects of the former and thereby bring them under the influence of both individual and collective forms of deliberation and reflection. Its "steer" approach sought to avoid the paternalistic implications of nudge by aiming to "change the subject" (Grist 2009): that is, to steer individuals to engage in programs of transformative learning so that they will knowingly change their own behaviors rather than responding unconsciously to the behind-the-scenes manipulations of choice architectures by self-appointed experts. The methods of "steer" are those of liberal government in Michel Foucault's sense of equipping individuals with the capacities that are needed to freely govern themselves. The Social Brain project thus aimed to disseminate the perspectives of the neurosciences "in a form that has salience and practical relevance for the people who want to change their own behavior on their own terms" (Rowson 2011, 5)—a requirement driven by the increasing need for "flexibility" in the modern world.

My interest here is in the role that the Social Brain project accorded sociological accounts of reflexivity as a model for the kinds of neural processes required to produce self-adapting flexible subjects. It thus called on the concern with "our capacity to reflect on the conditions of our action, and thereby shape our own lives and identities," associated with the "reflexive modernity" tradition in sociology to be integrated with "'neurological reflexivity'—the capacity to reflect upon and directly to shape our mental processes" (Rowson 2011, 19)—in reshaping the dynamics of contemporary selfhood. Represented most notably by the work of Ulrich Beck, Anthony Giddens, and Scott Lash (1994), the reflexive modernity tradition that Rowson refers to is one that, in purportedly unpinning the defining antinomies of classical sociology, has arguably perpetuated them with the consequence that, far from escaping the illiberal exclusions of nudge tactics, it has merely redefined them. Charles Camic (1986) has shown how, in Émile Durkheim's work, human action is divided between two poles—that of habit, interpreted as an anatomical-physiological sedimentation of our instinctual inheritance, and that of elected forms of conduct flowing from conscious decisions. While assessing the former as the stronger force, Durkheim assigned sociology the task of cultivating the latter so that it might prevail in bringing habits under conscious direction. At the same time, we find a familiar schism in Durkheim (1964) between the sections of the population judged to be capable of acquiring this capacity (by and large, the elite attendees of secondary schools who acquire a capacity to transcend habits by translating them into moral imperatives through a process of continual reflection) and those who lack it (those whose schooling is restricted to the primary level, where discipline instills a regime of routine habits). The "reflexive modernity" literature similarly, as Paul Sweetman (2003, 547) shows, always generates a distinction between "reflexivity winners" and "reflexivity losers," a distinction that, just as it did for Durkheim, largely replicates that proposed by early modern aesthetic theory in interpreting reflexivity as an attribute that is cultivated among those in liberal occupations but much less so among those in mechanical or routine occupations.[3]

The Social Brain project echoes these conceptions. While it aspires to "steer" people into freely transforming themselves through the mechanisms of neurological reflexivity, this turns out to be a possibility that is not open to everyone—at least not yet. On the one hand, reflexivity is a form of "self-awareness in action" that is necessary if we are to "achieve the forms of agency or autonomy that are implicitly or explicitly demanded of us to adapt to modern challenges" (Rowson 2011, 19). On the other hand, the levels of self-awareness needed for the exercise of such neurological forms of self-governance are not yet sufficiently broadly distributed to apply to everyone. Indeed, "only around twenty per cent of the population" (21) meet the required standards of reflexivity. The task of the Social Brain Centre was thus to disseminate this capacity as broadly as possible by bringing those who lack it under the tutelary wing of sociologically informed reflexivity managers.

Reflexivity in service of flexibility: there are, as Victoria Pitts-Taylor (2010) shows, many versions of how each of these concepts might be interpreted, of how the relations between them should be construed, and of the respects in which they press contemporary conceptions of neural plasticity into the service of neoliberal economic imperatives. Callard and Margulies (2011), for example, point to the radical transformation of earlier conceptions of the significance of those moments when the brain's activities are temporarily paused that have been developed within the neuroscientific field of "resting-state" research. The significance of such moments in late nineteenth-century psychological and social theory echoed the more everyday usages of the concept of rest, defined by the *Oxford English Dictionary* as "a natural repose or relief from activity; the intermission of labor or exertion . . . ; freedom from distress or trouble; quiet or tranquility of mind; . . . the opposite of: activity, busyness, labor, movement, restlessness and agitation" (quoted in Callard and Margulies 2011, 241). William James, for example, contrasted such moments to the brain's attentiveness as constituting a state of distraction or absentmindedness. By contrast, resting-state research includes "absentmindedness or mind-wandering as a form of introspective attention" (246) as a part and parcel of the actions of the resting brain, which is thus "characterized by ceaseless activity, exertion, industriousness and movement" (249), a flexibility constantly available to its own interventions. In other formulations, the discourse of flexibility echoes the contrast that Georges Simmel drew between the conservative minds of rural folk, governed by "the steady rhythm of uninterrupted habituations," and the agile intellectuality of the city dweller prompted by the "*intensification of nervous stimulation*" enjoined by the rhythms of the metropolis (Simmel 1950, 410). Pitts-Taylor identifies a similar set of contrasts in a contemporary journalist's contention that neural flexibility is dependent on the brain being subject to the constant stimulation of city environments, "with many people constantly moving around, extensive infrastructure, and plenty of lights," a scene that is counterposed to the lethargic underuse of the brain's capacities associated with "an abandoned village where a handful of elderly people are living out their time" (Y. Kokurina quoted in Pitts-Taylor 2010, 642).

It is, however, less the specific forms taken by the translation of neural plasticity into particular orderings of the relations between reflexivity and flexibility that Malabou has in view than the role such orderings accord different kinds of authority in giving plasticity a direction by guiding it along preferred pathways. In aspiring to liberate plasticity from such authoritative forms of direction, Malabou interprets the gaps, cuts, and intervals that she attributes to the synaptic relations between neurons as the locus for aesthetic forms of rupture that pave the way for entirely free and self-directed forms of development. In doing so, she follows the well-worn path of post-Kantian aesthetics as, in the terms proposed by Theodor Adorno, a form of commentary that seeks to engender free and self-reflective forms of individuality that will "stand free of any guardian" (Adorno 1963, 281)—except, that is, for that of the philosopher-aesthetician who, operating as freedom's navigator, exercises a distinctive form of authority, but one that occludes itself by attributing its effects to the intrinsic properties of the artwork (T. Bennett 2011a). This is the role that Malabou assumes in her account of the dynamics of what might best be called "habitus interruptus."

## Habitus interruptus

The root of Malabou's objection to programs that, taking their cue from the neurosciences, aim to inculcate new forms of flexibility via the production and management of neuro-reflexivity derives from their interpretation of flexibility as "the ideological avatar of plasticity—at once its mask, its diversion, and its confiscation" (Malabou 2008, 12). As normalizing practices that annex flexibility to a docility-obedience nexus, their central weakness is that they "grasp only one of the semantic registers of plasticity: that of receiving... a form or impression, to be able to fold oneself, to take the fold, not to give it." What flexibility lacks "is the resource of giving form, the power to create, to invent or even to erase an impression, the power to style. Flexibility is plasticity minus its genius" (12). The genius that Malabou has in mind is that of the aesthetic as exemplified by her interpretation of neural plasticity as essentially sculptural. The brain's capacity "to adapt itself, to include modifications, to receive shocks, and to create anew on the basis of this very reception" is the manifestation of a plasticity that "makes us, precisely in the sense of a work: sculpture, modelling, architecture" (7). Plasticity thus opens up the prospect that we might all become the authors of both our neuronal futures and ourselves as works of art.[4] "Plasticity," as Malabou puts it, "thus adds the functions of artist and instructor in freedom and autonomy to its role as sculptor" (24); it constitutes a view of the brain "not only as the creator and receiver of form but also as an agency of disobedience to every constituted form, a refusal to submit to a model" (6). The possibility of realizing this potential for neuronal autocreation as the brain swivels on itself to redirect the processes regulating its own formation depends on the logic of gaps. If the structure of neural tissue is discontinuous, then the pathway along which a habitus moves beyond the constraints of habit is an interrupted one: "The 'chain' that leads from elementary life to the autonomy of a free self, capable not only of integrating the disturbances arriving from the exterior without dissolving itself but also of creating itself out of them, of making its own history, is a movement full of turbulence" (75).

Malabou models this turbulence on the explosions Bergson attributes to the "energy of life producing a capability for free actions," explosions that rupture and interrupt the pathways of habit's repetitions by effecting "the transformation of one motor regime into another, of one device into another, a transformation necessitating a rupture, the violence of the gap that interrupts all continuity" (Bergson cited in Malabou 2008, 73). This influence of Bergson is mediated via Deleuze's engagement with the neurosciences. "And the brain is nothing but this," Deleuze writes, "—an interval, a gap between an action and a reaction" that functions as a "centre of indetermination . . . between a perception which is troubling in certain respects and a hesitant action" (Deleuze 1986, 65–67). This Deleuzian interpretation of the Bergsonian gap has been invoked in a variety of claims about its potential to serve as the locus for a capacity for radical self-transformation that is inherent to our constitution as human animals—but a locus that is lodged in the materiality of the brain, and of brain-body-environment relations, rather than in the abstraction of the mind. It provides the basis for Brian Massumi's relocation of the "higher functions" of consciousness and volition in the "autonomic, bodily reactions occurring in the brain but outside consciousness, and between brain and finger but prior to action and expression" (Massumi 2002, 29), where the gap between brain and finger is that "mysterious half second" between stimulus and reaction evidenced by Benjamin Libet's laboratory experiments. And it is invoked by Jill Bennett's account of the aesthetic as an example of "the 'affection image,'" which, dwelling in the Deleuzian interval between "a troubling perception and a hesitant action," untangles its operations—"the links—and blockages or 'hesitations'—between apprehension and action, between feeling and believing, appearing, saying and doing" (J. Bennett 2012, 4). It is, Bennett argues, this capacity to suspend or hover perception that confers on the aesthetic its true value rather than activist or other social and political demands to make art more serviceable by subordinating it to nonaesthetic imperatives. This follows the line of reasoning of Deleuze and Félix Guattari in locating the operations of art in "the deepest of the synaptic fissures, in the hiatuses, intervals, and meantimes of a nonobjectifiable brain," where its creative force disrupts the ready-made paths they attribute to the sedimentations of opinion (Deleuze and Guattari 1994, 209).

The distinctiveness of Malabou's position consists in her melding of the perspectives of indetermination and plasticity. There are, however, variations in how this melding is fashioned. Thomas Wormald argues convincingly that Malabou's polemical interpretations of neuroplasticity in *What Should We Do with Our Brain?* are somewhat untypical of, and less nuanced than, her longer-term commitment to develop an ontological conception of plasticity as constitutive of being as such. This ontology, he argues, constitutes a "new materialism of immanence" (2014, 1) in which the processes through which existing material forms are de-formed and re-formed are said to derive from the nature of being itself. Sebastian Rand similarly stresses the respects in which Malabou's concepts of form and plasticity are intertwined: "Insofar as plasticity designates both form-receiving and form-giving, it must be thought of as destructive. In receiving form, it destroys its old form, and in giving form it destroys the form of the thing to which it gives a new form. What is plastic thus destroys form generally, both its own and others'" (2011, 351n35). Change here does not require the production of a pure outside from which a micropolitics of resistance might be produced in the face of a totally unmalleable and repressive reality; it is rather an inherent outcome of the constitutively malleable set of relations that constitute the real.

Malabou is clear on her intentions in this regard in *The Future of Hegel*, in which she rethinks time through the concept of plasticity. This entails jettisoning the conception of time as a succession of moments, and of the future as one such moment, in favor of its conception as "an *anticipatory structure* operating within subjectivity" (Malabou 2005, 12). It is through this structure of anticipation—that of "*le voir venir*," to "wait and see" (but not to know) what is coming—that "subjectivity *projects itself* in advance of itself, and thereby participates in the process of its own determination" (Malabou 2000, 213). It is habit that provides the operative principles of this structure of anticipation as, in Hegel's terms, "a work of art of the soul" (Hegel quoted in Malabou 2005, 24), effecting its transition from nature to spirit as the "second nature" that constitutes the place proper to the human, between the animal and the divine. In thus placing a Hegelian grid on the Aristotelean concept of habitus, habit is presented as a process through which the psychic and the somatic are interactively engaged in a dynamic plasticity by means of which aptitudes are shaped via the ongoing giving of new form alongside the destruction of previously acquired form. The generative work of habit consists in its transformations of the repetitions set off by the previous phase of the spirit's formation. It is, in this respect, a virtuality, suspending the regular chronological ordering of time as a succession of moments through the simultaneity it forges between the three times produced by its mode of action: "the past (habit is prior to its being put to work), the present (habit is itself a modality of presence), and the future (habit takes the form of a task which must be fulfilled, of an expectation that rules the direction of what it is to come)" (Malabou 2005, 56).

The more explicitly political position that Malabou takes up derives its force from her fusion of her philosophical conception of plasticity and its currency in the neurosciences. In making this point, Tobias Rees argues that the philosophical gloss she places on the neurosciences aims not just to critique flexibility theory but also to recruit the neurosciences for a philosophical mediation of the relations between matter and mind, nature and freedom. This is a mediation that interprets the plasticity of neuronal synapses as "the cerebral locus of a revolutionary moment in which nature (necessity) is transcending itself," thereby effecting "the revolutionary transformation of necessity into (natural) freedom" (Rees 2011, 266). If this philosophical grounding of Malabou's position differentiates it from voluntaristic forms of resistance, the same is true of the role she accords philosophical aesthetics in guiding the interruptions, arising from the explosive and disruptive force of plasticity, that mark habit's passage along the pathways to freedom.

For in asking how plasticity is to be imbued with genius, Malabou's answer is to invoke aesthetics as a force that intervenes to inflect how the opportunity for free self-shaping that the gaps, cuts, and voids that she imputes to the organization of cerebral space is exercised. In doing so, she constitutes aesthetics as a form of authority that is to be exercised in the gapped time produced by moments of indetermination. The issues at stake here are foregrounded in a later essay in which Malabou draws on Foucault's "What Is Enlightenment?" (Foucault 2007b) to interpret the sculptural plasticity generated by the indeterminacy of synaptic gaps as a model for the free self-creation of humanity as a subject of reason. The chief lesson she draws from Foucault is his interpretation, via Baudelaire, of "modern man" as being compelled "to face the task of producing himself" (Foucault 2007b, 109) and his related endorsement of Immanuel Kant's conception of enlightenment as the moment when humanity will "put its own reason to use, without subjecting itself to any authority" (104). For Foucault, Kant's essay serves as a summation of the position informing his three *Critiques*, including the *Critique of Judgement* (Kant [1790] 1987). The autonomy that Kant established for the sense of beauty in freeing it from its previous subordination to concepts—most immediately in the relations between Christian Wolff's aesthetic and the *polizeiwissenschaften* of the Prussian state (see Caygill 1989; Chytry 1989)—opened up the aesthetic as a zone of freedom, a way of working on the self independently of the forms of tutelage to the truths promulgated by moral or epistemological authorities.

In their subsequent development, however, the trajectories of post-Kantian aesthetics have witnessed the development of a range of positions in which philosopher aestheticians have brought aesthetic dispositions under the new and distinctive forms of direction constituted by the hands-off forms of authority they claim as freedom's self-appointed guides.[5] As such, philosophical aesthetics has tended to occlude its role in guiding conduct along the particular paths opened up by the freedom imputed to aesthetic encounters as being intrinsic to such encounters rather than a product of its own activities in mediating them. Marc De Kesel (2016) pinpoints the bearing of these issues on Malabou's position in calling attention to how frequently she uses the motif of "we do not know it." In her bid to displace the authority claimed by reductive forms of brain research that interpret neural determination as a denial of freedom, Malabou claims that we are free, we are the subjects of our own autocreation, we are the authors of ourselves—but we do not know it. "Humans make their own brain," she says, "but they do not know that they make it" (Malabou 2008, 1). The full realization of their potential in this regard thus depends on their being led by others to a consciousness of the brain's historicity and, thereby, to a realization of the possibility for free self-creation that arises from the gaps, clefts, voids, and so on that neuronal synapses introduce into the relations between the brain's cells. The use of aesthetic conceptions and imagery to interpret the possibilities opened up by synaptic gaps means that the philosopher aesthetician operates as no more and no less a guardian of such gaps, pointing to a path out and across them, than do sociology's reflexivity theorists. What is at stake in such relations are contestations over the constitution of habit's pathways, the directions in which conduct should be led along or out of them, and who should do the leading.

What is perhaps more noteworthy, however, are the respects in which, in reviving the currency of the Bergsonian gap, Malabou, like so many who have slip-streamed in his wake in the radical potential they attribute to this gap, fails to engage with the discriminatory political history that it has enacted. We can see this in the consequences of Malabou's abstraction of plasticity from its practical histories, and in the equally historically abstracted nature of the aesthetic qualities she attributes to it. "Plasticity acts like a sculptor," she writes, "and we can speak of a plastic art of and in the brain" (Malabou 2016, 28). This attribution of plasticity to the brain abstracted from the fleshiness of bodies ignores the respects in which conceptions of plasticity have been tied up with those of the body's impressibility and malleability, and the respects in which—as we saw when discussing Kyla Schuller's work in chapter 2— the differential distribution of varied forms and degrees of the malleability-plasticity couplet across raced, gendered, and classed bodies has been tangled up with biopolitical forms of governance. Schuller and Jules Gill-Peterson make the same point when including Malabou in their critique of a range of contemporary politics of subversion that, interpreting plasticity as "a resource for the disruption of normalizing systems of power," neglect the respects in which "malleability is already an enlisted feature of state power through the biopolitics of plasticity" (Schuller and Gill-Peterson 2020, 2). Generally, they continue, "plasticity is equated with potential and assigned to whiteness" to be "protected and nurtured by the state," while blackness "is characterized by a quality of stolidity that at best can be pressed into a new shape, but can never self-transform," and Indigeneity lingers as "a remnant of past growth that froze in time many centuries ago" (2).

The association of plasticity with the sculptural qualities that Malabou attributes to the arts has also by no means been a constant one. In his significant reworking of the narratives of art history, Éric Michaud shows how the categories of the sculptural and the painterly have been variably interpreted with regard to the form-making and form-breaking capacities attributed to them and how, in the most distinctive tendencies of its nineteenth-century development, sculpture was viewed as the more conservative of the two. He also emphasizes the racial dimensions that informed sculpture's assignation to what was interpreted as the moribund legacy of Greek and Roman classicism that distinguished the art of southern Europe from the dynamism of the painterly orientation that characterized the art of northern Europe as a significant aspect of racialized conceptions of cultural differences that had a marked influence on twentieth-century Caucasian conceptions of whiteness (Michaud 2019, 155–59).

These, then, are the issues that Malabou's account of the relations between habit and plasticity fails to register, owing to the respects in which it seals off in advance any consideration of how those relations have been differentially distributed through their inscription across different practices of governing. There are, however, broader issues posed by her severance of the dynamics of subjectivity from the findings of empirical disciplines concerned with the forces—be they psychological, neurological, or social—bearing on the shaping of conduct. These are the issues that Malabou acknowledges in *Morphing Intelligence*, where, drawing on Bourdieu's critique of scholastic reason, she turns her back on the wayward tradition to dismantle the "protective shield" that it had constructed, particularly in Bergson's work, as a means of blocking off the implications of the scientific concept of intelligence in favor of more traditional philosophical conceptions of spirit, reason, and the intellect. She does so by advancing a reading of the literature on AI that inverts the logic on which differentiations of human and machinic intelligence have depended by reading the qualities of the former, the logic of "habitus interruptus," into the latter—where it operates as a form of what I shall call "automaticity interruptus"—and then back again. "The critical task," she argues, "is to rediscover the pathway for interrupting automaticity so as to better emancipate automatisms" (Malabou 2019, 133). I turn next to look at what this involves.

## Automaticity interruptus

"One of the commonest phenomena in the living world," W. Ross Ashby argues, "occurs when an organism given an innocuous and unvarying stimulus or disturbance repetitively, reacts briskly at first, then less actively and finally perhaps not at all." He argues that this phenomenon, known variously as "habituation" or "adaptation," has been "recognized from time immemorial" but "still lacks explanation" (Ashby 1959, 95–96). However, the account he offers of the "mechanism of habituation" provides less an explanation of this mechanism, or that of dishabituation, than its extension beyond the neurophysiological operations of living organisms to the procedural capacities of any dynamic mechanical system. He had illustrated this logic several years earlier in imagining a machine, a conceptual incubator for his later homeostat, consisting of a frame with a number of heavy beads on it joined together through a network of elastic bands (Ashby 1945). Positing a distinction between static and dynamic equilibrium, he imagines two scenarios: one in which one of the bands is stretched, setting off reverberations throughout the network but with an eventual return to the initial state; and a second in which one of the bands breaks—and perhaps others too as a consequence—setting off reverberations that lead to a new and altered state of the network. There is no need, he argued, to suppose any vital life force to account for the shift from a condition of static to dynamic equilibrium: all that is needed is the intervention of a disturbance—and whether it is a neuronal or a mechanical one makes no difference—that will dislodge habituated responses to repeated stimuli and effect a reset that will initiate a path toward a new equilibrium.

I have, in presenting this experiment, drawn on Andrew Pickering's interpretation of it as emblematic of the reconceptualization of the brain as an "*acting* machine" rather than a "thinking machine" (Pickering 2010, 6). He associates this conception with the importation of the logic of the gap—the moment of indetermination—into the field of automation that informed the early development of cybernetics and AI to which Ashby contributed. The "cybernetic brain," as Pickering puts it, was not "representational but performative, . . . and its role in performance was *adaptation*" (6), a role fulfilled through the process of dis- and rehabituation as activated through mechanisms of interruption. As such, it undid the "modern settlement"—which, as we have seen, Foucault signed up to in endorsing Baudelaire's call to modern man to face up to the challenge of producing himself—by staging a nonmodern ontology in which machines, like people, are to be understood as dynamic realities always in the process of being made in ways that incorporate their own activities. This opens up a complex dance of agency—an "ontological theatre"—that "destabilizes any clean dualist split between people and things" (42). David Bates, taking a similar tack, highlights the role accorded to intelligence in early postwar cybernetics and AI in modeling computer design on the significance accorded acts of intellectual creativity in progressive trends in 1930s psychology rather than on conceptions of machinic automaticity. He cites the Swiss psychologist Edouard Claparède to the effect that it is "intelligence which takes on the task of readapting us," overcoming the "rupture of equilibrium, when reflexes or habits are not available to intervene, and we are momentarily disadapted" (Claparède quoted in Bates 2016, 205).

Taking her cue from Bates's further contention that this reciprocal modeling of brains and machines on one another provides a basis for grounding resistance in the critical history of automaticity rather than in a modern ontology of ourselves (Bates 2016, 197), Malabou significantly revises her earlier understanding of neural plasticity. Far from being opposed to mechanisms of biological and psychological determination, or arising from a human logic fundamentally at odds with that of machinic automaticity or cybernetic reasoning, she argues that neural plasticity constitutes a form of intelligence that, like that of the machine, operates through a process of interruption. Repetition, its interruption, and the processes of self-reorganization that this gives rise to constitute the dialectical relation that both humans and machines have with themselves. Both can become authors of themselves through the exercise of intelligence as the mechanism that governs their regenerative plasticities. The route by which Malabou arrives at this conclusion involves—indeed, requires—the removal of what she calls the "protective shield" that Bergson had placed between the biological and psychological sciences, on the one hand, and the creativity of spirit and the intellect or critical reason, on the other, in order to insulate the capacity for freedom of the latter from the assault of behavioral determinisms he imputed to the former. Key aspects of her argument here include, first, the contention that the twenty-first-century development of the epigenetic paradigm in biology has displaced the force of genetic determinisms and the role these accorded inheritance by opening up the phonotype to the influence of environmental and lifestyle factors; and second, the incorporation of a capacity for synaptic plasticity into the vocabularies of computing as a result of the manufacture of computer chips able to transform themselves.

It is in the light of these considerations that Malabou turns to Piaget, Dewey, and Bourdieu for readings of intelligence that, rather than opposing it to spirit or critical reason, or to conceptions of biological, technological, or social determination, set out to inscribe freedom in the relations that intelligence has with itself through the mediating effects of the relations between home, school, and environment. Both Dewey and Bourdieu, it is worth noting, were pretty scathing in their assessment of Bergson. For Dewey, opposing "spirit" and "life" to "matter" and "body," attributing to the former a force that "outruns habit" so that "nothing remains to spirit, pure thought, except a blind onward push or impetus," was sufficient reason for questioning the separation of "soul and habit" on which Bergson's position rested. A spiritual life "which is nothing but a blind urge separated from thought," he concluded, "... is likely to have the attributes of the Devil in spite of its being ennobled with the name of God" (Dewey 2002, 73–74). He returns to this theme a little later in rejecting the Bergsonian division of the universe into two portions, "one all of fixed, recurrent habits, and the other all spontaneity of flux" (245). For Bourdieu, similarly, Bergson's underwriting of the authority of saints, geniuses, and heroes as the authors of conscience in opposition to Durkheim's stress on the shaping role of impersonal social forces had made him an emblem for those whom he lampooned for seeing themselves as "unique 'creators' of singularity" (Bourdieu 2000, 132).

Malabou is particularly drawn to Bourdieu's conception of "conditionability" in providing a basis for an understanding of the grounding of intelligence in the body that does not reduce it to its biological determinations. Conditionability, as Bourdieu defines it, "is a natural capacity to acquire non-natural, arbitrary capacities" (Bourdieu 2000, 136). Intelligence, Malabou thus argues, is rooted in the body's physiological makeup but exceeds it: it is "the natural aptitude of an organism to produce itself as a second nature ... as a result of a first cultivation of the self" (Malabou 2019, 58). The locus for this aptitude, Malabou continues, is the brain's plasticity, since it is this that generates the potential for "neuronal architecture to be shaped by the influences of environment, habit, and education" (58)—and, it should be added, to creatively reshape those influences. What Malabou derives from her interpretation of Bourdieu's conception of conditionability is "the capacity to form a 'habitus,' that is, a way of being that is simultaneously permanent and fluid" (65). She turns to Piaget for an account of intelligence that inscribes its dynamics as unfolding along the relations between subject and object, the mind and things, through the relations between the processes of assimilation (of reality into inherited intellectual schemas) and accommodation (of such schemas to specific situations). If these dynamics describe pathways toward an equilibrium, those pathways—like those of Ashby's machine— are interrupted by blanks, blocks, or breaches that set off new processes of assimilation-accommodation. It is the invention of the synaptic chip that extends the productive power of the assimilation-accommodation couplet to AI and computing, thereby extending the potential for the production of singularities from human to machinic plasticities.

It is at this point that Malabou introduces habit's pathways into her argument, interpreting their dynamic via Dewey's conception of the relations between habit and intelligence. Drawing on the semantic ambiguities of the Greek concepts of automatism (an involuntary movement) and *automatos* (that which moves by itself), she interprets these as incorporating "a double valency of mechanical constraint and freedom" (100). For Dewey, intelligence is the method that pits the second meaning against the first in opposing "the power of the automatism to the automatisms of power" (101). Intelligence, understood as inextricably connected to action rather than as an abstracted form of reason, is, in this reading of Dewey, inherently dynamic. Its movement transforms indeterminate situations into determinate ones in order that provisional configurations of relations permitting pertinent forms of action might be arrived at, while acknowledging that what has thus been rendered provisionally determinate will later be subjected to disturbances and conflicts that will render it indeterminate again. The relations between habit and intelligence—between old answers that have become habitual and in need of new ones that only intelligence can provide—thus describe a distinctive pathway, one that, as Malabou puts it, "does not break violently with the past but rather proceeds through a constant reconfiguration of the past in the movement of a negotiated taking leave" (104). This is a pathway that has an accumulating logic as intelligence converts past experience and habits into projects oriented toward the current situation that will affect the future trajectories of experience, understood as "the continuum of life which moves forward thanks to various specific experiences that extend it every day, like raindrops constantly filling and regenerating a river" (106–7).

This is a sharp departure not only from the ruptural formulations of *What Should We Do with Our Brain?* but also from the "deviating form" and "explosive plasticity" that Malabou attributes to her aquatic presentations of habit's pathways in *Ontology of the Accident*. Called on now to carve an accumulating course for experience, the dialectic of habit and intelligence works through mechanisms of interruption that, more akin to James's formulations, retain the links between past and present, redirecting their trajectories rather than breaking from them. But there are no guarantees that this progressive potential will be realized. It is because the "plastic dispositions of subjects" are always also the gateways through which normalizing forms of power might be brought to bear on them, blocking the potential for the creative transformation of lifestyles and behavior through the "uniformizing processes of a reactionary positivism" (132–33), that Malabou urges the need to "rediscover the pathway for interrupting automacity so as to better emancipate automatisms" (132). This argument is made via a new reading of Foucault's essay "What Is Enlightenment?," which, considered in the light of the neurosciences, Malabou interprets as opening up the possibility for a "*biologization of the transcendental*" (130) understood as the capacity to adopt the perspective of another to oneself, and thus become an object of reflection to oneself. This possibility is one that she works through and animates by restating the positive potential of the aesthetic in this regard. She does so by taking issue with a neurohumanities project that purported to demonstrate that neural plasticity favors tonality and melody over serial and atonal music in view of the ways in which it builds on the listener's expectations to further develop music intelligence. This is contrasted to the passive response allegedly elicited by serial and atonal music owing to its failure to appeal to any sense of musical progression. "The brain," Malabou objects, "is not 'made' for tonal music or figurative painting" but is open to "dissymmetries and disharmonies, irregular and destabilizing forms," pinning her hopes on these—on there being "no biological programming for the aesthetics of reception" (137)—as counters to the normalizing forces of automation.

It's here that the connections Malabou makes between machinic and human automaticities lead her into an unnecessarily polarizing opposition— "the power of the automatism" versus "the automatisms of power"—in, once again, singularizing bodies. However, it is not only the variable malleabilities of raced, classed, and gendered bodies that are overlooked here. So are the implications of the ways in which, for Bourdieu, bodily habitus are differentiated by virtue of their positioning in intersecting fields of social relations. Toward the end of his discussion of bodily knowledge in *Pascalian Meditations*, Bourdieu proposes a different account of the ways in which "habitus has its 'blips,' critical moments when it misfires or is out of phase." These are moments that, in suspending relationships of adaptation to given social conditions, introduce "an instant of hesitation into which there might slip a form of reflection" (Bourdieu 2000, 162) through which practice is redirected and the habitus refashioned. These blips might be related to a variety of social circumstances, ranging from the traumas of colonization to the differences associated with intra- and intergenerational trajectories of social mobility, but their effect is to generate "contradictory positions, which tend to exert structural 'double binds' on their occupants," giving rise to "destabilized habitus, torn by contradiction and internal division" (160).[6] Their occurrence is in all cases, however, the product of a social logic rather than that of a general opposition between the "power of automatism" and the "automatisms of power." Such blips have, indeed, been argued to be the norm rather than the exception to the social logic of habitus by those who have criticized Bourdieu for—as he undoubtedly did in his earlier work—attributing an overly unifying power to different class habitus. Bernard Lahire, for example, argues that social actors are always placed at the intersections of different and sometimes contradictory social worlds so that Bourdieu's blips, mismatches, misfirings, and discordances of habitus are the rule:

> Once an actor has been placed, simultaneously or successively, within a plurality of social worlds that are non-homogeneous, and sometimes even contradictory, or within social worlds that are relatively coherent but present contradictions in certain aspects, we are dealing with an actor with a stock of schemes of action or habits that are non-homogeneous, non-unified; and with practices that are consequently heterogeneous (and even contradictory, varying according to the social context in which they are led to develop). (Lahire 2011, 25–26)

It is, then, surprising that Malabou should, while enlisting Bourdieu as an ally, at the same time overlook the social logic that informs his position. The consequences of this are evident in her invocation of the aesthetic represented by atonal music—as well as cinematic and painterly forms of abstraction—as a deus ex machina in view of the significant role that Bourdieu's work has played in relativizing aesthetic dispositions. This is not to discount the potential critical force of the kinds of aesthetic practice that Malabou pins her hopes on. But this is a force that is, by and large, available only to those with certain aptitudes already acquired by particular, socially restricted forms of training. For it is clear that the class distribution of involvement in such practices is significantly tilted toward the professional middle classes and is thereby also implicated in the organization of class relations and the role of the education system in the mechanisms of inheritance through which such relations are reproduced.[7] It is her neglect of such considerations that allows Malabou to accord avant-garde aesthetic practices a privileged place as plasticity's mentors against the overunified force that she attributes to automatisms. The capacity she accords such practices to reshape habitus fails to register the respects in which socialized body-brains differ in terms of their degrees and forms of plasticity and corresponding susceptibility to aesthetic forms of self-fashioning.

### Aesthetics and the dynamics of habit

In her postscript to the English translation of *Morphing Intelligence*, Malabou argues that the challenges presented by the development of cybernetics and AI not just to the conditions of thought, knowledge, and expertise but to every aspect of the human psyche and field of activity have made her aware of society's "deep and urgent *need for philosophy*" (2019, 144). The extent to which, in addressing this need, she distances herself from her earlier subscription to the "protective shield" that the wayward tradition erected between philosophy and the psychological disciplines, while welcome, is not as far-reaching as it needs to be. There have been two main aspects to my argument in this respect. The first is that, while dismantling the operations of the protective shield insofar as they relate to behaviorist strands in the neurological and psychological disciplines, Malabou leaves many of its ramparts intact so far as the relations between philosophy and more recent developments in the social sciences are concerned. In failing to register the implications of contemporary forms of race theory, she also, in her selective use of Bourdieu, fails to register the significance of his insistence on the differentiation of bodily habitus and their capacities effected by their social placement. The second leg of my argument has been that it is the continuing operation of the "protective shield" in these regards that underlies the radical potential Malabou attributes to specific aesthetic forms without regard to the differential social distribution of different aesthetic dispositions.

There has, however, been a third aspect to my concerns, one that underlies the foregoing lines of argument. It has to do with the blind spots of Malabou's pointed engagement with habit's pathways. It's worth recalling again Bruno Latour's assessment of the hiker's relief, on coming to a crossroads, at not having to choose which path to follow because "he can finally put himself 'in the hands' of others" (Latour 2013, 265). This assumes that, when habit's pathways are interrupted, individuals either are entirely bereft of guidance or already know whom to trust rather than being faced with competing signals as to whom to follow, which authorities to place themselves in the hands of. This is clearly not the case. Indeed, the point of Malabou's interventions has been to put aesthetics in contention with other forms of expertise at such moments of hesitation just as, for Elizabeth Grosz, it is philosophy that assumes this burden. She does so, however, without adequate regard for the checkered history of the role that aesthetics has been summoned to play in this respect. This is not solely in view of the social variability of aesthetic dispositions. It also has to do with what Sianne Ngai calls "the hypertrophy of the 'aesthetic function'" associated with the recent histories of the aesthetic categories of the zany, the cute, and the interesting. For it is these, she argues, that "speak to the most significant objects and socially binding activities of late capitalist life—our affectively complicated relation to commodities, information, and performing, the ways in which we labor, exchange and consume" (Ngai 2012, 242). It is in the attention she pays to the ways in which these categories bridge the relations between avant-garde and more popular, thoroughly commercialized, cultural practices that Ngai opens up to consideration the different ways in which an expanded set of aesthetic categories, operating through different institutional connections in relation to different publics, audiences, and consumers, are active in the socially differentiated everyday dynamics of habit.

There are also limits to the ways in which Bourdieu engages with these questions via his interpretations of the relations between those habitus that are reanimated by blips and misfirings, and those that stay on the same course. Having peeped over Malabou's shoulders at some similarities between Dewey's and Bourdieu's approaches to habit, I take a closer look at these, alongside other socialized approaches to habit's pathways, in the following chapter. This will help set the scene for my discussion, in the final chapter, of the relations between the rival forms of authority that have been invoked as habit's guides along its contested pathways.

# 7

## Progressive
## Pathways

THERE ARE MORE SUBSTANTIAL SIMILARITIES between John Dewey and Pierre Bourdieu than their shared disdain for Henri Bergson's putative lording of spiritual forms of authority over empirical disciplines. Bourdieu recognized the striking "affinities and convergences" between his conception of habitus—reminding us that he always "said habitus so as *not* to say habit" in order to distinguish it, as "an *ars inveniendi*," from mere mechanism—and Dewey's understanding of habit as "an active and creative relation to the world" (Bourdieu and Wacquant 1992, 122). These "affinities and convergences" also involved the forms of progression they attributed to habit's modern pathways. Bourdieu distinguished these from the stasis he attributed to "archaic habitus." The same was true of the contrast Dewey drew between the conception of habit's pathways that he applied to "savages" owing to the preponderant influence of custom, which, he argued, held in check the impulse for innovation and differentiation that characterized its modern pathways. In these regards both Bourdieu and Dewey were, like Gabriel Tarde, influenced by the doctrine of survivals, albeit interpreting it differently both from Tarde and from each another. They also differed in their conceptions of the capacities for dynamic change that they attributed to modern habitus/habits, and especially in how they envisaged the relations between state action and market forces in the pathways they mapped out for their future direction.

In exploring these and other questions, I look first at Dewey. His contention that habits should be understood as capacities that are distributed across the relations between individuals, social groups, and the sociomaterial environments and infrastructures that connect them has been widely influential in recent debates, and rightly so.[1] That said, such assessments of his work have often depended on abstracting selected aspects of his remarks on habit from their place within the architecture of his thought more generally. Relatively little attention has been paid to how Dewey's conception of habit was shaped by his understanding of its relations to the other factors at play in the shaping of conduct. Yet it is this broader question—and not habit in isolation—that defines his concerns in *Human Nature and Conduct*, where he sees conduct as being shaped by the relations between impulse, habit, and intelligence. While his account of the relations between habit and intelligence has attracted attention—including, as we saw in the last chapter, from Catherine Malabou—the role of impulse has been mostly left out of the picture.[2] This has been accompanied by another area of neglect: of the significance that Dewey assigned to anthropology among the new social sciences of sociology and social psychology, which, alongside physiology and biology, he accorded a key role in "the establishment of arts of education and social guidance" (Dewey 2002, 10). He viewed this guidance as necessary if habits were to escape the pull of what he called "the routineers road" in order to be directed along the pathways that he viewed as appropriate to the advanced stages of civilization he associated with a capitalist modernity that stood in need of modifying forms of state action. The wider implications of the role that Dewey accorded intelligence in superintending the direction of conduct cannot be properly appreciated unless such considerations are taken into account.

I shall, in interrogating the similarities and differences between Bourdieu's and Dewey's versions of habit's pathways, interpose a third version of those pathways: that constituted by Shannon Sullivan's (2006) account of their rocky course, which she attributes to the undoing of the racial habits of white privilege. I do so partly for the light her discussion throws on the racial underpinnings of Dewey's account of habit and partly in view of how her account of the tortuous pathways that must be negotiated in undoing the "transactional unconscious" that subtends the habits of white privilege brings a socialized conception of the unconscious into the picture. I also take the use that Sullivan makes of Maurice Merleau-Ponty's conception of the relations between habits and bodily schemas as a point of entry into a broader discussion of how the relations between this aspect of Merleau-Ponty's work and Bourdieu's account of habitus are commonly viewed. This provides a springboard for my consideration of the role that Bourdieu assigned to what he called the "historical unconscious" in the progressive trajectory he attributed to the unfolding of the relations between different habitus. However much he might have said "habitus" in order not to say "habit," I shall argue that Bourdieu by no means escaped the tension between the two concepts. It is, in particular, in his account of the relations between archaic and modern habitus that the conception of habit as mere mechanism continues to haunt his conception of habitus as "an *ars inveniendi.*"

### Habit, impulse, innovation, and the dynamics of modernity

In *Multitude,* Michael Hardt and Antonio Negri relate Dewey's conception of habits as necessarily socialized to their concern with the production of the common as the basis for the subjectivity of the multitude. In going beyond a conception of habits as "simply rote repetition of past acts, following the grooved routes in which we walk every day," they argue that Dewey defines them as forming "a nature that is both produced and productive, created and creative—an ontology of social practices in common" (Hardt and Negri 2006, 197–98). They go on, though, to identify the limitations of Dewey's conception of habit arising from its close association with early twentieth-century conceptions of modernity, placing particular stress on the tension between his commitment—manifest in his support for the New Deal—to the development of democratic forms of political planning and his relative lack of interest in extending these to the economy. The result, they argue, was a duality that, leaving the economy largely to its own devices as a realm in which "habit only appears as dumb repetition," figured the political as the primary realm in which there might be realized "the democratic promise of the pragmatic notions of habit and social conduct" (199).

These were not the only respects in which the intellectual coordinates of modernity shaped Dewey's conception of habit. This was also true of the racialized conceptions that shaped his understanding of the relations between impulse, innovation, and civilization. His account in *Democracy and Education* of the different relations to the environment associated with "savage" and "civilized" societies provides a point of entry into these issues: "A savage tribe manages to live on a desert plain. It adapts itself. But its adaptation involves a maximum of accepting, tolerating, putting up with things as they are.... A civilized people enters upon the scene. It also adapts itself. It introduces irrigation; it searches the world for plants and animals that will flourish under such conditions; it improves, by careful selection, those which are growing there. As a consequence, the wilderness blossoms as a rose. The savage is merely habituated; the civilized man has habits which transform the environment" (Dewey 1916, loc. 794–95).

And in the process, of course, "civilized man" transforms himself, whereas "the savage" does not. Dewey does not attribute this difference to a lower intelligence or a defective moral sense on the part of the savage. It is rather an effect of institutions that "limit the stimuli to mental development" (loc. 627). In *Experience and Nature*, he attributes this limitation to the subjection of individuality, and therefore a suppression of the potential for innovation, to the inhibitive power of custom. "Custom," as he put it, "is Nomos, lord and king of all, of emotions, beliefs, opinions, thoughts as well as deeds" (Dewey 1929, 266). While innovative breaks with habituated practices do occur, they are infrequent and invariably the result of individual initiatives, usually generated by rivalries that impel individuals to break the hold of custom. Their effects are also temporary. If, even in "cultures most committed to reproduction, there is always occurring some creative production through specific variations, that is, through individuals" (266–67), such variations, once adopted, "become automatic group habits" (268) as the force of individuality is brought back under the inhibitive control of custom. Dewey identifies many other types of societies and practices in which individuality is similarly inhibited through the force of fixed norms: artists and artisans who "merely observe ... ready-made models and patterns," and "the mechanic who follows blueprints and a procedure dictated by his machine in the production of standardized commodities" (269). Greek art and philosophy are taken to task for subscribing to a metaphysic of the individual as "something complete, perfect, finished, an organized whole of parts united by the impress of a comprehensive form" (269). Dewey assesses this as lacking the dynamism of diverse individualities that he attributes to modern individualism, when individuality came to be prized as "something moving, changing, discrete, and above all initiating instead of final" (270).

Dewey's sense that a set of dynamic connections between individualism, capitalism, and innovation are necessary for the ongoing breaking and remaking of habits to become the norm is underlined in a later political inflection of habit's pathways. Invoking William James's contention that habit, in economizing on muscular and intellectual energy, frees us up to develop new capacities, Dewey interprets the state as a public reserve that, by saving energy on previous innovations that have become habitual, frees up private initiative for more entrepreneurial ventures. Developing his argument with reference to America's railway system, he links it to the circulation of capital between the state and private enterprise. It takes the vigor of the latter to develop economic innovations in face of the resistance of the "organized community." The most that can be expected of the state here is not to interfere. Only when an innovation has become old and familiar, habituated through regular use—and Dewey cites railways as a case in point—might it properly fall within the orbit of state ownership as something requiring only settled forms of management (Dewey 1991, 58–62).

In *Human Nature and Conduct*, the plasticity that Dewey attributes to initiative, resourcefulness, and ingenuity as the virtues of a capitalist individualism are pointedly contrasted to the inertia of savage society. Endorsing evolutionary conceptions of the contribution that the transgenerational transmission of habits makes to the advancement of civilization, Dewey calls on the imagery of paths used and unused to make his point. "A savage," he says, "can travel after a fashion in a jungle." But civilized activity requires the intervention of the state to modify the conditions governing activity in order to provide "smoothed roads . . . signals and junction points; traffic authorities and means of easy and rapid transportation. It demands a congenial, antecedently prepared environment" (Dewey 2002, 20). He returns to the problem of savagery when, discussing the relations between plasticity and impulse, he identifies two contrasting views of savage life: the popular one of the savage as a "wild man . . . who freely follows his own impulse, whim, or desire whenever it seizes him or wherever it takes him," and the anthropological view of "savages as bondsmen to custom" (103). The truth, he argues, lies in the combination of these two views, in a conception of savage life as governed by elements of both "undirected instinct and over-organized custom" (103). Where custom exists, its grip is powerful but not total; however, what slips outside its grip is guided only by "appetite and momentary circumstance," with the result that "enslavement to custom and license of impulse exist side by side" (104). And this legacy of the savage, Dewey tells us, still exists within civilization, where—as an instance of those "hang-overs" that "the student of culture calls survivals" (99)—it is manifest as a tendency for a "degree of oscillation between loose indulgence and strict habit" (104).

These assessments reflected Dewey's close association with the Boasian school of cultural anthropology, and particularly Franz Boas's (1911) account of "the mind of primitive man."[3] This lent a particular inflection to Dewey's departure from the conception of habits as practices rooted in the interiors of atomized subjects, conceiving them rather as being distributed across the relations between minds, bodies, and environments. This had significant consequences for the position he adopted in relation to questions concerning the governance of habits.[4] In reviewing the place of habit in conduct, he thus includes the social environment alongside the natural environment as jointly dispelling as illusory the view that habits might be interpreted as "belonging exclusively to a self . . . isolated from natural and social surroundings" (Dewey 2002, 15–16). Habits are "not private possessions of a person" but "working adaptations of personal capacities with environing forces. All virtues and vices are habits which incorporate objective forces" (16). This leads Dewey to urge that questions concerning the governance of habits should shift from a focus on the purely internal dynamics of personhood to encompass actions on the milieus that condition such dynamics. "To change the working character or will of another," he says, "we have to alter objective conditions which enter into his habits" (19).

The key questions this poses concern habit's relations to the contradictory pulls of custom and impulse, and the role of intelligence, appropriately guided, in regulating the relations between these to give a fitting direction to conduct. It is never, Dewey argues, habit in and of itself that is a conservative force; it is so only when subjected to custom. Although strongest in "savage society," custom is also an operative force in modern society. Developing an effective counter to its influence requires attending to the ways in which custom has been, so to speak, weaponized to reinforce the power that it exerts over habits. For Dewey this involved considering how schools, rather than cultivating the acquisition of intelligence, too often pervert learning "into a willingness to follow where others point the way, into conformity, constriction, surrender of scepticism and experiment" (64). Dewey is severely critical of how, rather than, as his ideal, promoting a democratic dynamic through which intelligence, impulse, and habit interact so as to interanimate each other, the guiding role accorded intelligence in this mix is monopolized by some in ways that simultaneously deny it to others, binding them to the unthinking docility of a particular custom-habit nexus. In developing this view, Dewey anticipates significant aspects of Bourdieu's account of the role of cultural capital in reproducing class divisions.[5] He puts the matter as follows:

> Intellectual habits like other habits demand an environment, but the environment is the study, library, laboratory and academy. Like other habits they produce external results, possessions. Some men acquire ideas and knowledge as other men acquire monetary wealth. While practicing thought for their own special ends they deprecate it for the untrained and unstable masses for whom "habits," that is unthinking routines, are necessities. They favor popular education—up to the point of disseminating as a matter of authoritative information for the many what the few have established by thought, and up to the point of converting an original docility to the new into a docility to repeat and to conform. (69–70)

Where there are no democratic means for spreading the guiding role of intelligence, Dewey looks to the force of impulse—of primary and secondary emotions—for a source capable of breaking the hold of any particular habit-docility nexus and to open up the possibility of new courses of action. In doing so, however, he bemoans the randomness of the ways in which, in earlier history, this force has been made manifest. Typically held in check by powerful social mechanisms of inhibition, impulse had previously only been untethered from these by the "accidental upheavals" (101) occasioned by war, revolution, and mass migrations. Random in their occurrence and consequences, such releases of impulses from the hold of routinized habits had rarely resulted in their being brought under the influence of intelligence to bring about any continuous reconstruction of habit. Dewey was equally concerned by the diminishing prospect, in twentieth-century societies, that such external prompts might intervene to release impulses from the grip of habit given that "the stock of fresh peoples" capable of dynamizing the "petrifying rigidity" of congealed habits is "approaching exhaustion" (102). He therefore looks to the increasing internal complexity and diversity of modern societies as a counterbalance to this. The abrasion of conflicting patterns of conduct this engenders gives rise to "internal frictions and liberations" (128), prompting the development of "antagonistic impulses" and "contrary dispositions" (129) among the members of society. If left to themselves, however, such frictions divide habits against one another in a random and ad hoc fashion, leading to a disruption of personality in which "the scheme of conduct is confused and disintegrated" (130). The resulting social and psychological strife can only be halted if "released impulses are intelligently employed to form harmonious habits adapted to one another in a new situation" (130). Or, as he puts it later, if a breach "in the cake of custom releases impulses . . . it is the work of intelligence to find ways of using them" (170).

## Escaping the pull of the "routineer's road"

The place of habit in Dewey's thought, then, is fully elaborated not in what he says about habit or impulse but in how he construes their relations to the role of intelligence in human conduct. It is here that Dewey draws on the currency of habit's pathways to distinguish the "routineer's road" from that produced when the interactions between habit and impulse are brought under the direction of intelligence. On the routineer's road, habits—much as for Bruno Latour's hiker, except for being appraised negatively—are "blinders that confine the eyes of the mind to the road ahead." The routineer's road is a "ditch out of which he cannot get, whose sides enclose him, directing his course so thoroughly that he no longer thinks of his path or destination" (Dewey 2002, 173). It is only when this "path of least resistance" is "thwarted by untoward circumstances" that efficiency "in following a beaten path has then to be converted into breaking a new road through strange lands" (173). This disruption of a particular set of habit-environment relations produces "a hitch" in the unconscious workings of habit, an interruption of an established equilibrium of forces that gives way eventually to a new accommodation of "the old habit and the new impulse" (179).

The course of habit thus constitutes a pattern of "interruptions and recoveries" that Dewey likens to James's "stream of consciousness" as an "alteration of flights and perchings" (179).[6] It is what happens in such moments of "interruption and recovery" that Dewey turns to when considering the role of intelligence in relation to conduct. Comparing life to "a traveler faring forth" along a path that he initially "marches on giving no direct attention to his path, nor thinking of his destination," Dewey argues that his unthinking course will eventually be abruptly "pulled up, arrested" by an unforeseen obstacle, producing shock and uncertainty: "For the moment he doesn't know what hit him . . . nor where he is going." If the habits that are now blocked "give him a sense of where he *was* going, of what he had set out to do, and of the ground already traversed," those habits are given a new direction "as they cluster about the impulse to look and see" (181). It is then that "the clew of impulse" that is always "in a hurry," rushing us "off our feet," is brought under the influence of intelligence: "the clew of reason … to stop and think." It is in this moment of "delay, of suspended and postponed overt action" (197), that deliberation, which "has its beginnings in troubled activity," leads to a "course of action which straightens it out" (199).

But what is to direct intelligence in its deliberations along habit's conflicted pathways? This is the question Dewey poses in concluding *Human Nature and Conduct*, where, countering the tendency for conduct, "when distributed under heads like habit, impulse and intelligence," to be shredded into isolated elements, he reflects on the organization of "conduct as a whole" (278). It is a question that comes down to which authorities should guide those moments of deliberation when habit is temporally stalled before being set off on a new course. Dewey disqualifies a range of previous authorities that have contended for this role in order to clear a space for its occupancy by the "sciences of man." Ruling out those authorities that enjoin us, in such moments of hesitation, to pursue "remote and elusive perfection" or to "obey supernatural command" (280), he rejects those versions of habit's pathways that interpret them as steps on the way to "an exhaustive, stable, immutable end or good" (287). The logic of such pathways, he argues, depends on a contrast between the infinity of the goal and the limitations of man's empirical and finite nature, a disjunction that, explaining why man constantly falls short of such a goal, serves only to keep conduct under its continuing tutelage to the authorities of the infinite. Dewey thus dismisses the very form of the "office of inspiration and guidance" (288) that such conceptions entail. "Instruction in what to do next," he argues, "can never come from an infinite goal, which for us is bound to be empty. It can be derived only from the study of the deficiencies, irregularities and possibilities of the actual situation" (289).

The targets of Dewey's criticisms here move across idealist philosophies, theological versions of habit's pathways, and those associated with cumulative conceptions of evolution exemplified by Herbert Spencer. Dewey argues that their place needs to be taken by the "judgements on conduct by the method and materials of a science of human nature" (321). Only the light that such a science throws on how habits are formed "under the influence of the conditions set by men's contact, intercourse and associations with one another" (323) can furnish forms of guidance that "enable an individual to see for himself what he is doing, and which put him in command of a method of analyzing the obscure and usually unavowed forces which move him to act" (321). It is this "science of man," forged from a combination of modern disciplines—chemistry, biology, physiology, anthropology, sociology, and social psychology—that is called on to displace the earlier forms of authority that had ruled over habit's pathways. Its role is both to provide the forms of empirical knowledge that will guide the intelligence of social and political authorities in manipulating the social milieus in which habits are formed and to equip individuals with a capacity for the intelligent direction of their own habits in the light of their awareness of the factors determining them.[7]

Dewey's position in these regards differs significantly from that of the "wayward tradition." Indeed, his criticisms of the forms of spiritual authority over habit's pathways whose exertion depends on infinitely deferrable ends could—with some tweaking—apply equally well to the current retrieval of the wayward tradition in the name of philosophies of becoming. However, this does not let Dewey off the hook of the racial assumptions that underpinned his account of habit. It is in view of the further light that it throws on these aspects of his work, as well as her own distinctive account of habit's pathways, that I turn now to the work of Shannon Sullivan.

## Refashioning the habits of whiteness:
## A course of tricks, disguises, and evasions

In discussing what is involved in changing human nature, Dewey questions the exaggerated conception of its alterability that he attributes to John Locke, who, "magnifying . . . the accomplishments of acquired experience[,] . . . held out a prospect of continuous . . . improvement without end" (Dewey 2002, 106). Sullivan also refers to Locke, albeit implicitly, in her discussion of the habits of white privilege. "How," she asks, "can a person be unaware of her experience if she is the one experiencing it?" (Sullivan 2006, 189). The question echoes one put by Locke in his critique of innate ideas: How could anyone have ideas without being conscious of them? But Sullivan's answer, in seeing no contradiction in the idea of unconscious experience, points in the opposite direction: toward the force of a socialized conception of the unconscious that occupies pride of place in her account of the barriers that impede and deflect attempts to shed the habits of white privilege.

Distinguishing this from the more overt and conscious forms of white supremacy, Sullivan argues that the less strident forms of racism characterizing white privilege had become increasingly prevalent in the post–civil rights and pre-Trump period. Given a legislative and policy environment in which explicit forms of racial discrimination had been formally, albeit not always effectively, discouraged, white privilege continued to thrive as a form in which more explicit racist habits were obliged to take refuge underground. Sullivan's primary concern is thus with how the subjects of white privilege can counter the habitual forms of oppression they practice but that have become hidden to them through a range of evasions effected by the "transactional unconscious" that conditions their relations to their environments.

This is not to discount the significance of how various forms of governmental action on environments—via schooling, housing, and so on—might serve as a counter to racist habits. However, Sullivan's attention is focused on how, and to what extent, such environments might be internalized as principles of action: not, though, in order to set up an internal psychological drama in which the will might be pitted against unconscious habits, but rather to explore how the subjects of white privilege might counter those habits by placing themselves in a different position relative to the external environments that condition them. "Whatever significant control over unconscious habits exists," she says, "is found in the indirect access one has to them via environment," leading to the contention that "a white person who wishes to change her raced and racist habits would do better to change the environments she inhabits than (to attempt) to use 'will power' to change the way she thinks about and reacts to non-white people" (9).

If this involves a significantly different interpretation of how environmental factors influence habits from that proposed by Dewey, Sullivan also distances herself from Dewey's aversion to racial diversity. This stood in marked contrast to the positive value he placed on the social complexity of modern societies and their internal diversity as a source capable of disrupting established habits and setting them off on new paths. For Dewey, as for the Boasian school of anthropology, which shaped his views on these matters, those forms of racial difference (notably African American and Native American) that stood outside the course of a potential assimilation into a white nativist culture served rather to reinforce the racist habits characterizing the latter. Whereas other forms of difference might set habits off on new tracks, Dewey attributed a certain unavoidability to racial prejudice in interpreting it as arising from an "instinctive aversion to what is new and unusual, to whatever is different from what we are used to, and which thus shocks our customary habits" (Dewey quoted in Sullivan 2006, 34). For Sullivan, Dewey's position on race serves as an instance of W. E. B. Du Bois's interpretation of white privilege as a set of unconscious habits, an interpretation that extended the Freudian unconscious beyond the traumatic dramas of the nuclear family to encompass the forms of repression and resistance to change characteristic of dominant races.

The fact that such habits are, as Sullivan puts it, sociocultural rather than biologically constituted "does not change the fact that transforming them will take a great deal of patience and time, in large part because of habit's ability to actively undermine its own transformation" (Sullivan 2006, 22). Far from being based on an accidental and unintentional ignorance of the dynamics of race, the unconscious habits of white privilege are an active, albeit duplicitous, agent in those dynamics. Such habits not only obstruct their own improvement. They also conceal such obstructions, with the result that "habit does not appear at all complicit in the blockage of its own transformations" (62). Shaped by their transactions with their environments, the habits of white privilege become active parts of such environments, refashioning the social world in operating as "psychosomatic machines" that function in collaboration with other racialized social machineries.

Although Sullivan presents her account of the transactional unconscious as a counter to Sigmund Freud's atomistic conception of the unconscious, the pathways that are constituted by their dynamics have much in common. Freud's interpretation of the relationship between repetition and repression, Gilles Deleuze argues, gives rise to a pathway for the psyche shaped by "the relation between repetition and disguises" (Deleuze 2004, 18); a pathway in which the force of repetition is maintained through the evasions the psyche constructs to shield itself from its continuing effects. "The disguises and the variations, the masks or costumes" that characterize the theater of the unconscious "do not come 'over and above'" but are "the internal genetic elements of repetition itself, its integral and constituent parts" (19). Similarly, if overcoming the habits of white privilege requires that those who are the bearers of such habits resituate themselves in relation to the social environments responsible for such habits—moving from white into black neighborhoods, for example—there are a range of subterfuges through which those habits are repeated in disguised forms that reinforce their hold. Pretensions to color blindness, as if the effects of color could be simply whisked away, thus merely fuel "white privilege by strengthening its obsessional desire to be rid of everything that would contaminate white purity" (Sullivan 2006, 191). Romantic appropriations of the cultures of Native Americans in narcissistic forms of cross-cultural identification "reinforce oppressive stereotypes about those cultures that sustain white privilege" (91). Each well-intentioned step toward a progressive reform of racist habits runs the risk of repeating the unconscious habits that it seeks to suspend. That risk is reduced if such steps are guided by critical race theory—not, to be sure, on a voluntaristic, one-step-at-a-time basis, but through the incorporation of its insights into the environments that shape their course by spreading an awareness of the pitfalls they might encounter. Only then might practices oriented toward the self-overcoming of the unconscious habits of white privilege lead to the development of "habits of resistance" with a cumulative dynamic.

There is another aspect to Sullivan's interpretation of habits as "psychosomatic machines." This draws on the conception of habits as bodily schemas that orient the body's actions in relation to both objects and others within and across varied sociomaterial worlds and institutional regimes. Sullivan draws on the use to which Frantz Fanon puts this concept—attributable initially to Maurice Merleau-Ponty—in *Black Skin, White Masks* (Fanon 1967) to foreground the consequence of the different ways in which black and white bodies experience the "historico-racial schema" (Sullivan 2006, 103) assumed by the institutions of whiteness: disrupting and challenging for the black person, confirming and enabling for the white-skinned. Merleau-Ponty's work has also generated a more widespread literature examining the political consequences of the different ways in which not just raced but classed, sexed, and gendered bodies experience the implicit bodily schemas of dominant institutions: as confirming existing and enabling of future practices for those whose bodily schemas are in tune with such institutionalized schemas; as troubling forms of dissonance and oppression for those whose schemas are out of sync.[8] In turning now to look more closely at the influence of Merleau-Ponty's work in this regard, I do so primarily as a prelude to identifying how, in spite of his best intentions to the contrary, Bourdieu inscribed a familiar version of habit's pathways in his account of the relations between different habitus.

### Habits in the body:
### From inert to dynamic capacities

In introducing his discussion of habit in his *Phenomenology of Perception*, Merleau-Ponty registers his difference from "traditional philosophies." The chief shortcoming of these, he argues, consists in the difficulty they have in coming to terms with the "acquisition of habit as a rearrangement and renewal of the corporeal schema," owing to their inclination to "conceive synthesis as intellectual synthesis" (Merleau-Ponty 2002, 164). In displacing such concerns, he departs from approaches that "see the origin of habit in an act of understanding which organizes the elements only to withdraw subsequently"—a view he attributes to Bergson's conception of habit as "the fossilized residue of a spiritual activity"—insisting instead that the acquisition of habit has to be understood as "the motor grasping of a motor significance" (165).[9] He underlines the point in contending that habit is "neither a form of knowledge nor an involuntary action" but "a knowledge in the hands, which is forthcoming only when bodily effort is made" (166).

In discussing this aspect of Merleau-Ponty's work, Helen Ngo emphasizes the conjunction of the spatial and temporal dimensions it lends to habit's pathways. In commenting on the former, she interprets Merleau-Ponty's discussion of passing through a door without feeling any need to compare "the width of the door to that of my body" (Merleau-Ponty 2002, 165) as a habitual movement through a particular space made possible by a "knowledge in the hand" that hovers in a "hazy space between conscious and non-conscious being" (Ngo 2017, 3). However, insofar as habit represents a form of knowledge that has become sedimented in our bodies through the accumulation of past experience, the enlivening of that knowledge in any particular set of present circumstances involves an anticipatory relationship to what is to come. Bodily habits are thus "laden with histories that precede them while, at the same time, beholding *and* foreclosing possibilities of new ones to follow" (5). They make some futures readily available and others less so depending on whose bodies are in question and the contexts in which their actions are at issue.

I have already touched on the issues opened up by this perspective in my discussion, in chapter 1, of the new inflection that Merleau-Ponty lent to the epistemological figure of the blind man and his stick in viewing this as an expression of "our power of dilating our being-in-the-world, or changing our existence by appropriating fresh instruments" (Merleau-Ponty 2002, 166). The same is true of his discussion of another of habit's well-established figures: the musician, represented, in his case, by the organist. Merleau-Ponty's reading of this figure is best understood in terms of the position it takes up in relation to previous uses of musical figures as stand-ins for habit. Robert Whytt's discussion, also introduced in chapter 1, of the difference between the "young player upon the harpsichord," who is "at first very thoughtful and solicitous about every motion of his fingers," and the "masters" of the art, who "perform the very same motions, not only more dexterously, with greater ability, but almost without any reflexion or attention to what they are about," is especially instructive in this regard (Whytt quoted in Fearing 1970, 79). In presenting this as one of the earliest accounts of involuntary action that anticipated the later development of the reflex arc, Franklin Fearing calls attention to an ambiguity in Whytt's work in this regard. This consisted in Whytt's subscription to what he called the sentient principle—in effect, a reworking of the concept of mind or soul—as the ultimate source responsible for the direction of involuntary acts performed via the nervous and muscular systems, but a principle whose operations were too rapid to permit the intervention of the will directed by reason. Whytt's example of the harpsichord player was meant to serve as a roundabout way of confirming the operation of the sentient principle: to overturn, as Whytt put it, "the objection against the mind's being concerned in the vital and other involuntary motions" (79). We should not be too surprised if we are not conscious of the mind having played a role in such motions when we are in the midst of performing them, Whytt argues, given that the same is true of a host of voluntary actions—such as walking or playing the harpsichord—which, the more frequently we perform them and the greater facility we have acquired in their execution, "we become less sensible of any share or concern the mind has in them" (79).

Merleau-Ponty's example of the organist points in a different direction, and for two main reasons: first, because of the attention he accords to playing a musical instrument as an embodied practice; and second, in the significance he attaches to the particularity of the instrument in question. The issue he sets up concerns how an experienced organist is able, quite quickly, to play an organ he is unfamiliar with and whose component parts are differently arranged from those of the instrument he is used to playing. In ruling out a series of possible explanations for this—that the organist does so by reflex action, by implementing an elaborate plan, from memory, or through the force of custom—he notes instead the various steps which, before his performance, the organist takes to get "the measure of the instrument with his body," to incorporate "within himself the relevant dimensions," settling "into the organ as one settles into a house" (Merleau-Ponty 2002, 168). These adjustments of the relations between body and instrument during rehearsal constitute the mediations through which the relations between the organist and the musical score he performs are enacted.

Ngo interprets this as an instance of the process of habituation through which, in becoming at home in relation to the organ, the organist relates to it as "an open-field of possibility" (Ngo 2017, 6). She does so primarily with a view to exploring the ways in which the racialized bodies of people of color are not "at home" in the dominant institutions of white society. However, she also marks a difference between Merleau-Ponty's account of habit and the more socialized accounts of habitus proposed by Bourdieu. On the one hand, Ngo welcomes the social dimension that Bourdieu's concept of habitus offers in grounding what Merleau-Ponty called "stable dispositional tendencies" (Merleau-Ponty 2002, 169) in the social relations that differentiate body-minds in terms of the social positions that individuals occupy, the social collectives that they are able to enter into, and the institutions of education and training through which their dispositions are acquired. On the other hand, she takes him to task for a tendency to an overdeterministic construal of such processes that, in contrast to Merleau-Ponty's phenomenological account, pays insufficient attention to "how habits are *in*habited ... taken up, actively, and *held*" (Ngo 2017, 11) but always in a dynamic of self-surpassing. The result, she argues, is that Bourdieu tends toward a more passive account of the processes through which dispositions are formed than is implied by the terms in which he distinguishes the concept of habitus from that of habit in order to avoid the mechanistic associations of the latter. Nick Crossley reaches a similar conclusion, arguing that Bourdieu fails to match Merleau-Ponty's "dynamic account of the process in which habits are formed, reformed and, in some cases, extinguished across time" (Crossley 2013a, 147). Crossley also interprets Bourdieu's account of those momentary "blips" when habitus is out of sync with itself to suggest that he views "habit as a constraint upon freedom which the actor is only liberated from during periods of crisis, and even then only temporarily" (153).[10]

While there is some textual justification for these assessments, they do not engage adequately with the level at which questions concerning the relations between the social conditioning of conduct and freedom are most distinctively posed with Bourdieu's work. His project, as he summarizes it in *Pascalian Meditations*, is with how "there can be thought about the social conditions of thought which offers thought the possibility of genuine *freedom* with respect to those conditions" (Bourdieu 2000, 118). His answer, as well as differing from Merleau-Ponty's, is sharply at odds with those proposed by the wayward tradition in which a generalized potential for free acts, available to all social agents, arises out of the repetitions of habit. Rather, Bourdieu argues, the potential for practices of freedom to move beyond the social conditions that give rise to and cohere practices into distinctive habitus is a selective one, differentially distributed across different habitus in accordance with a social logic in which it is the conditions that condition the formation of some habitus that make possible the transcendence of those conditions.

To see how this is so, we need to look not just at Bourdieu's account of the relations between specific social conditions and the habitus they give rise to but also at the account he offers of the relations between fields and habitus and, more crucially, of the unfolding logic governing the historical relations between different habitus. This provides the setting for his conception of the role of collective intellectuals as our emancipatory guides along the historical pathway leading from habitus bound by the force of habit to a condition of freedom. These issues are connected to what Bourdieu had to say about what he called the historical unconscious, which, like Sullivan's concept of the transactional unconscious, inflects the Freudian conception of the unconscious in a social and historical direction, but a different one. If the pathways produced by attempts to escape the pull of Sullivan's transactional unconscious describe a course full of disguises and evasions, the pathway associated with Bourdieu's historical unconscious is plagued rather by the setbacks and reversals produced by the drags of time.

### Guiding the forth-comings of habitus

In discussing the processes through which an agent grows into an instrument so as to be able to use it comfortably, with an ease of action, Bourdieu adds a new aspect to Merleau-Ponty's discussion in noting that this facility also amounts to letting "oneself be used, even instrumentalized by the instrument" (Bourdieu 2000, 143). Being "at home" also includes a process of being adjusted to a social order. Where this order takes the form of a particular field—the cultural field, say—this adjustment is effected via the "implicit collusion" through which the participants in that field exert pressure on one another to fall into line with the demands of a shared habitus. Disciplinary forms of training, by contrast, "institute between the group and the body of each of its members a relation of 'somatic compliance,' a subjection by suggestion which holds bodies and makes them function like a kind of collective automaton" (145). It is not, then, only the case that the body, in becoming at home with an instrument, relates to that instrument as an open field of possibilities; the same process also opens up the body to be worked on to effect its subordination to the forms of power that give a direction to the instrument in question. A body that has become "at home" in relation to a given set of instruments is also one imbued with a set of capacities that can be triggered to act "like springs" (169), calling forth an ease of action—a way of doing things that, through habituation, has become inscribed in the body—that is central to the exercise, and productivity, of different forms of power.

Bourdieu returns to this theme of triggering when discussing the temporality of the habitus as an "encounter of two histories." For Bergson, the force of the past in the present constitution of the habitus is the outcome of a habit-memory inscribed in the body as the accumulated legacy of the mechanisms of organic evolution. For Bourdieu, it is a result of the social mechanisms through which the inheritor is conditioned by the heritage that they inherit while also being conditioned by their social milieu as to how to inherit that inheritance. It is this historical constitution of the habitus that accounts for the potential openness of its possible futures. "Habitus," as Bourdieu puts it, "is that presence of the past in the present which makes possible the presence in the present of the forth-coming" (211). Deriving its dynamic from its constitution as the result of an encounter between two histories, the habitus possesses a degree of freedom with respect to the force of determination exercised by the present circumstances that, in triggering the capacities that the habitus possesses, activates its past in a manner that introduces and orients the agent toward a possible forth-coming.

Not all habitus, however, are equally open to this possibility. The extent to which they are, and the different forms that such forth-comings take, depends on the "relationship between expectations and chances" (216). This, in turn, depends on the relations between the agents of different habitus and the different kinds of capital (economic, social, cultural, political) that govern the "field of the possible"—that is, the scope of present and possible future actions, and of the relations between them—that are available to them. The opportunities afforded by the possession of different kinds and degrees of capital give rise to different ways of temporalizing the self that, in turn, open up—or close down—the pathways generated between the here-and-now constitution of different habitus and their possible forth-comings. And the pathways that are open to some are premised on mechanisms that entail their closure to others. "Capital in its various forms is a set of pre-emptive rights over the future; it guarantees some people the monopoly over possibles" (225). The right to an education, the trajectory of a career, and the relation to time of a poetic disposition that projects "a pure openness to the world" (224) are examples of the effects of different kinds of cultural capital. For others, possible forth-comings constitute "a signposted universe, full of injunctions and prohibitions... obligatory routes or impassable barriers" (225). Bourdieu cites the case of Algerian subproletarians for whom the "link between the present and the future seems to be broken" (222), precluding any sense of a possible forth-coming, and thus setting them off down a path governed by a flat temporality. In order to "escape from the non-time of a life in which nothing happens and where there is nothing to expect," Bourdieu argues that those who are dispossessed of all forms of capital, and therefore lack any investment in the fields of the possible that such capitals generate, frequently resort to varied types of gambling as a form of fabricated time in which existence is momentarily enlivened by the temporal vector that points expectations forward toward the "finalized time" (222) of the game's end.[11] No matter whether the path of habitus generates a possible forth-coming or closes down any such prospect, conduct is subject to the effects of a habitus ordered by the position of the agent in relation to the distribution of capitals in the present and the modes of appropriation of the dispositions inherited from the past that that position produces.

A different set of issues is opened up by the significance Bourdieu attributes to "mismatches, discordance and misfirings" in the dynamics of habitus. These are not all of one piece. If the "principle of the transformation of habitus lies in the gap, experienced as a positive or negative surprise, between expectations and experience" (149), the extent to which such a gap is opened up and its consequences vary across habitus. There is no such gap where there is "an unproblematic agreement between the position and the dispositions of its occupant, between heritage and the inheritor": the case, for example, of those who, "in their right place" in the social world, can abandon themselves to the automaticity of their dispositions, as illustrated by "the 'ease' of the well-born" (163). It is only where such concordances are prized apart by individual social trajectories or structural social transformations that a gap arises as some agents are placed "'out on a limb,' displaced, out of place and ill at ease" (157). This is the case for "those who occupy awkward social positions, such as the *parvenus* and the *déclassés*," who are more likely to "keep watch on themselves" (163) so as to correct actions that are out of place in the new social spaces in which they find themselves.

It is where such experiences are generalized that Bourdieu sees the possibility for a "margin of freedom for political action aimed at reopening the space of possibles" (234). The case he cites is that of the frustrations associated with the generalization of access to education and the resulting discrepancy between the levels of qualifications attained, the social positions aspired to, and those actually occupied given the predominance of the power of economic capital over the holders of cultural capital. In such circumstances, symbolic struggles intervene to introduce "a degree of play into the correspondence between expectations and chances and open up a space of freedom" in the form of utopian plans, projects, and programs characterized by varying degrees of improbability. Such projects are, in their turn, countered by orthodox symbolic practices oriented toward the stoppage of time, the closing down of the space of possibles, in order to rebind habitus to the existing social order. It is in these terms that Bourdieu proposes a distinctive politics of gapped time in which when—for whatever reason—the automaticity attributed to habit is stalled, conduct is opened up to a series of competing interventions. It is the "margin of freedom" opened up by this gap that "is the basis of the autonomy of struggles over the sense of the social world, its meaning and orientation, its present and future" (235).

For Dewey, the disruption of the routineer's pathway brought about by the internal complexity of modern societies gives rise to a dialectic between impulse and intelligence in the direction of conduct. For Bourdieu, the disruptions constituted by the gap between expectations and chances generate a field of symbolic struggles regarding the directions in which the possibilities opened up by such gaps are to be developed or shut down. In taking issue with those forms of political action that seek to insert themselves in such gaps via a politics of consciousness—a position he attributes to traditional Marxist conceptions of ideological struggle—Bourdieu argues that a progressive politics of the gap must rather aim to give a direction to "dispositions which previous processes of inculcation have deposited in people's bodies" (235). Where Dewey looked to the "sciences of man" to give a direction to the development of conduct through and across the successive moments of its disruption, Bourdieu charges the collective intellectual with the responsibility for directing conduct along a path to freedom. This, for Bourdieu, is not a potential rooted in individuals but an accumulating and collective set of historical possibilities whose realization requires an alertness to the limitations that existing dispositions impose on the innovative imagination and openness to the possibilities generated by the suspension of the regularities of habitus tied to oppressive forms of power.[12]

As we have seen, habitus are not uniform in the manner of their formation or functioning. Some allow a greater capacity for reflexively modifying the force of the determinations that condition them than do others. They are also variable in terms of the positions they occupy in relation to what Bourdieu calls the "two states of history" (Bourdieu 1980). There is, first, the objective history deposited in "things, machines, buildings, monuments, books, customs." And then there is "history in its embodied state, having become habitus," where habitus is interpreted as the "product of a historical acquisition which permits the appropriation of that acquisition" (6). While this appropriation takes place mostly through the mechanisms of inheritance, Bourdieu assigns artists and intellectuals the responsibility for bringing to collective consciousness the cumulative value that has been stored up by the interactions between these two states of history within the literary, artistic, and intellectual fields. As the subjects of dissonant habitus by virtue of their critical relations to the fields of economic and political power entailed by their production and defense of the relative autonomy of literary, artistic, and intellectual fields, it is artists and intellectuals—forged into a collective by their struggles—who articulate the claims of a "historical universal" as an accumulating set of values that, since it has yet to be realized, heralds a collective forth-coming.

Bourdieu concludes his essay on the two states of history with an account of how the sociologist, in accounting for the capacity of habitus to be reshaped through an understanding of the forces that shape them, makes possible a certain "mastery of the self" for both individuals and collectives. This is so to the extent that "the scientific knowledge of necessity contains the possibility of an action aimed at neutralizing it, and thus a *possible* liberty" (Bourdieu 1980, 14). A similar role is accorded to the practice of historical anamnesis—the selective recollection of the past tilted toward the concerns of the present—in *Pascalian Meditations*. It is through this practice that the collective intellectual brings to light the hidden forces that have shaped the path of social and cultural development to open up a space for a practice of freedom that will place those forces under the direction of a self-reflexive collective historical agent. In calling on the collective intellectual to act in the gaps produced by the misfirings of habitus, Bourdieu interprets its role as that of an authority of freedom charged with the responsibility of directing the margin for freedom produced by such gaps in ways that will lead to the conditions required for its universalization as a collective historical accomplishment. The same is true of the postscript to *The Rules of Art*, where Bourdieu urges intellectuals to accept responsibility for a project of historical anamnesis as part of a politics of freedom through which writers, artists, and intellectuals will seek, first, to recover the history of the struggle for a collective universal that is implicated in the struggle for artistic and intellectual autonomy and, second, to defend that autonomy against the state and market while simultaneously seeking to extend its social reach through what he calls a "corporatism of the universal" (Bourdieu 1996, 339–48).[13]

## Archaic habitus: Haunted by habit

There is, however, another aspect to the relations between time and habitus in Bourdieu's work, one that points in quite a different direction. In his account of the choice of the necessary that, in *Distinction*, he imputes to working-class tastes, he argues that this principle is most evident when it is "operating out of phase, having survived the disappearance of the conditions which produced it" (Bourdieu 2010, 375). This is typically the case, he argues, of socially mobile people who, having risen from lowly origins to higher positions in the class structure, are unable to adjust their tastes and expenditure patterns to the new positions they occupy.[14] If this constituted an example of the cleft habitus—the *habitus clivé*, as Bourdieu called it—and of the "mismatches, discordance and misfirings" to which such habitus give rise, these mismatches differ from those that he attributes to artists and intellectuals in the respect that they are due to the operation of a lag through which a set of superseded past conditions continue to exert their force in the present.

Bourdieu (1962) had earlier cited a similar example of such a habitus in his study of the Kabyle, who, as rural Algerians faced with the dislocations of colonial rule and capitalist modernization, remained committed to their traditional ways of life. This was a habitus whose division derived from its being out of time, a survival of the past in the present, generating what Bourdieu called the "hysteresis of habitus," which, as George Steinmetz summarizes it, "turns habitus into a memory of an earlier socio-historical formation which no longer exists" (Steinmetz 2013, 122). Somewhat lost as to how to account for this being out of time that was exhibited by some sections of Algerian society (its rural peasantry) but not others (its urban *lumpenproletariat*), Bourdieu draws on the doctrine of survivals to account for this anomaly. He also invokes this doctrine in *Masculine Domination*, where he expands its scope, arguing that in contemporary "Mediterranean societies," the survival of archaic habitus is evident in the persistence of ritualized forms of gender stereotyping associated with earlier forms of masculine domination (Bourdieu 2001, 6, 54–55). And in comparing the forms that masculine domination takes in the peasant society of the Kabyle and in the Bloomsbury circle, as revealed by a symptomatic reading of Virginia Woolf's *To the Lighthouse*, Bourdieu takes the further step of treating the forms of masculine domination evident in contemporary Kabyle society *as if* they were an archaic forerunner of 1930s Bloomsbury. This interprets present-day Kabyle society as one in which, "abstracted from time," archaic social relations have "survived" into the present

(6). From this Bourdieu moves to construe the forms of masculine domination evident among the Kabyle, as well as in Bloomsbury, "as the instruments of an archaeological history of the unconscious which, having no doubt been originally constructed in a very ancient and very archaic state of our societies, inhabits each of us, whether man or woman" (54).

Archaic habitus thus persist not only in still-extant "archaic societies"; they also haunt modern habitus as a legacy of their deep, archaeological past, an inheritance that operates within us as a level of unconsciousness, but one requiring a collective form of socioanalysis rather than an individualized form of psychoanalysis if we are to be freed from its hold. We are here, then, in a similar territory to Sullivan's account of the transactional unconscious of white privilege, but one that generates its own distinct set of problems. Steinmetz identifies a crucial shortcoming in Bourdieu's assumption that the persistence of "archaic traditions" among the Kabyle is attributable to a conservatism of habitus rather than a consequence of how colonial strategies of indirect rule or, in the French case, of "associationism" often engaged selectively with Indigenous modes of life and the forms of power internal to them, cultivating some as essential conduits for the exercise of colonial governance while eliminating others that frustrated it.[15] And in settler colonial contexts, Indigenous peoples have developed sophisticated political articulations of the concept of survival in the value they place on the preservation of preconquest traditions in rebuttal of colonial strategies of elimination. This has entailed a critique of the anthropological doctrine of survivals in the stress placed on how those traditions have always been creatively developed and adapted to changing circumstances both in preconquest histories and, subsequently, in serving as a resource for resisting the practices of settler colonial states.

What, then, are the implications of the different pathways that Bourdieu constructs for the transformation of habits? These vary depending on whether his concern is with the elimination of survivals that, as we saw in chapter 2, depend on an assessment of the failure of the dynamic potential attributed to the ease of action of habitual forms of repetition to kick in, thus binding the groups in question to an endless repetition of the same; or whether it is with enlarging the scope for freedom imputed to the gap between experience and opportunity, present conditions and future possibilities, associated with certain kinds of modern cleft habitus. The differences between these pathways reflect the operation of two kinds of historical reasoning. The first, interpreting the forms of unconscious symbolic violence of the kind associated with masculine domination as a "historical transcendental," requires that analysis focus on the mechanisms through which particular dispositions developed in particular historical circumstances are perpetuated through time via unconscious mechanisms of social reproduction. In interpreting masculine domination as a historical transcendental, Bourdieu thus invokes the procedures of historical anamnesis to account for the incessant labor of reproduction through which its effects are produced. Bourdieu's method here is focused on "the historical labor of dehistoricization" effected by religious and cultural institutions through which the force of the historical transcendental has been organized and reproduced. To this end, Bourdieu's focus is on *stabilities* through time produced by historical processes of reproduction: an anamnesis of hidden constants, as Bourdieu calls it. It is when it comes to the development of the literary and artistic fields and the role of the collective intellectual in leading habitus along a path toward greater degrees of freedom that Bourdieu's second principle of historical reasoning is brought into play. In such cases, the practice of anamnesis is invoked to analyze *cumulative changes* through time by tracing the development of the historical universal as a set of enduring values that accumulates and deepens through time.

When, then, Bourdieu tells us that he always "said habitus so as *not* to say habit," we need to take what he says with a pinch of salt. Albeit in different ways, a recurring theme in his work consists in the contrast he proposes between habitus that, lacking any generative capacity, are nailed into a time that portends an endless repetition of the same, and habitus whose blips and misfirings open up a glimpse of freedom. Some of Bourdieu's habitus, to put the point differently, look a good deal more like the Aristotelian *consuetudo* than the Aristotelian *habitus*.

# 8

# Contested
# Pathways

I INDICATED AT THE OUTSET OF THIS STUDY that I would avoid the temptation to sign up to any particular version of habit's pathways. While I may have erred from this course from time to time, I have mainly stayed on track in keeping the primary focus of my attention on the varying political histories of habit that have characterized different interpretations of its pathways across a range of discourses. This has involved an examination of the association of those discourses with different regimes of truth and their inscription in the procedures of different apparatuses across different systems of power. My main concern, in addressing these questions, has been to review some of the ways in which habit has been operationalized by different authorities as a means of acting on conduct via the constructions of the relations between bodies, minds, and environments that those discourses propose. This has involved showing how the terms in which such questions have been posed have varied depending on exactly whose bodies and minds are at issue, how their internal architectures are configured, the environments in which they are placed, the apparatuses in which their conduct is inscribed, and the trajectories along which its governance is directed. While there have been significant mutations in the discourses in which habit has functioned as a key term, there are also continuities and connections between them, yielding a mobile balance of "similar but different" mobilizations of the concept that I have illustrated by discussing the varied ways in which the governance of the relations between habit and repetition has been envisaged across different versions of habit's pathways.

These excursions into the history of habit's pathways suggest that the concept of habit has operated somewhere between, or athwart, the two options that Michel Foucault presents in *The Archaeology of Knowledge*, which, in chapter 1, I drew on in outlining the theories and methods I have adopted in this study. Warning against the assumption that "statements different in form, and dispersed in time, form a group if they refer to one and the same object" (Foucault 1972, 32), he urges instead the need to attend to discontinuities in the functioning of apparently similar objects produced by their dispersal across different discursive formations. On the one hand, a certain continuity is detectable in how the concept of habit has straddled a tension between forms of repetition destined to endlessly reproduce themselves and those generative of a capacity for new and relatively free actions. On the other hand, discontinuities are evident in how the constitution and mechanisms of habit have been conceived in the light of highly mutable conceptions of their relations to changing understandings of the operations of the other aspects of personhood with which habit has been aligned or to which it has been opposed.

I put the matter in this way in order to open up avenues of inquiry that will question the force that long-standing conceptions of habit's duality have exerted in impelling us to think of the relations between repetition, power, and conduct as veering between either grinding us in limitless forms of repetition or glimpsing the prospect of freedom. It is with this end in view that, in this chapter, I probe a set of current debates—some theoretical, others more directly political—that, in the light they throw on the main strands of argument developed in the previous chapters, highlight the different positions that habit has been accorded in the processes though which the governance of conduct has been both effected and contested across different regimes of power.

My first probe places Bruno Latour's account of the blessings that habit's well-trodden pathways confer on the hiker in the context of the more varied set of roles that he attributes to habit's pathways in his account of modes of existence. This will serve as a means of drawing together the various threads of argument that I have developed in criticizing the tendency to abstract questions of habit from questions of power. I then look at some of the different positions that Gilles Deleuze took up in relation to the version of habit's pathways—"we are habits, nothing but habits, the habit of acquiring habits"—that he derived from his readings of David Hume and Henri Bergson. I have, as the reader will no doubt have noticed, been a little flirtatious in the plays on this interpretation that I have offered from time to time. But Deleuze's own relationship to this motto was also quite mobile, as he quoted it to varying effect at different stages in his work. I shall, then, look at the distance that Deleuze puts between the position he adopts in his earlier reading of Hume and the limits that, in *Difference and Repetition*, he places on habit's repetitions relative to those associated with modernist artworks that, in his estimation, lead out from and beyond those repetitions. In doing so I note the significance of Foucault's initial subscription to, but later departure from, similar assessments of the disruptive potential of modernist art practices. My third probe engages with recent literatures exploring the positions accorded the unthinking repetitions of habit in new forms of algorithmic governmentality. This will identify how the force attributed to habit in such accounts, and suggestions as to how that force might be modulated or avoided, draws on earlier orderings of the relations between power, repetition, and conduct and the counterorderings of such relations associated with their contestation. My fourth and final probe explores the implications of a politics of "gapped time" that goes beyond its most usual association with individual subjects to examine its currency in relation to the divided temporalities that characterize the relationships between the governance of habits in emergencies and the countertemporalities of "slow emergencies."

### Staying on track or taking the path of alteration

Latour's account of the lost hiker, freed by habit from the need to hesitate over which step to take next, is only one of the pathways he invokes in the place he accords habit in his "anthropology of the moderns," where, cast in the role of one mode of existence among others, habit is also viewed as providing the underpinnings of all modes of existence. Interpreting such modes of existence—those associated with science and technology, the arts and fictions, and religion, for example—as instituted streams or continuities of action, Latour argues that where the "existents" involved in such streams of action encounter unexpected problems of arrangement, they periodically have to adjust their course in order to deal with such moments of hiatus. Before introducing his hiker, Latour sings his praise of habit in relation to those existents who exemplify the virtues of its unthinking repetitions in relation to the courses of action associated with different modes of existence: the worker who, "once the subtle arrangements of muscle and nerve reflexes in relation to each tool and material have been established," lines up "the sequence of works and days without even being aware of it"; or the priest who, unless routinized to the moment of transubstantiation at his daily celebration of the Mass, would be "so stunned by what he is celebrating that he would never get beyond the first words of the Canon" (Latour 2013, 265). The hiker, as the example specific to habit's mode of existence that Latour invokes as a parallel to these figures, also stands as a counter to Double Click. Modeled on the instant retrieval of information effected by double-clicking on the mouse device, Double Click is Latour's figure for those existents for whom habit has become so effective in aligning discontinuities with established courses of action that they fail to respond to the need for a radical restart presented by moments of hiatus when the dizzying quantity of mediations bearing on action have gotten out of their accustomed line.

This prompts Latour to invoke a second figure of habit, one able to respond to such moments of hiatus by drawing on a force that is constantly available for reawakening beneath the forgetfulness of blessed habit: a capacity for attentiveness able to respond to the circumstances when habit's unthinking repetitions are disrupted. If habit protects us from what would otherwise be an endless series of discontinuities by allowing our unthinking navigation along a regular path, this virtue would degenerate into mere "mechanical gestures and routines" (269) were its power extended so as to veil or inhibit the power of attention. Habit's familiar duality is thus reinscribed: habit "either knows how to find the path of alteration" by yielding to the power of attention when brought to bear on the circumstances that prompted its current course or it loses "all traces of that path and begins to float without signposts" (269).

In outlining his reasons for the significance he attributes to habit, Latour brings a generational dimension to his concerns. Identifying himself as a baby boomer, he questions the legacy of the May '68ers for its misleading conjunction of the critique of habit with the critique of institutions. Although not explicit as to whom he has in mind, the negative conceptions of habit that prevailed in the Sartrean and critique of everyday life traditions that dominated French debates in the 1960s are the most likely candidates. The resulting polarity, pitting "initiative, autonomy, freedom, and invention" against institutions as "routinised, artificial, bureaucratic, repetitive, and soulless," was one that committed a "sin against blessed habit" (278) as a mechanism for the relay from one set of institutionalized practices to another. This, Latour argues, has deprived succeeding generations of the capacity to connect critiques of institutions to their renewal through the production of a new set of instituted truths. Giving rise instead to a metaphysics of alterity, it has grounded identities and knowledge on a terrain of pure outsides that, lacking the "scaffolding of habit," affords no vestige of continuity. The radical distinction proposed by critique between "what is true and what is instituted" reflects a further misunderstanding of habit that, if properly appreciated, teaches that *there is nothing true except what is instituted* (280). Habit is thus doubly relative: relative "to the weight, the thickness, the complexity, the layering, the multiplicity, the heterogeneity of institutions," and relative "to the always delicate detection of the leap, the threshold, the step, the pass" (280) that is necessary for it to serve as a mechanism for the rejuvenation of institutions.

Putting Latour's generational concerns to one side, the account he offers here is a nuanced rendition of the relations between the consolidations and breaches of habit's repetitions, between its gaps and their closure, as a relay mechanism in the change of dispositions. The ease of action made possible by the force of its accumulated repetitions has its virtues, until it doesn't; but when those repetitions become a constraint that needs to be broken with, its virtues come to the rescue in establishing a new set of instituted practices. All well and good, except that this neglects the respects in which institutionalized regimes of truth are also regimes in which distinctive forms of power are produced and exercised. It also neglects the different ways in which habit's pathways have been operated on by different authorities with regard to both the allowance of any scope for the operation of a gap in its repetitions that might be accorded a renovative significance and the denial of any such scope in the enforced perpetuation of habit's repetitions. It consequently mistakes the enforcement of mechanical repetitions on others for a lack of attention on their part. In short, Latour's account of habit's roles in relation to his modes of existence neglects the forms of authority that are in contention regarding the conduct of conduct.

If Latour's concern is with habit's role in the renovation of institutions, De-leuze's interest in the relations between habit and repetition focuses on their role in the production, constitution, and transformation of the self. It's worth noting, as a preamble to discussing these matters, the terms in which the Institut de France put the question for the prize that was awarded to Maine de Biran in 1802. In posing this as concerning the "influence of habit upon the faculty of thinking," entrants were required to "show the effect which the frequent repetition of the same performances produces upon each of our intellectual faculties" (Maine de Biran 1929, 41). Maine de Biran opens his entry with a quotation from the Comte de Mirabeau—"No-one reflects about habit" (47)—and then proceeds to do so: "Reflect upon what is habitual!... who could or would wish to begin such reflection?... This host of modifications which succeed each other, of performances which repeat each other and accumulate since the beginning? This *me*, which escapes itself in the apparent simplicity and extreme facility of its own acts, which ceaselessly eludes itself... how should one *reflect* on its habits, the most intimate, the most profound of all?" (47).

Deleuze's concern with habit similarly pivots on its role in relation to the part played by processes of repetition in the formation of the self. There are, however, differences between the terms in which he answers this question in *Empiricism and Subjectivity* and in the later *Difference and Repetition*. In the former, it is Hume's account of the role played by the social ordering of the passions in the mind's operations, and of the ways in which ideas come to be associated with one another in the imagination, that Deleuze interprets as providing a basis for an empiricist conception of the mind as a subject endowed with a capacity for surpassing its conditionings that is not dependent on the intervention of a transcendent force. He thus places particular emphasis on Hume's contention that the mind would revolve endlessly around the ideas derived from sensations without being able to generate any new original ideas "*unless nature has so fram'd its faculties*, that it feels some new original impression arise from such a contemplation" (Hume quoted in Deleuze 1991b, 31). It is, for Hume, habit—"the habit of contracting habits," which, as "one of the principles of nature," derives "all its force from that origin" (Hume quoted in Deleuze 1991b, 66)—that plays this role. And it is the interactions between experience and habit that account for the dynamism of the self. In elaborating the relations between habit and experience, Deleuze quotes the following passage from Hume's *Enquiry*: "Experience is a principle, which instructs me in the several conjunctions of objects for the past. Habit *is another principle*, which determines me to expect the same for the future; and both of them conspire to operate upon the imagination" (Hume quoted in Deleuze 1991b, 67).

Since the essence of experience is the repetition of similar cases, this does not enable inferences to be drawn from such repetitions that would provide a basis for future action. The form of repetition involved here is one in which the only difference between the second and the first case is that "the second comes after without displaying a new idea" (Deleuze 1991b, 67). Habit provides a counter to such a "mechanics of quantity" (67) in relating to repetition not with regard to the objects repeated but from the position of the mind that contemplates those repetitions, thereby producing a new impression in a "determination to carry our thoughts from one object to another... to transfer the past to the future" (Hume quoted in Deleuze 1991b, 68). It is in view of the synthesis that it thus effects that habit enables the mind to take up a dynamic relation to time, installing the subject in the midst of the process of "duration, custom, habit and anticipation" (Deleuze 1991b, 92) in which habit and anticipation are paired as a dynamic couplet that goes beyond the synthesis of time effected by memory. It is not, then, habits that are natural; rather, after Bergson, "what is natural is the habit to take up habits" (44), the mechanism through which the subject is set off down the road leading to the development of a second nature. "Habit," as Deleuze puts it, "is the constitutive root of the subject, and the subject, at root, is the synthesis of time—the synthesis of the present and the past in the light of the future" (93–94). As such, its road and that of the development of culture and morality are one and the same.

If this is the point to which, in Hume's account, habit's repetitions lead, these are, for the later Deleuze, the repetitions that must be broken with in order that what he calls true repetition might begin. This is his starting point in *Difference and Repetition*. "Repetition," he writes of true repetition, "is a necessary and justified conduct only in relation to that which cannot be replaced.... To repeat is to behave in a certain manner but in relation to something unique or singular which has no equal or equivalent" (Deleuze 2004, 1). The repetitions of habit propel the development of a second nature and, with it, the formation of conscience interpreted as the outcome of "the habit of acquiring habits (the whole of obligation)—which is essentially moral or has the form of the good" (5). Habit's repetitions thus subject conduct to the regulative force of a generality, to the role of equivalences, just as much as is involved in its regulation by natural law. True repetition, by contrast, "is by nature transgression or exception, always revealing a singularity opposed to the particular subsumed under laws, a universal opposed to the generalities which give rise to laws" (6). As such, true repetition derives its force from the "difference" that "inhabits repetition," establishing it as "the differenciator of difference" (97). Following Hume again, this capacity for repetition is due not to its effects on the object repeated—where it changes nothing—but to its ability to *change something in the mind which contemplates it*" (90). In *Difference and Repetition* this capacity for contemplation is brought down from the mind of an abstracted self to be nested in the organic constitution of the body's cellular and muscular systems.[1] As Deleuze puts it in his famous passage on our constitution as larval subjects, "Selves are larval subjects; the world of passive syntheses constitutes the system of the self, under conditions yet to be determined, but it is the system of a dissolved self. There is a self wherever a furtive contemplation has been established, whenever a contracting machine capable of drawing a difference from repetition functions somewhere" (100).

The differentiating dynamic that true repetition derives from our organic constitution can only be realized if conduct is rescued from those habitual forms of repetition—the "sad repetitions of habit" (366), as Deleuze calls them—generated by the requirement of obedience to some particular social law or code of behavior: in other words, to the effects of power. This requires, as Brian O'Keefe puts it, philosophy's intervention into the relations between the inner core of the self and its outer shell. The former is made of the pathways constituted by the multiple contractions of habits on the part of the many souls (cells, muscles, neurons) that are dispersed throughout the body, contractions that are made in the moments of detached contemplation produced by the pause or gap between one such action or perception and another. The outer shell of the self cloaks these dynamics of inner repetition in its mechanical automatisms: "The Deleuzian self seethes and fluctuates as beliefs and convictions jar against the verifiable truths and facts it also knows; appetites prompt that dynamic of craving and then satisfaction; sundry habits coalesce and ultimately wreathe outwards, from the kernel to the shell, to the outside, where a crust forms—sterile routine, stale automatism" (O'Keefe 2016, 82).

Bare repetition, repetition of the same, "is like a skin which unravels, the external husk of a kernel of difference of more complicated internal repetitions" (Deleuze quoted in O'Keefe 2016, 87). This conception of a "quilted self," as O'Keefe puts it, is one that has "gaps and holes" in its weave, and it is through these gaps and holes that there flow the energies that Deleuze—

whom O'Keefe aptly characterizes as "the pathfinder for all that flows and commingles" (2016, 93)—seeks to liberate from the forces that block them. O'Keefe argues that Deleuze performs this role—one that "takes the Humean moral subject so far along the path of true repetition that he exits morality altogether" (80)—through his advocacy of a particular kind of learning in which true repetition, as a "ceaseless adaptation to difference" (81), will be facilitated by a particular kind of teaching: "We learn nothing from those who say: 'Do as I do.' Our only teachers are those who tell us to 'do with me,' and are able to emit signs to be developed in a heterogeneity rather than propose gestures for us to reproduce" (Deleuze 2004, 26). This involves what O'Keefe calls a distinctive form of "semiotic apprenticeship," one that entails the ceaseless adaptation to difference that is the course of true repetition rather than the automatic repetition of the same. It is a course that, rather than enjoining pupils "to heedless repetition, where they automatically follow the example set in stone by the magister," points toward the cultivation of "otherness, singularities and the heterogeneous" (O'Keefe 2016, 81). Its guides are those exemplary teachers who nurture not followers but individuals able to set forth alongside their mentors but down their own paths.

In thus juxtaposing "doing with me" to "doing as I do," Simone Kotva (2015) argues that Deleuze pointedly takes issue with the role accorded to "mimetic discipleship" (Kotva 2015, 110) in Christian *paideia*, where "doing as I do" enjoins the imitation of Christ as an aspect of both the gift of grace and the means of achieving it. This is, in other words, the form of pastoral authority that Foucault summarized as obeying the law exemplified by "someone because he is someone" (Foucault 2007a, 175). The contrary form of the pedagogic relationship between teacher and pupil that Deleuze advocates as "doing with me" is merely one of the many ways in which, throughout *Difference and Repetition*, he establishes a distance between his position and different versions of the role of repetition in the direction of conduct along the pathway to grace. While citing Søren Kierkegaard, along with Friedrich Nietzsche, as a model for his conception of the "thinker-comet and bearer of repetition" versus the "public professor and doctor of law" (Deleuze 2004, 7), and praising him for opening up a path of repetition leading beyond the repetitions of habit and memory, Deleuze consistently sides with Nietzsche in differentiating his position from Kierkegaard's reworkings of Christian theology.[2] The difference between "Nietzsche's Dionysius and Kierkegaard's God," he says, is "insurmountable" (9), a point he returns to in criticizing the terms in which Kierkegaard equates the path of repetition with that of faith as inviting us to "rediscover *once and for all* God and the self in a common resurrection," thereby realizing "Kantianism by entrusting to faith the task of overcoming the speculative death of God and healing the wound in the self" (118).[3] He similarly invokes Karl Marx, as a stand-in for conflict and struggle, as a counter to readers who might be tempted to convert his account of the relations between difference and repetition into "the discourse of beautiful souls: differences, nothing but differences, in a peaceful coexistence in the Idea of social places and functions" (259). Although dependent on habit and made possible by it, true repetition leaves it behind, embarking on a multitude of unguided paths—unguided, that is, except for the power of the mystic, which, no longer the preserve of spiritual elites, has been implanted by the philosopher in the pulses and contractions of cellular matter as they poke through the gaps and holes they make in the fabric of our quilted selves.

There are, of course, many aspects of Deleuze's relations to Christian theology that go beyond the focus of his account of habit that is my concern here. There is, however, a substantial literature addressing the ways in which Deleuze's formulations redeploy the authority of the mystic. The same is true of aspects of Foucault's early work.[4] It is, then, quite likely that the early Foucault might have rapped me over the knuckles for taking issue with Deleuze's account of the relations between habit and repetition as constituting a bid to bring the direction of conduct under authority of the mystic. This is especially likely given the enthusiasm that Foucault expressed for *Difference and Repetition* in his 1970 essay "Theatrum Philosophicum," celebrating its account of repetition for freeing it from "the dreary succession of the identical" to become, instead, "displaced difference" (Foucault 1998d, 356). Foucault also, at this stage in his work, signed up to the role that Deleuze assigned to modernist aesthetic practices in nudging us along the pathways that lead beyond habit to pure repetition. Toward the end of *Difference and Repetition*, Deleuze urges that there is "no other aesthetic problem than that of the insertion of art into everyday life" (Deleuze 2004, 367), where, by virtue of its ability to repeat and, in doing so, to play with and decenter the repetitions that make up the standardized life of the society of controlled consumption, it points the way toward a liberating ungrounding of habitual repetitions. The visual artist to whom he accords pride of place in this regard is Andy Warhol, who, in pushing the painterly forms of repetition associated with copying to an extreme, is said to have conjugated varied forms of repetition—of habit, memory, and death—to insert a moment of freedom between them. Foucault was equally enthusiastic, interpreting Warhol's canned food series as one whose "boundless monotony" generates "the sudden illumination of multiplicity itself . . . a flickering of light that travels even faster than the eyes and successively lights up the moving labels and the captive snapshots that refer to each other to eternity" (Foucault 1998d, 362).

I dwell on the role that Deleuze and the early Foucault attributed to art and the aesthetic as a force potentially capable of freeing us from, as Deleuze put it, the "sad repetitions of habit" (Deleuze 2004, 366) by way of underscoring a difference between what I have drawn from these aspects of their work and what, albeit not without significant qualification, I have taken from Pierre Bourdieu. There is, of course, little in common between the approaches of Bourdieu and those of Deleuze, and relatively little intellectual traffic between those who have followed in the traditions they initiated. This is less true of the relations between the traditions of inquiry opened up by Bourdieu and Foucault. Although Foucault did not comment on Bourdieu's work, Bourdieu took a serious, albeit critical, interest in Foucault, and there have been numerous subsequent explorations of lines of both convergence and divergence between their work (T. Bennett 2010). It is, however, the divergences, particularly with regard to aesthetic matters, that are my concern here. It's not so much the assessments of Warhol that I have in mind, though one would be hard put, today, to find many who would echo Deleuze's and the early Foucault's unreserved attribution of a critical force to his work. When viewed in terms of the changing relations between the American and French art fields that developed apace in the postwar period; the links that have been established between the difference generated by Warhol's repetitions and the cycles of capitalist innovation; the subsequent unfolding of the relations between Pop Art and commerce; and its mobilization in the contestations of the Cold War, the credibility of such assessments seeps away (see Menand 2021, 512–41). It is, however, the more general procedure of attributing to particular works of art a force that operates independently of their position within the mutating institutional relations that govern the organization of art fields and their relations to economic and political forms of power that is at issue here. This derives from the ascription to art, as a general category, a force that acts on or in relation to the force of habit, again as a general category, in an invariant way irrespective of its institutional articulations and how different groups are placed in relation to the world of art constituted by such articulations. To inscribe the modernist enthusiasms of the 1960s as an invariant staging post on the role played by repetition in the trajectories of the self between habit and true repetition is only possible when both art and habit are abstracted from their varied social and political histories.

These, then, are positions that find little support from a critical history of either art or habit, or of the relations between them. They are also positions that find little support from the concern with the institutional and technological embedding of discursive and artistic practices that, as the predominant signature of Foucault's work from the early 1970s onward, have for me always trumped the significance of many of his earlier philosophical and aesthetic enthusiasms. This is not to suggest a Chinese Wall between these different phases of Foucault's work. There are, as I noted in chapter 2, undoubted continuities between Foucault's earlier archaeological concerns and his later genealogical analyses of the operations of different kinds of power.[5] However, while aspects of his earlier commentaries on selected literary texts and paintings anticipate and, indeed, illuminate his later analyses of power, Kenneth Berger (2018) convincingly argues that Foucault put to one side his earlier ascription of a positive political force to avant-garde aesthetic practices.

It is also worth noting that, while intense for a period, the collaborations between Foucault and Deleuze peaked around 1972, waning thereafter as their intellectual trajectories diverged. This was especially so, Paul Patton (2014) argues, with regard to Deleuze's tendency to exempt philosophy from the analysis of the truth/power effects of knowledge practices, whereas, in his later work, Foucault insisted on the need to interrogate the procedures governing the formation of philosophical discourses and their institutional inscriptions and effects (Scott 2014, 167–68). This was not the direction taken by Deleuze and Félix Guattari's conception of philosophy, in being uniquely engaged with the creation of concepts, as essentially liberatory, preparing the way for "a new earth and a people that do not yet exist" (Deleuze and Guattari 1994, 108). For this also exempted philosophy from its implication in the exercise of those forms of power characterized by "action upon the action of others" that Foucault attributed to liberal forms of governmentality and that, as we have seen, inform the place accorded habit in the processes of becoming that have been superintended by philosophy's pastorate within the wayward tradition.

## Computational pathways:
## The procedural dynamics of automation

Let me go back, in introducing my third probe, to Andrew Pickering's assessment of the significance of Ross Ashby's discussion of machinic forms of automation as staging a nonmodern ontology in which machines, like people, are understood as dynamic realities, changing and developing in ways that feed off their own activities. The dance of agency this opened up in destabilizing "any clean dualist split between people and things" (Pickering 2010, 42) has since developed apace as the practices of cybernetics and artificial intelligence (AI) have fed into the procedural dynamics of computational systems. These not only undercut any essentialist distinction between human and machinic forms of agency. They have also, as Carolyn Pedwell (2021) puts it, served to "re-mediate the human": that is, to alter the constitution and functioning of various aspects of our intellectual and affective makeup. The forms of automation that are involved here go beyond those associated with the nineteenth-century development of machinofacture. Brett Neilson and Ned Rossiter, reflecting on Marx's discussion of automation in the *Grundrisse*, thus argue that the issue is no longer that of labor being reduced to the level of an accessory to machinic forms of automation. Rather, the consequences of AI and machine learning mean that the role that Marx reserved for labor in providing the "conscious linkages" that those forms of automation required can now be to some degree dispensed with as the limited forms of intelligence to which the inputs of labor have been reduced mean that these too can now be artificially emulated. And in forms that sever the association of automation with repetition—performing "the same action over and over again"—as automation now "lives by adapting to its environments" through its machinic repatterning of the inputs-outputs that mediate such relations (Neilson and Rossiter 2019, 199). Mark Andrejevic (2020) similarly stresses the respects in which automated media go beyond earlier forms of machinic automation that were brought to bear only—or at least mainly—on the regulation of production processes and, thereby, on the disciplining of labor. In extending from the organization of physical labor to that of informational and communication practices, the operations of computational systems also have consequences for practices of consumption, forms of sociality, and modes of political action. Disrupting the operations of the knowledge practices that characterized earlier forms of disciplinary power, they pose a profound challenge in requiring the development of counterknowledges that go beyond the traditional symbolic forms of critique (Andrejevic 2013).

Habit has, unsurprisingly, been a significant point of reference for debates concerning the implications of what Luciana Parisi calls "*the automation of automation*" (2019, 90) in the sense that it is now the "meta-level of algorithmic function"—that is, the automated generation of new algorithms—that engenders new forms of nonconscious cognition capable of developing accumulating capacities for acting on varied forms of conduct. It has been invoked in various ways in relation to the role played by computational systems in the operations of the new logistical infrastructures, which, through the institution of virtual systems of control over the movement of people and goods, have extended the reach of capital beyond the disciplinary enclosures of the factory walls. Liam Magee and Ned Rossiter's concern with what they call the "habits of data"—that is, with "the routine and repeatable processes through which digital data circulate within and across logistical operations" (Magee and Rossiter 2021, 132)—encompasses not only the part they play in relation to the impact of the new circuits of capital on the habits of labor in the warehouse settings of platform companies like Amazon but also their roles in the coordination of habit regimes across the relations between home, office, warehouse, and data center. They are particularly concerned with how such "routines of data" might narrow behaviors into ever more rigorously monitored routines that can then be channeled in the direction of varied forms of hyperproductivity in the practices of consumption, management, and labor. If consumers are rewarded "the more they purchase—and review"—and white-collar workers are encouraged "to produce friction and critique" with a view to enhancing the regulatory capacity of the logistical systems they are a part of, warehouse laborers are inveigled into "a complex choreography of supervision, surveillance, maintenance and co-operation with the robots whose workspace they cohabit" (144). This is a choreography that involves an intensification of the forms of routine earlier associated with Taylorist and Fordist forms of assembly-line factory production.

There is another aspect to Magee and Rossiter's concerns. The relations between the "habits of data" and those of both labor and consumption under the conditions of "cognitive capitalism" subject our somatic and cognitive lives to new forms of proceduralism that militate against the production of gaps in the temporal regimes they impose. "Robots," as they put it, "dream of nothing" (139). This is a concern that we encountered, at the close of chapter 5, in Wendy Chun's (2016) argument that the procedural dynamics of new media tend to close down the forms of undecidability—and thence the opportunity to initiate new courses of action that depart from congealed habits—associated with gapped time. And it is one that Jonathan Crary shares in his contention that the loss of sleep associated with the factory, symbolized by Joseph Wright of Derby's *Arkwright's Cotton Mills by Night*, is compounded by the omnipresence of today's media, which go one step further in also robbing us of "the interval before sleep" as a moment of "suspended time" in which the "perceptual capacities that are nullified or disregarded during the day" (Crary 2014, 126) might be recovered. For Andrejevic, Crary does not go far enough because he fails to register not only how the refuge of sleep is lost but also how sleep is invaded, folded into the circuits of capital, by digital monitoring devices that mine marketing data even from sleepers (Andrejevic 2020, 105). This is, however, but one aspect of the ways in which the operational logic of computational systems mutes the force of human agency. The automated responses that they harvest from consumers not only detach them from the systems of representation from which they derive their meaning; they also close down the gap between sign and referent that, according to the prognoses of critical semiotics, generates the desires that give a new impetus and direction to the will. For Parisi, the self-regulating systems of cybernetic feedback that constitute the habitual time of automata are an instance of the capacity of "instrumentality to entrap time" (Parisi 2017, 6), folding the past into the present and thereby depriving memory of any possibility of gapping the time of the present.

These, then, are some of the ways in which, in "re-mediating the human," computational media have been said to reconfigure the relations between cognition and memory, for example, as aspects of the makeup of persons in relation to which the action of habit has been variably configured. These formulations also go beyond those associated with earlier accounts of automatism—from René Descartes through the reflex arc to nineteenth-century forms of machinofacture—in suggesting that the accumulative dynamic of habit has been transferred from persons to computational systems. If, in post-Lockean accounts, the accumulation of a set of skills sedimented in the mind or body—or mind-body—through the repetitions of habit facilitates the acquisition of new competencies, so "the habits of data" of computational systems enhance their capacity to enroll the new data acquired along their pathways into more forceful forms of action on their human coactors. This suggests a transference of the dynamics of habit from persons to machines according to which it might be said of the latter that "we are habits, nothing but habits, the habit of acquiring your habits, detaching them from your development and inscribing them in ours—is there any better account of the machinic self?" Indeed, this might well have served Deleuze as a suitable aphorism for his account of what he characterized as "societies of control" in which the disciplinary technologies informing the operations of institutions of enclosure—prisons, factories, schools—have progressively given way to the regulative effects of code, which, in effecting a differential distribution of access to information, now typify contemporary systems of corporate power (Deleuze 1992).[6]

Prompted by these concerns, a good deal of contemporary critical engagement with computational media has focused on the role of repetition as enacted across the relations between human and nonhuman actors in the operations of the assemblages through which varied forms of power are constructed. This is part of a broader theoretical terrain in which both Latourian and Deleuzian traditions of assemblage theory have been brought into critical dialogue with Foucauldian perspectives on the workings of different knowledge/power relations through the operations of different apparatuses. The Deleuze invoked in these debates is less the Deleuze of *Difference and Repetition* than a later Deleuze who, in his appreciation of Foucault, endorsed those aspects of *The Archaeology of Knowledge* from which I have taken my bearings in this study. In christening Foucault as "a new archivist," Deleuze took on board his warning that the conditions under which a statement may be repeated—in the sense of carrying the same meaning and operating to the same effect—are very strict. Where these conditions are not met, propositions— "species evolve" is the example he gives—have to be read as parts of different statements operating to different effect across different discursive formations: in this case, those of eighteenth- and nineteenth-century biology (Deleuze 1988, 10–11). His appreciation of the later Foucault of *Discipline and Punish* as "a new cartographer" who treats the statements of different discursive formations as parts of the diagrams that structure the operations of the concrete assemblages—schools, workshops, prisons—as proceeding through relations between forces that "take place 'not above' but within the very tissue of the assemblages they produce" (37) points in the same direction.

What needs to be stressed here are the consequences of the multiple forms of interaction between statements in which the concepts of habit, routine, and conduct are implicated and different diagrams of power, and their translation into particular techniques of governance—and the ways in which these are contested—through the operations of the concrete assemblages they form a part of. For it is through such interactions that a range of effects—some pulling in complementary directions, others in contradictory ones—are produced. These are matters that Engin Isin and Evelyn Ruppert raise in considering the role played by a range of epidemiological knowledges during the COVID-19 pandemic in exercising new forms of intervention into conduct in concert with the development of new systems for monitoring bodily movements afforded by the procedural dynamics of computational systems. They suggest that the pandemic highlighted the development of a new form of "sensory power" that has been under way since the 1980s. They call it sensory power in view of its dependence on the operations of "different technologies of detecting, identifying and making people sense-able through various forms of digitized data (text, number, image, sound, signal and so on) about their conduct such as transactions, movements, searches, clicks, and so on" (Isin and Ruppert 2020b, 8). As such, they argue, endorsing a principle Foucault always insisted on, sensory power has to be considered in its relations to the continuing operation of earlier modes of governing conduct.

Isin and Ruppert thus urge the need to attend to the strategies of different forms of power in terms of the effects on conduct they aim to secure; the technologies they deploy to this end; the knowledges that order the relations between technologies and strategies; the assemblages through which knowledges, technologies, and strategies are brought together; the objects to which different forms of power are applied; and the forms of resistance they give rise to. If the strategy of discipline is to secure submission to the norm through the application of technologies of confinement, correction, and punishment superintended by the sciences of medicine, nosology, psychology, and sociology, it brings these to bear on bodies through the assemblages of camps, prisons, schools, hospitals, and workhouses, giving rise to varied forms of subversion. Sensory power, by contrast, effects changes in conduct via technologies that aim to modulate our bodily performances exercised under the superintendence of the computational social sciences, cryptography, data science, and web science.[7] The object to which it is applied, Isin and Ruppert argue, is a new one: not that of territories characteristic of sovereign power, or the bodies characterizing the anatamo-politics of disciplinary power, or the populations of governmental and biopower, but that comprising the performances of bodies in the clusters, such as bubbles and hotspots, produced by the sensory assemblages of apps, devices, and platforms. And the form of resistance that sensory power gives rise to is that of a range of calculated forms of opacity effected by the means of various techniques—of encryption, anonymization, and noncompliance—calculated to disrupt the tracing and tracking of bodily movements and performances.

There is, though, no consideration in this account of either the historical or continuing role of the discourses, techniques, and apparatuses of pastoral government. Yet, as Rosalind Cooper (2020) shows, there are a number of ways in which the algorithmic processing of our existences echoes and incorporates aspects of the "shepherdic technologies" of pastoral governance. The digital prizing of our everyday practices into its algorithmic operations effects a transparency of conduct to power—be it that of the state or of capital—

that reworks the techniques of the confessional. Algorithmic power also harnesses a set of anticipatory techniques through which the tracking of past events, coded into data, endows capital with the ability to direct our conduct along selected routes without the need to enlist our awareness or agreement. "The anticipatory techniques undergirding the software-mediated conducting of souls," as Cooper puts it, "thereby extend and intensify the twin pastoral concerns to produce obedient servitude and foreclose upon the human will" (2020, 40). Cooper also notes the respects in which community-based forms of activism that seek to limit algorithmic power, or to inflect its operations in new directions, resonate with the respects in which the types of counter-conduct developed in early forms of Protestantism took issue with the binary structure of pastoral power by invoking shared communal norms and practices in rebuttal of priestly forms of authority.

This is in accord with the central argument of Isin and Ruppert's (2020a) earlier and broader analysis of the politics of "digital citizenship," in which they draw on Foucault's work to account for the distinctive fusion of obedience, submission, and subversion characterizing engagements with contemporary forms of algorithmic governmentality. Interpreting cyberspace as a technological mediation of the relations between embodied practices, they concern themselves with the different forms of "action on the actions of others" or the "conduct of conduct" that are at stake within this space. This is an issue that centers on the different types of performativity associated with state and corporate forms of digital action on, and the harvesting of, our everyday habits on the one hand and, on the other, the resistance to and subversion and contestation of these arising from the new ways of conducting ourselves and our relations to others in cyberspace produced by varied forms of digital activism. In relating these concerns to "the figure of the citizen we inherit" (Isin and Ruppert 2020a, 18), Isin and Ruppert place a Foucauldian gloss on Étienne Balibar's conception of the "citizen subject" (Balibar 1991) as a figure that is "not merely *subject to power* or the *subject of power* but embodies both" (Isin and Ruppert 2020a, 19).

Fashioned by an inheritance of multiple forms of power (sovereign and disciplinary, for example) producing a composite of diverse dispositions (obedience, submission, subversion), the citizen subject is the locus for contesting directions for the conduct of conduct. If being *subject to power* reflects the legacy of obedience required by sovereign power, being the *subject of power* "means *submission* to authority in whose formation the citizen participates and its potential *subversion*" (20). The citizen subject is not the one or the other of these but the site of their conflicting potentialities. As such, the inheritances that are coded into the citizen subject reach back beyond both the Enlightenment and sovereign power to the stress Foucault placed, in his analysis of the forms of pastoral governance, on the "acts of truth" about the self that were promoted by the confessional, which, in cultivating an active orientation to both faults and merits, made it possible for "the subject to constitute himself or herself as a subject of power" (20). These, then, are among the resources drawn on by those forms of digital and data activism that, premised on the development of new ways of acting both with and on the actions of others, prize open the putative closures—around race, gender, xenophobia—effected by corporate and state forms of algorithmic governmentality.

Heidi Rae Cooley's account of how the governance of habits effected by the computational tracking of our movements, social connections, and consumption practices is countered by the dynamics of community-based habits points in the same direction. Drawing on the pragmatist philosophy of Charles Sanders Peirce, she interprets his conception of habit as being forged in shared semiotic perspectives derived from communal styles of life as providing a counter to mechanical responses to technical instructions. While thus invoking the communal formations of habit as a possible mechanism for change, Cooley is equally insistent that these cannot be viewed as an outside to the mechanisms of computational governance. "To imagine an outside to these conditions of being 'on,' connected, and on grid in the twenty-first century," she argues, "would be a mistake" (2014, 52). The issues at stake in mobilizing the communal forms of habit are not, therefore, those of an accumulating second nature along habit's pathway to freedom but rather ones concerning the direction and political forms in which conduct is to be regulated.

The same is true of the issues posed by my final probe, which returns to the questions raised by my discussion, at the end of chapter 2, of the distribution of different temporalities along the different forms of habit's pathways associated with the governance of emergencies.

### Habit, emergency government, and the politics of "gapped time"

To recap briefly, in elaborating what they mean by "racializing emergency," Ben Anderson, Kevin Grove, Lauren Rickards, and Matthew Kearnes identify how the governance of emergencies—occasioned by floods or pandemics, for example—frequently operates through a division between the strategies directed at liberal white (or whitened) subjects, on the one hand, and black and Indigenous subjects, on the other. Strategies directed toward white liberal subjects are predicated on an anticipatory structure that, in both placing limits on and working through habitual norms of individualized self-control, projects a future of "growth, change, development and becoming" (Anderson et al. 2019, 623) in which those norms are fully restored. By contrast, the strategies brought to bear on black and Indigenous subjects depend on techniques of racialization that suspend black and Indigenous subjects in "a durative temporality of decline, stagnation, decay, *and* a repetitive temporality of recurring plantation violence" (623). What is at stake in emergency governance, they argue, is "the relation between emergency and the everyday" in which "everyday habits, practices and events" (625) are related to as possible sources of emergencies, as what have to be addressed in plotting a route through them, and as what have to be restored or refashioned once the emergency is declared to have been overcome. But these engagements with habit are shaped by racially differentiated logics.

The reference Anderson and his coauthors make to "the repetitive temporality of recurring plantation violence" is not meant to be taken literally any more than the form of blackness invoked is that of a phenotypical category. It is rather a reference to blackness as "a political, juridical and philosophical category" that has "constructed certain spaces as unlivable and marked those inhabiting these areas as less-than-human," spaces that have to be understood in terms of their differential relation to spaces of whiteness governed by the European conception of modern time as an "open-ended domain of progressive change, growth and betterment, amenable to human intervention and calculated improvement" (626). If the temporality of plantation violence was initially dependent on the dead-end time produced by the enforced repetitions of the plantation system, then so its continuing operation is also dependent on those revisions of plantation violence exemplified by the "slow violence" associated with the production of new spaces of segregation—the prison-industrial complex, segregated inner-city areas, Indigenous reservations—that characterize the contemporary forms of Achille Mbembe's "necropolitics" (Mbembe 2003).[8]

It is only the counterlogic constituted by the projects of "slow emergencies" that promises a break with the dead-end time of such enforced repetition. The political logic of slow emergencies has several dimensions. In contrast to those state-initiated forms of emergency governance that work to secure a return to the free and open-ended futurities of white subjectivities, campaigns for slow emergencies seek to bring transformative attention to bear on the "un- or barely-bearable conditions" (Anderson et al. 2019, 623) that characterize the lives of those trapped in the durative temporalities of decline, stagnation, and decay. If such circumstances are ones in which "the intersection of stalled time and disastrous time foreclose capacities to become otherwise" (632), the campaigns for change that characterize slow emergencies typically depend on the mobilization of collective and communal forms of authority that seek to construct future pathways shaped by a different logic from "individualism's individualized, open-ended futurity of limitless growth" (632). The politics of slow emergencies also depend on the production of an interval that interrupts the stalled time constituted by racializing forms of necropolitics. Not, though, an interval in the internal dynamics of the self but one produced by public forms of political and artistic activism that aim "to make situations of attritional lethality into events that demand some form of urgent response" (633).

The contradictory placement of the repetitions of habit in the relations between these two different forms of emergency has been an aspect of the Northern Territory Intervention. Triggered by the Northern Territory National Emergency Response Act of 2007, this brought the daily lives of Indigenous Australians in Australia's Northern Territory under exceptional forms of control and direction. While these were supported by some Indigenous Australians, others took issue with them on a variety of grounds. For Aileen Moreton-Robinson, the logic of the Intervention depended on its mobilization of colonial discourses of Indigenous pathology—of Indigenous people as "nomadic, sexually promiscuous, illogical, superstitious, irrational, emotive, deceitful, simple minded, violent and uncivilised . . . as living in a state of nature that was in opposition to the discourse of white civility" (Moreton-Robinson 2009, 65)—in order to bring about the disciplined subjection of Indigenous people to the habitual codes of white civility. Ostensibly occasioned by a report addressing high levels of child sex abuse in a number of Indigenous communities of the Northern Territory, the Intervention installed a set of rules that, in contradistinction to the purely case-by-case treatment of child sexual abuse on the part of white Australians, went beyond punishing those found guilty of such offenses to subject whole communities to a new set of requirements and restrictions aimed at addressing an alleged collective and racialized shortfall in the operation of individualized forms of self-control and responsibility.[9] In addition to placing a large number of Indigenous communities under martial law, a range of the regulative measures introduced by the Intervention—restrictions placed on alcohol consumption, the auditing of computers to detect pornographic material, quarantining income support payments for basic necessities such as food, clothing, and shelter to ensure they were not spent otherwise—reflected the widespread conception of those communities as locales for "the undeserving poor who lack effort, proper money management skills, a sense of morality, the ability to remain sober, the ability to resist drugs and a work ethic" (70).

While not using the vocabulary of slow emergencies, Moreton-Robinson evokes its logic in her criticism of the Intervention for deflecting attention from the deep and systemic impoverishment and disadvantages that afflict Indigenous communities—and urges the need to mobilize communal forms of action to attend to this—by interpreting it instead as the result of a deficiency of character on the part of Indigenous Australians. Similar views were evident in the contributions many members of the Indigenous communities brought under the jurisdiction of the Intervention made, in 2011, to a program of consultations conducted by the Senate before a legislative review of the Intervention in 2012.[10] Two themes stood out. The first concerned the resentments occasioned by the undermining of the limited degrees of community autonomy and self-control that the Intervention introduced in restricting the "capacities to become otherwise" that these had fostered. Valerie Martin, eschewing the emergency logic predicated on the cultivation of individualized forms of self-control that bypassed, indeed dismantled, community forms of governance, singled out this aspect of the Intervention for "ruining our lives and spoiling our future. We want self-control in our own communities" (quoted in Harris 2012, 37). The second concerned the Intervention's deadening consequences for the dynamics of daily life. Mr. Oliver of the Malabam Health Board evoked these when he pointedly asked the visiting Senate committee, "Do you all know what a lorrkon is? It is a hollow log. We use logs for coffins. Since the intervention and since this new policy has come in that is all we are seeing. We are seeing hollow people walking around" (quoted in Harris 2012, 33). By implementing a new set of relations between the repetitions of habit, power, and the direction of conduct, the Intervention imposed a new set of intersections between "stalled time and disastrous time." These were, though, as we have seen, not without precedent. Albeit different in its social and institutional forms, it was a historical replay of the late nineteenth-century forms of coercive rule that were applied to "primitive peoples" for having failed to follow the dynamics of habit's liberal pathways through to their proper, individualized, self-civilizing ends.

# Conclusion

OURS, THEN, IS INDEED A TIME when questions of habit have been placed on the line politically across a wider range of concerns than at any moment in its earlier histories. Many of these are continuations of the roles it played in relation to what Mike Savage (2021) calls the categorical divisions of inequality of race, gender, class, and colonialism that I discussed in the opening chapters of this study. Although the dominant forms of its earlier operations in relation to those inequalities have been challenged in many of the traditions of habit theory discussed in later chapters, their legacies are still very much in play in relation to the escalating inequalities that mark the early twenty-first century. Other contentions over habit's political implications are more distinctly contemporary: the urgencies attaching to the redirection of the everyday habits that have given rise to the already evident ecological disasters attributable to climate change; the consequences—still unfolding—of new regimes of digital automation for our everyday habitual practices of labor and consumption; and the conscriptions of habit in programs of managed mindfulness prompted by new neuroscientific conceptions of mind-body-environment entanglements.

It is not surprising, then, that theories of habit should now also be on the line, in the sense of being renewed subjects of attention and critique. There are, I have suggested, a number of earlier periods when this has been so: the contentions over the role accorded habit in earlier forms of pastoral government that characterized the Reformation; the reworking of habit in early modern philosophy that accompanied the transition from sovereign power to liberal forms of governmentality; and the challenges to the forms for the guidance of conduct associated with earlier theological and philosophical accounts of habit that were mounted by the new empirical sciences in the late eighteenth and nineteenth centuries. In revisiting these earlier moments in habit's political histories via the concept of habit's pathways, my main purpose has been to show how the force attributed to habit has differed depending on the nature of the power relations within which that force has been harnessed, disciplined, or inhibited by the forms of authority that have been in contention regarding the ends to be pursued via the different ways in which they have fashioned its role in the guidance or direction of conduct.

In opening the previous chapter, I reaffirmed my commitment not to sign up to any of the particular versions of habit's pathways, or the definitions of habit on which they depend, that have provided my theoretical route into habit's political histories. However, I should, in concluding, like to chance my arm a little by outlining a perspective that, while not detracting from the variability of habit's definitions, will accord it a certain degree of constancy, but one that is able to encompass its varied intellectual and political histories. It is a perspective suggested by Pierre Bourdieu's concept of conditionability as "a natural capacity to acquire non-natural, arbitrary capacities" (Bourdieu 2000, 136). I referred to this at the end of chapter 6 when discussing Catherine Malabou's use of it as a basis for her conception of intelligence as a capacity grounded in the body but not reducible to its biological determinations. While this was a part of Bourdieu's concern, he also invoked the concept as a means of defending the principles of a dispositional sociology. In doing so he acknowledged a similarity between the concept of conditionability and the conception of the habit of acquiring habits that Gilles Deleuze derived, in *Empiricism and Subjectivity*, from his reading of David Hume's melding of habit and custom as natural and artificial forms of repetition that reinforce each other. But Bourdieu lent a different inflection to Deleuze's aphorism in interpreting habit as a capacity—that of acquiring new dispositions—that, derived from the constitution of living beings, is one to which there attaches a degree of arbitrariness regarding the nature of the further dispositions it generates, the mechanisms through which they are acquired, and the forms of authority to which they are subjected.

The sense of arbitrariness that is in play here is a limited and specific one. When referring to the arbitrariness of conditionability, Bourdieu meant that the further dispositions it makes possible are arbitrary with regard to the capacity of conditionability but not socially arbitrary. The acquisition of such dispositions is the work not of "a transcendental subject but of a socialized body, investing in its practice socially constructed organizing principles that are acquired in the course of a situated and dated social experience" (137–38). As we saw in chapter 7, Bourdieu was not entirely successful in sidestepping the theoretical effects of earlier conceptions of habit. Putting these considerations to one side, however, to think of habit as a form of conditionability that is open-ended with regard to the consequences that might follow from how it is acted on, operationalized, directed in different ways, and contested provides a way of engaging with the varied forms of force it has exercised in the different regimes of power that it has been entangled with across the course of its plural political histories.

This allows that habit's pathways will remain—and remain in contention—since they are a part and parcel of the arbitrariness of its constitution; only guided pathways are able to convert its indeterminacy into determinate directions. The question of habit thus always brings in tow issues concerning the direction of conduct. And this in turn engenders a series of further questions. Which authorities—instituted or oppositional—are to direct it? How, and to what degree, do these emerge from and enlist the active participation of those beckoned to tread the pathways in question? How do we deal with the consequences of the differential social distribution of different kinds of pathways—those encountering the possibility of changes of direction prompted by gaps, blips, and misfirings, and those that close such possibilities down? How are our guides along habit's myriad pathways to be held to account? And how might the forms of authority they exercise be challenged, displaced, or reconfigured? These are questions that the "wayward tradition" is not well equipped to deal with. For it has, in essence, already answered them through its revision of long-standing theological and philosophical conceptions of habit in ways calculated to take account of but, at the same time, trump the rival forms of authority that, since the eighteenth century, have been entangled in complex ways—sometimes in partnership with, at others in critique of—such philosophical inheritances. Our engagements with habit, both theoretical and political, will be better served by attending to the variable force that has been attributed to it through its inscription in different forms of power. For it is only in this light that we can understand how the arbitrariness constituted by the capacity to acquire new forms of action has constituted the locus for contestations over how that capacity should be guided, by whom, under what conditions, and toward what ends. Far from anticipating that these are matters that might soon be settled, all the signs point to the likelihood of their becoming increasingly fraught and embattled.

# NOTES

## INTRODUCTION

1. I do so with a primary focus on the Anglophone and French literatures and the exchanges between them. This is an artificial limitation, as both of these literatures have been significantly influenced by other national traditions. The influence of German thought—from Gottfried Wilhelm Leibniz through G. W. F. Hegel to Friedrich Nietzsche and Martin Heidegger—has been especially important in this regard. However, the French and Anglophone connections have been particularly strong with regard to the issues I examine over the period I am mainly concerned with. For what it's worth, the Google Ngram for *l'habitude* follows a roughly similar pattern to that for *habit*: increasing sharply toward the end of the eighteenth century and maintaining high levels throughout the nineteenth century, then dipping in the twentieth century—but by no means so much or so sharply as for *habit*—and then showing a very sharp rise from 2000 to the present. These differences probably reflect the attention accorded habit within the French phenomenological tradition throughout the twentieth century.

## CHAPTER ONE. POWERING HABIT

1. Parsons's argument here extended Weber's exclusion of crowd behavior from the field of social action proper on the grounds that its imitative logic did not meet the requirement that social action be meaningfully oriented toward others. See Borch (2012, 109–10).

2. Rita Felski has offered a trenchant critique of this aspect of Lefebvre's work, noting also its connection to his view—along with that of Julia Kristeva—that the strength of women's association with repetition emphasized "their connection to

nature, emotion, and sensuality and thus to biological and cosmic rhythms" (Felski 2000, 82).

3. This was the subject of Lukács's essay "Reification and the Consciousness of the Proletariat," later collected with other essays in *History and Class Consciousness* (Lukács 1977).

4. Bourdieu often stressed that the two concepts of habit and habitus should not be confused, usually drawing on the Aristotelian distinction between *consuetudo* and *habitus*. He often complained that commentators fudged the two concepts. He thus registered his irritation at François Héran's (1987) failure to appreciate that "I said habitus so as *not* to say habit" (Bourdieu and Wocquant 1992, 122). I return to this issue in chapter 7, where I discuss Bourdieu's failure to maintain a watertight distinction between the two concepts.

5. For an overview of critical engagements with the critique of everyday life tradition, see T. Bennett (2004a).

6. More recent work by Daniel Ussishkin (2017) suggests that, at least in the British context, the nineteenth century witnessed the development of new forms of military training that worked through the cultivation of morale as a collective capacity which provided a new means of normalizing individual conduct that, to a degree, displaced the mechanisms of discipline.

7. Recent work on the economic logic of the plantation system casts doubt on this claim. I return to this question in chapter 2.

8. I touch here on only a few aspects of the significance accorded the instincts across a range of practices of governing. Katherine Frederickson (2014) offers a more broad-ranging consideration of these questions.

9. Although they differ in particulars, Gary Shapiro (2003) and Joseph Tanke (2009) offer similar assessments of the relations between Foucault's archaeological and genealogical perspectives represented by different stages in his approach to the analysis of artworks.

10. This favored imagery of habit has a longer history: it is invoked, for example, by Thomas Hobbes in illustrating his conception of habit as a motion made easy by custom as a repeated form of endeavor. See Von Leyden (1981, 22–23) for an assessment of the place of habit in Hobbes's account of the role of endeavor in his science of mechanics.

11. For extended discussions of the place Bourdieu accords the tennis player in his theory of action, see Lahire (2011) and Noble and Watkins (2003).

12. Guston's series of Ku Klux Klan paintings occasioned a good deal of controversy in 2020 when the retrospective exhibition *Philip Guston Now* was postponed by the four major American art museums that had initiated it in the light of accusations that the series was racist. This decision prompted a widespread campaign, with significant contributions from African American, Asian, Persian, and Arab artists and curators whose contextual readings underlined the significance the series had played in critiquing white supremacism. The campaign resulted in the museums concerned revising their decision to postpone the exhibition to 2024, opening it instead in 2022.

See Schwendener (2020) for details of the campaign; J. Friedman (2020) for the background to, and unfolding of, this controversy; and Slifkin (2021) for a broader discussion of the political resonances of Guston's Klansmen series.

13. See Jones (2016, 8–22) for a probing account of the role played by the figure of the blind man in the debates concerning the relations between sight, touch, and knowledge from Descartes through Denis Diderot and on to the optical regimes of the nineteenth-century world's fairs.

14. See Barad (2007, 154–57) for an account of how earlier epistemic conceptions of the role played by the blind man's stick in mediating the relations between the subject and an independent external world were reworked by the physicist Niels Bohr in ways that resonated with Merleau-Ponty's account of its role in the contraction of bodily habits.

15. There are notable differences between Mill's position on habit in his 1843 text *A System of Logic* (Mill 1967) and his 1859 essay *On Liberty* (Mill 1969). I have discussed these in T. Bennett (2011b).

16. I won't labor the point any further. However, for an interesting discussion of the intersections between the concepts of habit and custom as applied to the routines of different forms of labor, see Shah (2017).

17. For a more detailed discussion of these issues, see T. Bennett (2021).

18. This aspect of Foucault's work has generated a considerable literature on the different historical forms in which freedom has been implicated in practices of governing. I have benefited greatly from the contributions that Patrick Joyce (2003) and Nikolas Rose (1999) have made to this literature.

CHAPTER TWO. DEAD ENDS AND NONSTARTERS

1. Although this passage is often quoted in favor of habit's virtues, the broader context from which it is lifted presents a more complicated picture. In discussing the role of habits of thinking in conjoining ideas "not allied by nature," Locke is clear that this can become a problem if it leads to their unthinking repetition. Of those who are unduly guided by, among other things, "the din of their party," he thus writes that "the confusion of two different *ideas*, which a customary connexion of them in their minds hath to them made in effect but one, fills their heads with false views and their reasonings with false consequences" (1965, 341).

2. The blacksmith is frequently cited as an example of how, in *The Nicomachean Ethics* (bk. 2, chap. 1), Aristotle accounts for the acquisition and development of the skills associated with particular arts and crafts as being attributable, alongside the acquisition of moral virtue, to their repeated use and exercise.

3. Kay's work is the site of a significant tension between different ways of conceiving and acting on the habits of the poor. Lauren Goodlad (2003) thus shows how his position on these questions shifted from a pastoral conception of the poor as subjects to be engaged in programs of voluntary self-reform under middle-class tutelage toward an increasingly statistical and environmental conception of them as needing to be improved by governmental forms of action on their milieus.

4. Marx's reference here is to Ure (1835), a classic eulogy to the factory system.

5. Thompson also applied this logic to what he called still-existing "primitive societies," as exemplified by E. E. Evans-Pritchard's work on the time consciousness of the Nuer and Pierre Bourdieu's discussion of the resistance to clock time among the Kabyle; see E. Thompson (1991, 355–56).

6. See M. Thompson (2019, 3–5) for an account of the rigorous clock time that was enforced on George Washington's domestic servants.

7. The authority of the overseer was differently constituted in different plantation systems. In his discussion of the regulation of slavery in late eighteenth-century Puerto Rico, Nicholas Mirzoeff identifies the respects in which that authority derived ultimately from the system of sovereign power within which it was inscribed as the final link in a "chain of authority" running "from God to king, king to governor, governor to planter, planter to overseer, and overseer over the enslaved" (Mirzoeff 2011, 118).

8. The dual relation to slaves as labor and capital is evident in George Washington's instructions to his overseers to ensure that his slaves worked diligently from dawn to dusk—admonishing that "lost labor is never to be regained"—while simultaneously admonishing that this should not be at the expense of their health or constitution and thus of their value (M. Thompson 2019, 77).

9. There is also an extensive literature exploring how the wastage of bodies associated with the coffle—and, indeed, the plantation system—was anticipated by that associated with the wastage of bodies in the slave ships of the Middle Passage. See, for example, Sharpe (2016) and Zieger (2021).

10. Schuller borrows the concept of "sociobiological indeterminism" from this characterization of Lamarck's work in Stocking (1982).

11. Cope devotes considerable attention to demonstrating that all automatic movements must have their origin in consciousness as part of his dispute with Darwinism and his interpretation of evolution as a divinely ordered process.

12. This association between channels and habit had a broader currency in Victorian literature; see Vrettos (1999/2000) for a discussion of its role in the work of Charles Dickens and Elizabeth Gaskell.

13. See Otis (1994) for a discussion of the wider currency of the concept of organic memory.

14. I have developed this concept more fully elsewhere: see T. Bennett (2011b, 111–13).

15. For a fuller discussion of this aspect of Bagehot's work, see T. Bennett (2004b, 89–91).

16. I draw here on the discussion of Max Müller's theory of language in Wolfe (1999). While drawing on Müller's work, Tylor was also critical of it: see Tylor (1994) for a review, published in the *Quarterly Review* in 1866, of a course of lectures delivered by Müller at the Royal Institution of Great Britain.

17. Particularly via Durkheim, who drew significantly on Spencer and Gillen's fieldwork in his account of "primitive" religions (Durkheim 1961), and via Freud, who referred extensively to Spencer and Gillen, alongside other Australian anthropologists, in his *Totem and Taboo* (Freud 1960, 114–21). See Frederickson (2014) for a discussion of

how the conceptions of primitivism proposed by Australian anthropology influenced Freud's account of the role of instincts in the composition of the mental structures of "savages" and "neurotics."

18. This is not to suggest that Indigenous peoples were not enslaved. Andrés Reséndez (2016) suggests that Native Americans were subjected to varying practices of slavery both in larger numbers and over a longer period than African Americans. Australia's Indigenous peoples also experienced slavery, albeit not in the specific form of the plantation system that is my concern here.

19. And these were, indeed, often symbiotic processes. The removal of Indigenous Australians from their lands was often accompanied by their disciplining as a source of rural labor tethered to the outback stations that constituted the outposts of the rural economy. Australia's sugar industry was also dependent on slave labor, though mainly through the importation of Pacific Islanders, resulting in plantation economies with strong similarities to, and developed through collaborative networks with, the Caribbean plantation economy (Sparrow 2022).

20. There is a substantial Indigenous literature addressing the conceptual underpinnings of these policies, focusing particularly on the relations between the practices of anthropological fieldwork and museums in the late nineteenth and early twentieth centuries. The work of Martin Nakata (2007) has been particularly influential in this regard. I also offer a more detailed discussion of these questions in chapter 6 of T. Bennett (2004b).

21. I touch here on only one aspect of Tarde's account of the relations between repetition, imitation, and habit. See Borch (2012) and Dibley (2021) for more broadranging discussions.

22. Gilles Deleuze (2004, 157–58n3) accords considerable significance to Tarde's work as an early harbinger of his own account of the relations between difference and repetition. Tarde's work on Maine de Biran also had a significant influence on both Henri Bergson and Deleuze: see Alliez (2004). The issues I draw attention to here are not typically discussed in accounts of the relations between Deleuze's and Tarde's work.

23. The consequences of racial and class differences for the different ways in which governments have sought to regulate habits have been evident throughout the COVID-19 pandemic. For a discussion of these and related questions concerning the governance of habits in the early stages of Australian responses to COVID-19, see T. Bennett , Dibley, Hawkins, and Noble (2021).


CHAPTER THREE. UNWILLED HABITS

1. For a shorter overview than that offered by Fearing, see Phillips (1971).

2. See Greenwood (2010) for a detailed discussion of the differences between Huxley's and Descartes's accounts of automata. See also Georges Canguilhem (2008), who, while acknowledging significant similarities between the two, shows how these were inflected differently in Huxley's work in the light of subsequent developments in the life sciences.

3. I draw here on the arguments developed in greater detail in Gaukroger (1995).

4. Tully's discussion relates to Locke's 1697 *Report of the Board of Trade to the Lords Justices respecting the Relief and Employment of the Poor.*

5. The use of the language of slavery in connection with drinking and other forms of addiction was a highly variable one. In early nineteenth-century Britain, the relations between the vocabularies of habit, addiction, and enslavement varied in their application across antislavery and temperance movements. In early nineteenth-century America, the slavery-addiction trope was mainly applied to whites on the basis that it implied a loss of control over the self, a capacity that was viewed as innately lacking among the actually enslaved. For a wide-ranging account of these variations as figured within literary genres—within both Britain and America, and between them—see Zieger (2008).

6. I draw here on a fuller discussion of these questions in T. Bennett (2001).

7. The most notable, perhaps, were those focused on the shock effects arising from the speeded-up rhythms of modern city life and their impact on the mentalities of city denizens arising from the condition of neuroanaesthesia. See Jackson (2013) for a discussion of the psycho-medical coordinates of this conception and Crary (2001) for a more extended discussion of the broader cultural impact of the condition and its distribution across different city populations. Georg Simmel's classic 1902–3 essay "The Metropolis and Mental Life" (Simmel 1950) approached similar issues from a different perspective in the contrast he proposed between city dwellers who had adjusted to the shocks of city life and newcomers to the city.

8. Canguilhem's discussion of milieu is more broad ranging, encompassing its mechanical conception within Newtonian physics to refer to the medium of action between bodies as well as its later Lamarckian conception as the ensemble of forces that act on living beings (Canguilhem 2008, 75–120). It is this latter usage that Foucault draws on.

9. See Walusinski (2020) for a more detailed discussion of Morel's account and an assessment of its place in its broader intellectual and political setting.


CHAPTER FOUR. PATHWAYS TO VIRTUE

1. I should stress, by way of signaling the limitation of my concerns, that the historical reordering of the relations between pastoral, sovereign, and governmental forms of power from the sixteenth century on raises questions that go far beyond my interest in the shifting place accorded habit in these transitions. See Schilling (1995) for a more wide-ranging discussion of the changing relations between church (across all confessions: Lutheran, Calvinist, Catholic, and Anglican) and state in the development of new and more far-reaching ways of both disciplining and governing populations as formerly elite spiritual practices were more broadly deployed in new forms of education and religious supervision.

2. These specific concerns entail that I chart a selective route through the immense literature on the role of habit in Christian theology and practice. I have also put to one

side the debates occasioned by Foucault's concept of pastoral government regarding the respects in which its account of different moments in the development of pastoral power and its imbrication with other governing practices might need to be qualified. Blake (1999) and Ojakangas (2012) provide some pointers to these debates.

3. The passage is from bk. 8, sec. 5. The translation is Heiner's.

4. This is a summary of a more intricate set of relations between different forms of habitus in Aquinas. See Darge (2018) for an account of the respects in which Aquinas reworked the Aristotelian *consuetudo/hexis* distinction into a distinction between two forms of habitus: the *habitus entitativus* and the *habitus operativus*.

5. Agamben's account of pastoral government differs from Foucault's in many respects (see Leshem 2015); however, these do not bear critically on the point at issue here.

6. See Porter (2018) for an extended discussion of this matter.

7. Sylvie Delacroix (2022, chap. 3) offers an insightful discussion of these two different senses of virtue considered with regard to the acquisition of both the technical skills and the nontechnical ethical capacities required across a range of contemporary professions.

8. Heinz Schilling (1995) underlines the significance of celibacy in this regard in discussing the consequences of the later permission of marriage for the Protestant clergy for the recruitment and training of Protestant ministers as a development that weakened the force of the trifunctional inequalities Piketty discusses.

9. First broadcast in 2000, *The Habits of New Norcia*, directed by Frank Rijavec, cowritten and narrated by Indigenous writer Harry Taylor, was funded by the Australian Film Finance Corporation and the broadcaster SBS Independent. For further details, see Laurie (2000).

10. See also Christina Petterson (2012), who sees the issues at stake in counterconducts as being the same as those in pastoral and governmental forms of power: how to direct the relations between forms of conduct and the forces of life.

11. I draw here also on Corey McCall's (2014) discussion of Foucault's concept of conduct.

CHAPTER FIVE. UNFOLDING PATHWAYS

1. I have discussed the significance of Maine de Biran's work in these regards, and also his influence on Ravaisson, in more detail elsewhere: see T. Bennett (2021). His departure from the Lockean tradition and its significance is richly illuminated by Jonathan Crary (1996, 2001). It should be noted, however, that there are varied accounts of what Ravaisson drew from the work of Maine de Biran and the implications of this for how the relations between his work and both earlier and later philosophical traditions should be read. Jeremy Dunham (2015) takes issue with the theoretical lens through which both Carlisle and Mark Sinclair interpret Ravaisson's work on these grounds.

2. I have elaborated the concept of "guided freedom" more fully elsewhere—see T. Bennett (2011a)—albeit tilting it in a different direction here. I offer a fuller discussion of these issues in chapter 6.

3. The reference here is to Weismann 1893 text *The Theory of Heredity*. Grosz (2004, 91–93) discusses the background to, and significance of, this text.

4. Bergson derives the impetus to life from solar energy, interpreting the force of life as one that is bound by the laws of inert matter while constantly working to limit such laws and to set itself free from them.

5. I draw here on Melanie White's (2013) discussion of the role played by the imagery of leaping in Bergson's work.

6. Ribot played a key role in translating the organic memory tradition from its Anglophone context into French debates. Émile Durkheim, for example, drew on Ribot's work in his account of the role of neurophysiological mechanisms of inheritance through which the unconscious is constituted (Durkheim 1964, 304).

7. Ribot presents this account as a corrective to the science of character that John Stuart Mill had proposed in his *A System of Logic* (Mill 1967). See White (2005) for a discussion of this aspect of Mill's work from a governmentality perspective.

8. See Sinclair (2011b) for a fuller discussion of the influence of Ravaisson's work on Bergson's conception of habit as a residue of spiritual activity.

9. Carlisle (2013b, 45), noting that Ravaisson does not mention Aquinas, argues that the Christian Aristotelianism that informs his text aligns him with the Catholic tradition most influentially represented by Aquinas.

10. This sense of an acquired virtuosity informs David Bissell's (2018) discussion of "habits of commuting." In recounting his experience in a Cycling in the City course in Sydney, he describes how, under the watchful eye of course instructors committed to the principle of "cycling graciously," he learned a new set of techniques for managing the relations between signaling, braking, and pedaling in city-center contexts. The terms that Bissell proposes for understanding the operation of such habits constitute a blend of Ravaisson's double law of habit—albeit largely shorn of its theological implications—according to which facility of action is increased with repetition, and the conception of habits as necessarily enacted across the relations between people and their social and material environments. While it is an issue that goes beyond the specific focus of Bissell's concerns, training programs aimed at teaching cyclists how to "cycle graciously" often have a marked social and racial bias. Melody Hoffmann (2016) addresses these questions in her study of similar programs in Milwaukee, Portland, and Minneapolis.

11. I have discussed these issues more fully elsewhere; see T. Bennett (2004b, 99–106).

12. See M. Bennett (2019) for a fuller discussion of Grosz's interpretation of Darwinian categories.

13. See chapters 7 ("Irigaray and the Ontology of Sexual Difference") and 9 ("Sexual Difference as Sexual Selection: Irigarayan Reflections on Darwin") in Grosz (2011, 100–12; 132–68).

14. There are, however, some difficulties with Butler's account of the role played by the repetition of regulatory practices in the organization of the forms of gender performativity through which sexed bodies are produced. Karen Barad (2007, 60–66,

193–94, 204) usefully identifies both Butler's and Foucault's failure to accord any specific role to the dynamism of matter in their accounts of the agential capacities of apparatuses. See also Patricia Clough (2018, 69–74) for a probing discussion of the relations between Butler's and Grosz's positions.

15. It is true of walking more generally that it is often invoked as affording the kinds of intervals that Grosz argues are central to the dynamics of habit change. See also Gros (2014) for a discussion of the role of walking as a form of repetition that has lent itself to distinctive forms of spiritual guidance and, for a more general discussion, Solnit (2014).

16. For fuller discussions of the relations between affect and habit in which the significance and limitations of affect are both acknowledged, see Pedwell (2017b, 2021).

17. The interpretations of memory that were developed in association with the development of evolutionary thought were quite varied. See T. Bennett (2004b) for a review of some aspects of its different forms and their implications. See Radstone and Hodgkin (2003) for a more general discussion of varied forms of memory practice.

## CHAPTER SIX. EXPLODED PATHWAYS

1. I offer in this and the next section of this chapter a revised and extended discussion of issues raised in T. Bennett (2016).

2. See Hawkes (2014) for a summary of Australian organizations offering industry and community leaders brain-training and flexibility management programs derived from recent positions in the neurosciences.

3. I refer here to the culture of civic humanism in which the aesthetic disposition was connected to the position of the landed gentry and the members of the professions that catered to its needs in late seventeenth- and early eighteenth-century England; see Klein (1994).

4. Neuronal pathways are thus not, for Malabou, as they were for James, most strongly marked by how they are distinguished from one another by the role played by social and occupational position in fixing, and limiting, our neurally embedded habits to particular stations in life. To be sure, Malabou says, we know that "the brain of a pianist is not strictly identical to that of a mathematician, a mechanic, or a graphic artist"; but, beyond the influence of "a person's 'trade' or 'specialty,' . . . the entire identity of the individual is in play" (Malabou 2008, 7).

5. I draw here on arguments developed at greater length in chapters 6 and 7 of T. Bennett (2013b). Chapter 6 engages with the different uses to which the "uselessness" attributed to the aesthetic in selected traditions of post-Kantian theory have been put; chapter 7 discusses how the aesthetic ethos of "guided freedom" informs the work of Jacques Rancière.

6. For further discussion of the implications of Bourdieu's account of divided habitus, see T. Bennett (2007) and S. Friedman (2016).

7. Bourdieu's (2010) account of musical tastes in *Distinction* pays particular regard not just to class but to the temporal dynamics of musical fields, emphasizing

how the interactions between these connect to the differential trajectories of age within social classes. The significance accorded classical music within practices of distinction is now markedly less than it was at the time of Bourdieu's study, and for a number of reasons. These include the increased significance accorded atonal musical forms on the part of the younger members of the professional and middle classes as a way of marking their differences from both their parallel age cohorts in lower social classes and the older branches of the professional and middle classes. For a discussion of these questions in the Australian context, see T. Bennett, Dibley, and Gayo (2021).

### CHAPTER SEVEN. PROGRESSIVE PATHWAYS

1. On the role of infrastructures in this regard, see Hawkins (2021).

2. MacMullan (2009) is an exception to this neglect of the role of impulse, as is Crossley (2013a).

3. I discuss these connections between Dewey and the Boas school more fully in T. Bennett (2015).

4. Shannon Sullivan initiated these debates (see Sullivan 2000, 2004, 2006), with an early response from MacMullan (2009). Crossley (2013a, 2013b) has also been influential, and I contributed an earlier perspective (T. Bennett 2013a). Pedwell (2017a, 2021) has since extended these debates in important directions.

5. See Holmwood (2022) for a discussion of some similarities between the terms in which Dewey and Bourdieu posed the relations between questions of class, morality, and habit(us).

6. The distinctiveness of Dewey's position here is highlighted by the role that his contemporary, the physiologist Walter Cannon, accorded homeostasis in fashioning a "wisdom of the body" that secured its operations from the destabilizing effects of external disruptions. Drawing on Claude Bernard's concept of the *milieu intérieur* as a set of internal bodily processes regulating the body's relations to its external natural and social environments, Cannon viewed the "involuntary nervous system"—in essence, an extension of the reflex arc—as "acting automatically, without direction from the central cortex," and thereby preserving "the fitness of the internal environment for continued extrofective action" (Cannon 1940, 250). It is the regular functioning of this system constituted by the condition of homeostasis that—in another corporealized version of the Lockean schema—serves as the engine of freedom. It is only the "automatic regulation of the routine necessities" that frees the brain for the "higher services" of "intelligence and imagination, insight and manual skill" (303). Like Dewey, Cannon invokes the pathway analogy to explore the political implications of what he calls the body's "autonomic system." He thus likens this to a "vast and intricate stream" (314) that regulates the flow of bodily fluids just as canals, rivers, roads, and railroads regulate the flow of goods and people within the nation-state. In contrast to Dewey, Cannon argues that disruptions of such flows are to be regretted. Freedom is acquired

not by escaping the "routineer's road" but by being bound to it. In entertaining the concern that "social stabilization would too greatly interfere with the free action of individuals," Cannon advises that, to the contrary, the production of "steady states in society" is essential for the "steady states in its members" that are required for the realization of their "higher freedom" (324).

7. The weight that Dewey placed on different disciplines within what he variously called the "science of human nature" or the "science of man" varied. In his later *Freedom and Culture* (1939), he assigns the anthropological concept of culture the coordinating role among these disciplines. In urging its virtues as providing a means for acting on the conduct of the collectives bound together by the cultures they share, he displaced the individualized approaches to the direction of conduct that he attributed to Western philosophical traditions and psychology.

8. Sara Ahmed (2007), addressing these questions from a phenomenological perspective inflected via her experience as a woman of color conducting diversity work in white institutions, questions the value of placing an undue stress on the agency of white people in overcoming the habits of whiteness. See also Iris Marion Young (2005) for an influential engagement with these issues from a feminist perspective.

9. Although Merleau-Ponty does not cite Maine de Biran, he made extensive notes on his work and was clearly influenced in these formulations by the significance Maine de Biran accorded to the sensory mediation of the body's motility in the development and transformation of embodied dispositions: see Duchêne (2005).

10. See also Crossley (2013b) for a fuller discussion of these issues.

11. The terms Bourdieu uses here closely resemble those, discussed in chapter 3, that Gareth Stedman Jones uses in relation to the urban poor of nineteenth-century London.

12. See Emirbayer and Schneiderhan (2013) for a related discussion of the differences and similarities between Dewey's positions on these questions.

13. This is a formulation of the politics of freedom that depends both on the role that Immanuel Kant envisaged for aesthetic judgment as a practice of freedom whose exercise involved the historical projection of a *sensus communis*, and on the terms in which Bourdieu reworked this project by "fighting at the same time against the mystificatory hypocrisy of abstract universalism" that he attributed to formalist aesthetics "and for universal access to the conditions of access to the universal" (Bourdieu 1998, 66), which he viewed as the task of a historical sociology. The significance of Bourdieu's subscription to this aspect of the Kantian aesthetic is often overlooked in view of his better-known critique of the Kantian ethos of disinterestedness informing the sense of distinction characterizing bourgeois tastes. I have discussed the broader cast of Bourdieu's engagements with Kant's aesthetic in T. Bennett (2005).

14. See S. Friedman (2016) for a fuller discussion of the tensions generated by divided habitus acquired through social mobility.

15. For a more fully developed set of arguments along this line, also see the essays collected in Goodman and Silverstein (2009).

1. A full elaboration of Deleuze's position here would require an extended consideration of his relations to Darwinism and post-Darwinian debates. Suffice it to say that Deleuze's conception of our organic constitution follows Bergson, and the work of August Weismann on which Bergson drew, in departing from the accumulating logic of the organic memory tradition. For further details on these questions, see Ansell-Pearson (1999), M. Bennett and Posteraro (2019), and Posteraro (2016).

2. Clare Carlisle takes the opposite position, drawing on Kierkegaard in her assessment of the limitations of Nietzsche's preference, in *The Gay Science*, for a radically nomadic way of life in which the adoption of "brief habits" constantly interrupts the tyrannous sway exercised by "enduring habits" (Carlisle 2014, 77–81). She does so as a prelude to endorsing the theological underpinnings of Félix Ravaisson's "dual law of habit." Carlisle's position thus differs from the critical trajectories that Elizabeth Grosz associates with the wayward tradition in aligning that tradition with conventional Christian conceptions of habit and the forms of spiritual intervention into its direction associated with Christianity and other world religions. Carlisle's background is at the intersections of religious and philosophical studies, to which she brings a long-standing commitment to spiritual forms of activism.

3. Deleuze's account of repetition is nonetheless profoundly influenced by Kierkegaard's conception of it as a form of transcendental motion. In distinguishing repetition from recollection as similar forms of motion but working in opposite directions— recollection as a form of repetition backward, and "genuine repetition" as carrying the force of recollection forward as a starting point for a transformative process of becoming—the space of existence, as distinct from that of everyday living, in which this process takes place is transcendentally constituted. For Kierkegaard, as Ionuț-Alexandru Bârliba puts it, "repetition is a subjective, spiritual movement that depends on the reality and becoming of the self, aspects that maintain its transcendence" (Bârliba 2014, 30). The role accorded repetition in relation to liberty, the development and transcendence of the self, is thus pregiven in its philosophical definition.

4. Petra Carlsson Redell (2014) discusses the currency of the mystic in the work of both Deleuze and Foucault, and its role in the relations between their two positions.

5. See on this, in addition to the studies by Shapiro (2003) and Tanke (2009) discussed earlier, David Panagia's (2019) discussion of the respects in which Foucault's studies of painting, and particularly of Manet's work, foreshadowed his later discussion of the principles of panopticism.

6. Brian Massumi's work has been influential here. Connecting Deleuze's account of "societies of control" to Foucault's discussion of the transformations of liberal forms of subjectivity effected by the neoliberal programming of economic life (Foucault 2008), he pays particular attention to the consequences of the coding of information effected by digitized marketing practices in producing automated forms of "deliberation without attention" through which rational forms of choice are "jammed." See, for example, the second part of Massumi (2014).

7. There are, in this respect, similarities between the approach of Isin and Ruppert and the "datalogical turn" advocated by Patricia Clough and her coauthors in urging the need for a shift from the "critique of governance based on a humanist sociology toward a critical sociology of a mathematically open sociality" produced by the synergies between "big data and algorithmic governance" (Clough et al. 2018, 112).

8. See McKittrick (2011) for an extended discussion of both the pertinence and limitations of superimposing the logic of plantation time on that of the prison-industrial complex or the forms of "urbicide" she associates with rundown inner-city black residential areas.

9. I say "ostensibly" since the report in question—*Little Children Are Sacred*—explicitly rejected any suggestion that the high level of sexual abuse it identified in Indigenous communities might be attributed to a diminution of individual responsibility owing to the influence of customary law. The state of emergency, moreover, was declared just six days after the report's release and before any adequate public consideration of its findings. For further details, see Douglas and Finnane (2012, 207–10).

10. Most aspects of the Intervention, however, remained in place until 2022.

# REFERENCES

Adorno, Theodor. 1963. *Critical Models: Interventions and Catchwords.* Translated by Henry W. Pickford. New York: Columbia University Press.

Agamben, Giorgio. 2013. *The Highest Poverty: Monastic Rules and Form-of-Life.* Translated by Adam Kotsko. Stanford, CA: Stanford University Press.

Ahmed, Sara. 2007. "The Phenomenology of Whiteness." *Feminist Theory* 8 (2): 149–68.

Ahmed, Sara. 2014. *Willful Subjects.* Durham, NC: Duke University Press.

Ahmed, Sara. 2019. *What's the Use? On the Uses of Use.* Durham, NC: Duke University Press.

Allen, Kristie M. 2010. "Habit in George Eliot's *The Mill on the Floss*." *Studies in English Literature* 50 (4): 831–52.

Alliez, Éric. 2004. "The Difference and Repetition of Gabriel Tarde." *Distinktion: Scandinavian Journal of Social Theory* 5 (2): 49–54.

Anderson, Ben, Kevin Grove, Lauren Rickards, and Matthew Kearnes. 2019. "Slow Emergencies: Temporality and the Racialized Biopolitics of Emergency Governance." *Progress in Human Geography* 44 (4): 621–39.

Andrejevic, Mark. 2013. *Infoglut: How Too Much Information Is Changing the Way We Think and Know.* London: Routledge.

Andrejevic, Mark. 2020. *Automated Media.* New York: Routledge.

Ansell-Pearson, Keith. 1999. *Germinal Life: The Difference and Repetition of Deleuze.* London: Routledge.

Ansell-Pearson, Keith. 2018. *Bergson: Thinking Beyond the Human Condition.* London: Bloomsbury.

Ashby, W. Ross. 1945. "The Physical Origin of Adaptation by Trial and Error." *Journal of General Psychology* 32:13–25.

Ashby, W. Ross. 1959. "The Mechanism of Habituation." In *Proceedings of the Symposium on the Mechanisation of Thought Processes*, edited by D. V. Blake and A. M. Uttley, 93–118. London: H. M. Stationery Office.

Bagehot, Walter. 1873. *Physics and Politics: Or Thoughts on the Application of the Principles of "Natural Selection" and "Inheritance" to Political Society*. London: Henry S. King.

Balibar, Étienne. 1991. "Citizen Subject." In *Who Comes after the Subject?*, edited by Eduardo Cadava, Peter Connor, and Jean-Luc Nancy, 33–57. London: Routledge.

Balibar, Étienne. 2013. *Identity and Difference: John Locke and the Invention of Consciousness*. Translated by Warren Montag. London: Verso.

Barad, Karen. 2007. *Meeting the Universe Halfway: Quantum Physics and the Entanglement of Matter and Meaning*. Durham, NC: Duke University Press.

Barandiaran, Xabier E., and Ezequiel A. Di Paolo. 2014. "A Genealogical Map of the Concept of Habit." *Frontiers in Human Neuroscience* 8:522.

Bârliba, Ionuț-Alexandru. 2014. "Søren Kierkegaard's *Repetition*: Existence in Motion." *Symposium* 1 (1): 23–49.

Bassiri, Nima. 2016. "Epileptic Insanity and Personal Identity: John Hughlings Jackson and the Formations of the Neuropathic Self." In *Plasticity and Pathology: On the Formation of the Neural Subject*, edited by David Bates and Nima Bassiri, 65–111. Berkeley: Townsend Center for the Humanities, University of California.

Bates, David. 2016. "Automaticity, Plasticity, and the Deviant Origins of Artificial Intelligence." In *Plasticity and Pathology: On the Formation of the Neural Subject*, edited by David Bates and Nima Bassiri, 194–218. Berkeley: Townsend Center for the Humanities, University of California.

Beaumont, Matthew. 2015. *Nightwalking: A Nocturnal History of London*. London: Verso.

Beck, Ulrich, Anthony Giddens, and Scott Lash. 1994. *Reflexive Modernization: Politics, Aesthetics and Tradition in the Modern Social Order*. Stanford, CA: Stanford University Press.

Beckert, Sven. 2014. *The Empire of Cotton: A New History of Global Capitalism*. London: Penguin Books.

Benjamin, Walter. 1970. *Illuminations: Essays and Reflections*. Translated by Harry Zohn. London: Jonathan Cape.

Bennett, Jill. 2012. *Practical Aesthetics: Events, Affects and Art after 9/11*. London: I. B. Taurus.

Bennett, Michael James. 2019. "Framing Sexual Selection: Elizabeth Grosz's Work on Deleuze, Darwin and Feminism." In *Deleuze and Evolutionary Theory*, edited by Michael James Bennett and Tano S. Posteraro, 59–74. Edinburgh: Edinburgh University Press.

Bennett, Michael James, and Tano S. Posteraro, eds. 2019. *Deleuze and Evolutionary Theory*. Edinburgh: Edinburgh University Press.

Bennett, Tony. 2001. "Acting on the Social: Art, Culture, and Government." In *Citizenship and Cultural Policy*, edited by Denise Meredyth and Jeffrey Minson, 18–34. London: Sage.

Bennett, Tony. 2004a. "The Invention of the Modern Cultural Fact." In *Contemporary Culture and Everyday Life*, edited by Tony Bennett and Elizabeth Silva, 21–36. Durham, NC: Sociologypress.

Bennett, Tony. 2004b. *Pasts Beyond Memory: Evolution, Museums, Colonialism*. London: Routledge.

Bennett, Tony. 2005. "The Historical Universal: The Role of Cultural Value in the Historical Sociology of Pierre Bourdieu." *British Journal of Sociology* 56 (1): 141–64.

Bennett, Tony. 2007. "Habitus Clivé: Aesthetics and Politics in the Work of Pierre Bourdieu." *New Literary History* 38 (1): 201–28.

Bennett, Tony. 2010. "Culture, Power, Knowledge: Between Foucault and Bourdieu." In *Cultural Analysis and Bourdieu's Legacy: Settling Accounts and Developing Alternatives*, edited by Elizabeth Silva and Alan Warde, 102–16. London: Routledge.

Bennett, Tony. 2011a. "Guided Freedom: Aesthetics, Tutelage and the Interpretation of Art." *Tate Papers* 15. https://www.tate.org.uk/research/tate-papers/15/guided-freedom-aesthetics-tutelage-and-the-interpretation-of-art.

Bennett, Tony. 2011b. "Habit, Instinct, Survivals: Repetition, History, Biopower." In *The Peculiarities of Liberal Modernity in Imperial Britain*, edited by Simon Gunn and James Vernon, 102–18. Berkeley: University of California Press.

Bennett, Tony. 2013a. "Habit: Time, Freedom, Governance." *Body and Society* 19 (2–3): 107–35.

Bennett, Tony. 2013b. *Making Culture, Changing Society*. London: Routledge.

Bennett, Tony. 2015. "Cultural Studies and the Culture Concept." *Cultural Studies* 29 (4): 546–68.

Bennett, Tony. 2016. "Mind the Gap: Toward a Political History of Habit." *The Comparatist* 40:28–55.

Bennett, Tony. 2021. "Habit, Attention, Governance." In *Assembling and Governing Habits*, edited by Tony Bennett, Ben Dibley, Gay Hawkins, and Greg Noble, 13–27. London: Routledge.

Bennett, Tony, Ben Dibley, and Modesto Gayo. 2021. "The Mark of Time: Temporality and the Marks of Distinction in the Musical Field." In *Fields, Capitals, Habitus: Australian Culture, Inequalities and Social Divisions*, edited by Tony Bennett, David Carter, Modesto Gayo, Michelle Kelly, and Greg Noble, 49–65. London: Routledge.

Bennett, Tony, Ben Dibley, Gay Hawkins, and Greg Noble. 2021. "Disassembling and Reassembling Habits in a Pandemic." In *Assembling and Governing Habits*, edited by Tony Bennett, Ben Dibley, Gay Hawkins, and Greg Noble, 217–35. London: Routledge.

Berger, Kenneth. 2018. "From the End of Man to the Art of Life: Rereading Foucault's Changing Aesthetics." *Foucault Studies* 24:125–50.

Bergson, Henri. 1935. *The Two Sources of Morality and Religion*. Translated by R. Ashley Audra. New York: Henry Holt.

Bergson, Henri. 1946. *The Creative Mind*. Translated by Mabelle L. Andison. New York: Philosophical Library.

Bergson, Henri. 1998. *Creative Evolution*. Translated by Arthur Mitchell. New York: Dover.

Bergson, Henri. 2004. *Matter and Memory*. Translated by Nancy Margaret Paul and W. Scott Palmer. New York: Dover.

Bissell, David. 2018. *Transit Life: How Commuting Is Transforming Our Cities*. Cambridge, MA: MIT Press.

Blake, Lynne A. 1999. "Pastoral Power, Governmentality and Cultures of Order in Nineteenth-Century British Columbia." *Transactions of the Institute of British Geographers* 24 (1): 79–93.

Blencowe, Claire. 2008. "Destroying Duration: The Critical Situation of Bergsonism in Benjamin's Analysis of Modern Experience." *Theory, Culture and Society* 25 (4): 139–58.

Boas, Franz. 1911. *The Mind of Primitive Man*. New York: Macmillan.

Borch, Christian. 2012. *The Politics of the Crowd: An Alternative History of Sociology*. Cambridge: Cambridge University Press.

Bourdieu, Pierre. 1962. *The Algerians*. Translated by Alan C. M. Ross. Boston: Beacon.

Bourdieu, Pierre. 1980. "Le mort saisit le vif: Les relations entre l'histoire réifée et l'histoire incorporée." *Actes de la recherché en sciences sociale* 32 (3): 3–14.

Bourdieu, Pierre. 1996. *The Rules of Art: Genesis and Structure of the Literary Field*. Translated by Susan Emanuel. Cambridge: Cambridge University Press.

Bourdieu, Pierre. 1998. *On Television*. Translated by Priscilla Parkhurst Ferguson. London: Pluto.

Bourdieu, Pierre. 2000. *Pascalian Meditations*. Translated by Richard Nice. Cambridge, UK: Polity.

Bourdieu, Pierre. 2001. *Masculine Domination*. Translated by Richard Nice. Cambridge, UK: Polity.

Bourdieu, Pierre. 2010. *Distinction: A Social Critique of the Judgement of Taste*. Translated by Richard Nice. London: Routledge.

Bourdieu, Pierre, and Loïc Wacquant. 1992. *An Invitation to Reflexive Sociology*. Chicago: University of Chicago Press.

Brenninkmeijer, Jonna. 2010. "Taking Care of One's Brain: How Manipulating the Brain Changes People's Selves." *History of the Human Sciences* 23 (1): 107–26.

Brown, Peter. 2000. *Augustine of Hippo: A Biography*. Berkeley: University of California Press.

Butler, Judith. 1999. *Gender Trouble*. New York: Routledge.

Bynum, William Frederick. 1974. "Time's Noblest Offspring: The Problem of Man in the British Natural Historical Sciences, 1800–1863." PhD diss., University of Cambridge.

Callard, Felicity, and Daniel S. Margulies. 2011. "The Subject at Rest: Novel Conceptualisations of Self and Brain from Cognitive Neuroscience's Study of the 'Resting State.'" *Subjectivity* 4 (3): 227–57.

Camic, Charles. 1986. "The Matter of Habit." *American Journal of Sociology* 91 (5): 1039–87.

Canguilhem, Georges. 2008. *Knowledge and Life*. Translated by Stefanos Geroulanos and Daniela Ginsburg. New York: Fordham University Press.

Cannon, Walter B. 1940. *The Wisdom of the Body*. Rev. ed. New York: W. W. Norton.

Carlisle, Clare. 2006. "Creatures of Habit: The Problem and Practice of Liberation." *Continental Philosophy Review* 38:19–39.

Carlisle, Clare. 2013a. "Between Freedom and Necessity: Ravaisson on Habit and the Moral Life." In *A History of Habit: From Aristotle to Bourdieu*, edited by Tom Sparrow and Adam Hutchinson, 153–76. Lanham, MD: Lexington Books.

Carlisle, Clare. 2013b. "The Question of Habit in Theology and Philosophy: From Hexis to Plasticity." *Body and Society* 19 (2–3): 30–57.

Carlisle, Clare. 2014. *On Habit*. London: Routledge.

Caygill, Howard. 1989. *Art of Judgement*. Oxford: Basil Blackwell.

Chun, Wendy Hui Kyong. 2016. *Updating to Remain the Same: Habitual New Media*. Cambridge, MA: MIT Press. Kindle edition.

Chytry, Josef. 1989. *The Aesthetic State: A Quest in Modern German Thought*. Berkeley: University of California Press.

Clough, Patricia Ticineto. 2018. *The User Unconscious: On Affect, Media, and Measure*. Minneapolis: University of Minnesota Press.

Clough, Patricia Ticineto, Karen Gregory, Benjamin Haber, and R. Joshua Scannell. 2018. "The Datological Turn." In *The User Unconscious: On Affect, Media, and Measure*, by Patricia Ticineto Clough, 94–114. Minneapolis: University of Minnesota Press.

Cole, Henry. 1875. "National Culture and Recreation: Antidotes to Vice." In *Fifty Years of Public Work of Sir Henry Cole, K. C. B., Accounted for in His Deeds, Speeches and Writings*, 357–69. London: George Bell and Sons.

Collini, Stefan. 1979. *Liberalism and Sociology: L. T. Hobhouse and Political Argument in England, 1880–1930*. Oxford: Clarendon.

Cooley, Heidi Rae. 2014. *Finding Augusta: Habits of Mobility and Governance in the Digital Era*. Hanover, NH: Dartmouth College Press.

Cooper, Rosalind. 2020. "Pastoral Power and Algorithmic Governmentality." *Theory, Culture and Society* 37 (1): 29–52.

Cope, Edward Drinker. 1886. *Origin of the Fittest: Essays on Evolution*. New York: D. Appleton.

Crary, Jonathan. 1996. *Techniques of the Observer: On Vision and Modernity in the Nineteenth Century*. Cambridge, MA: MIT Press.

Crary, Jonathan. 2001. *Suspensions of Perception: Attention, Spectacle and Modern Culture*. Cambridge, MA: MIT Press.

Crary, Jonathan. 2014. *24/7: Late Capitalism and the Ends of Sleep*. London: Verso.

Crossley, Nick. 2013a. "Habit and Habitus." *Body and Society* 19 (2–3): 136–61.

Crossley, Nick. 2013b. "Pierre Bourdieu's *Habitus*." In *The History of Habit: From Aristotle to Bourdieu*, edited by Tom Sparrow and Adam Hutchinson, 291–307. Lanham, MD: Lexington Books.

Cryle, Peter, and Elizabeth Stephens. 2017. *Normality: A Critical Genealogy*. Chicago: University of Chicago Press.

Cuntz, Michael. 2016. "On the Oddness of Habit." In *Reset Modernity*, edited by Bruno Latour with Christophe Leclercq, 215–23. Karlsruhe, Germany: ZKM / Centre for Art and Media; Cambridge, MA: MIT Press.

Danziger, Kurt. 1982. "Mid-nineteenth Century British Psycho-Physiology: A Neglected Chapter in the History of Psychology." In *The Problematic Science: Psychology in Nineteenth-Century Thought*, edited by William R. Woodward and Mitchell G. Ash, 119–46. New York: Praeger.

Darge, Rolf. 2018. "'As One Is Disposed, So the Goal Appears to Him': On the Function of Moral Habits (Habitus) according to Thomas Aquinas." In *The Ontology, Psychology and Axiology of Habits (Habitus) in Medieval Philosophy*, edited by Nicolas Faucher and Magali Roques, 143–65. Cham, Switzerland: Springer.

Darwin, Charles. 1881. *The Formation of Vegetable Mould through the Action of Worms with Observations on Their Habits*. London: John Murray.

Darwin, Charles. 1968. *The Origin of Species*. London: Penguin Books.

Darwin, Charles. 1981. *The Descent of Man, and Selection in Relation to Sex*. Princeton, NJ: Princeton University Press.

Davidson, Arnold I. 2011. "In Praise of Counter-conduct." *History of the Human Sciences* 24 (4): 25–41.

Deere, Don T. 2014. "Truth." In *The Cambridge Foucault Lexicon*, edited by Leonard Lawler and John Nale, 517–27. Cambridge: Cambridge University Press.

De Kesel, Marc. 2016. "The Brain: A Nostalgic Dream: Some Notes on Neuroscience and the Problem of Modern Knowledge." In *Neuroscience and Critique: Exploring the Limits of the Neurological Turn*, edited by Jan De Vos and Ed Pluth, 11–21. London: Routledge.

Delacroix, Sylvie. 2022. *Habitual Ethics?* Oxford: Hart.

Delbanco, Andrew. 2019. *The War before the War: Fugitive Slaves and the Struggle for America's Soul from the Revolution to the Civil War*. New York: Penguin Books.

Deleuze, Gilles. 1986. *Cinema 1: The Movement-Image*. Translated by Hugh Tomlinson and Barbara Habberjam. London: Continuum.

Deleuze, Gilles. 1988. *Foucault*. Translated by Seán Hand. London: Athlone.

Deleuze, Gilles. 1991a. *Bergsonism*. Translated by Hugh Tomlinson and Barbara Habberjam. New York: Zone Books.

Deleuze, Gilles. 1991b. *Empiricism and Subjectivity: An Essay on Hume's Theory of Human Nature*. Translated by Constantin V. Boundas. New York: Columbia University Press.

Deleuze, Gilles. 1992. "Postscript on the Societies of Control." *October* 59 (Winter): 3–7.

Deleuze, Gilles. 2004. *Difference and Repetition*. Translated by Paul Patton. London: Continuum.

Deleuze, Gilles, and Félix Guattari. 1994. *What Is Philosophy?* Translated by Hugh Tomlinson and Graham Burchell III. London: Verso.

Descartes, René. 2011. *Meditations and Other Writings*. Translated by Desmond M. Clarke. London: Folio Society.

Desmond, Adrian, and James Moore. 1992. *Darwin*. London: Penguin Books.

Dewey, John. 1916. *Democracy and Education: An Introduction to the Philosophy of Education*. Public domain. Kindle edition.

Dewey, John. 1929. *Experience and Nature*. London: George Allen and Unwin.

Dewey, John. 1939. *Freedom and Culture*. New York: G. P. Putnam's Sons.

Dewey, John. 1991. *The Public and Its Problems*. Athens, OH: Swallow Press/Ohio University Press.

Dewey, John. 2002. *Human Nature and Conduct: An Introduction to Social Psychology*. New York: Prometheus Books.

Dibley, Ben. 2021. "Habit, Suggestion, and the Paradox of the Crowd." In *Assembling and Governing Habits*, edited by Tony Bennett, Ben Dibley, Gay Hawkins, and Greg Noble, 44–61. London: Routledge.

Didi-Huberman, Georges. 2002. "The Surviving Image: Aby Warburg and Tylorian Anthropology." *Oxford Art Journal* 25 (1): 59–70.

Douglas, Heather, and Mark Finnane. 2012. *Indigenous Crime and Settler Law: White Sovereignty after Empire*. London: Palgrave Macmillan.

Douglass, Frederick. 1845. *Narrative of the Life of Frederick Douglass, an American Slave*. Boston: Anti-slavery Office.

Duchêne, Joseph. 2005. "Merleau-Ponty lecteur de Biran: À propos du corps propre." *Revue philosophique de Louvain* 103 (1–2): 42–64.

Duhigg, Charles. 2012. *The Power of Habit: Why We Do What We Do in Life and Business*. New York: Random House.

Dunham, Jeremy. 2015. "From Habits to Monads: Félix Ravaisson's Theory of Substance." *British Journal for the History of Philosophy* 23 (6): 1085–105.

Durkheim, Émile. 1961. *The Elementary Forms of Religious Life*. Translated by Joseph Ward Swain. New York: Collier.

Durkheim, Émile. 1964. *The Division of Labour in Society*. Translated by W. D. Halls. New York: Free Press.

Emirbayer, Mustafa, and Erik Schneiderhan. 2013. "Dewey and Bourdieu on Democracy." In *Bourdieu and Historical Analysis*, edited by Philip S. Gorski, 131–57. Durham, NC: Duke University Press.

Evans, Nick. 2012. "A 'Nudge' in the Wrong Direction." *Institute of Public Affairs Review*, December 2012. https://ipa.org.au/ipa-review-articles/a-nudge-in-the-wrong-direction.

Fanon, Frantz. 1967. *Black Skin, White Masks*. New York: Grove.

Faucher, Nicolas, and Magali Roques. 2018. "The Many Virtues of Second Nature: Habitus in Latin Medieval Philosophy." In *The Ontology, Psychology and Axiology of Habits (Habitus) in Medieval Philosophy*, edited by Nicolas Faucher and Magali Roques, 1–23. Cham, Switzerland: Springer.

Fearing, Franklin. 1970. *Reflex Action: A Study in the History of Physiological Psychology*. Cambridge, MA: MIT Press.

Felski, Rita. 2000. *Doing Time: Feminist Theory and Postmodern Culture*. New York: New York University Press.

Fosl, Peter S. 2013. "Habit, Custom, History and Hume's Critical Philosophy." In *The History of Habit: From Aristotle to Bourdieu*, edited by Tom Sparrow and Adam Hutchinson, 133–52. Lanham, MD: Lexington Books.

Foucault, Michel. 1972. *The Archaeology of Knowledge*. Translated by Alan Sheridan. London: Tavistock.

Foucault, Michel. 1977. *Discipline and Punish: The Birth of the Prison*. Translated by Alan Sheridan. London: Allen Lane.

Foucault, Michel. 1998a. *The History of Sexuality*. Vol. 1, *The Will to Knowledge*. Translated by Robert Hurley. London: Penguin Books.

Foucault, Michel. 1998b. "Nietzsche, Genealogy, History." In *Michel Foucault: Aesthetics, Method, Epistemology*, translated by Robert Hurley and others, edited by James Faubion, 369–92. London: Penguin Books.

Foucault, Michel. 1998c. "On the Archaeology of the Sciences: Responses to the Epistemological Circle." In *Michel Foucault: Aesthetics, Method, Epistemology*, translated by Robert Hurley and others, edited by James Faubion, 297–333. London: Penguin Books.

Foucault, Michel. 1998d. "Theatrum Philosophicum." In *Michel Foucault: Aesthetics, Method, Epistemology*, translated by Robert Hurley and others, edited by James Faubion, 345–68. London: Penguin Books.

Foucault, Michel. 2003a. *Abnormal: Lectures at the Collège de France*. Translated by Graham Burchell. London: Verso.

Foucault, Michel. 2003b. *Society Must Be Defended: Lectures at the Collège de France, 1975–76*. Translated by David Macey. New York: Picador.

Foucault, Michel. 2007a. *Security, Territory, Population. Lectures at the Collège de France, 1977–1978*. Translated by Graham Burchell. London: Palgrave Macmillan.

Foucault, Michel. 2007b. "What Is Enlightenment?" In *The Politics of Truth*, translated by Lysa Hochroth, edited by Sylvère Lotringer, 97–120. Los Angeles: Semiotext(e).

Foucault, Michel. 2008. *The Birth of Biopolitics. Lectures at the Collège de France, 1978–1979*. Translated by Graham Burchell. New York: Palgrave Macmillan.

Foucault, Michel. 2015. *The Punitive Society: Lectures at the Collège de France, 1972–1973*. Translated by Graham Burchell. London: Palgrave Macmillan.

Fox, A. Lane. 1875. "On the Principles of Classification Adopted in the Arrangement of His Anthropological Collection Now Exhibited in the Bethnal Green Museum." *Journal of the Anthropological Institute of Great Britain and Ireland* 4:293–308.

Frederickson, Katherine. 2014. *The Ploy of Instinct: Victorian Sciences of Nature and Sexuality in Liberal Governance*. New York: Fordham University Press.

Freud, Sigmund. 1960. *Totem and Taboo: Points of Agreement between the Mental Lives of Savages and Neurotics*. Translated by James Strachey. London: Routledge and Kegan Paul.

Freud, Sigmund. 1994. *Civilization and Its Discontents*. Translated by James Strachey. New York: Dover.

Friedman, Julia. 2020. "Philip Guston (Not) Now: The Impact Argument." *Athenaeum Review*, November 13, 2020.

Friedman, Sam. 2016. "Habitus Clivé and the Emotional Imprint of Social Mobility." *Sociological Review* 64 (1): 129–47.

Fullager, Simone. 2021. "Urban Habits of Walking in Women's Recovery from Depression." In *Assembling and Governing Habits*, edited by Tony Bennett, Ben Dibley, Gay Hawkins, and Greg Noble, 184–98. London: Routledge.

Gaukroger, Stephen. 1995. *Descartes: An Intellectual Biography*. Oxford: Clarendon.

Genovese, Eugene D. 1976. *Roll Jordan Roll: The World the Slaves Made*. New York: Vintage Books.

Giddens, Anthony. 1994. "Living in a Post-traditional Society." In *Reflexive Modernization: Politics, Tradition and Aesthetics in the Modern Social Order*, edited by Ulrich Beck, Anthony Giddens, and Scott Lash, 56–109. Cambridge, UK: Polity.

Glennie, Paul D., and Nigel Thrift. 1996. "Reworking E. P. Thompson's 'Time, Work-Discipline and Industrial Capitalism.'" *Time and Society* 5 (3): 275–99.

Goodlad, Lauren M. E. 2003. *Victorian Literature and the Victorian State: Character and Governance in a Liberal Society*. Baltimore: Johns Hopkins University Press.

Goodman, Jane E., and Paul A. Silverstein, eds. 2009. *Bourdieu in Algeria: Colonial Politics, Ethnographic Practices, Theoretical Developments*. Lincoln: University of Nebraska Press.

Greenwood, John. 2010. "Whistles, Bells, and Cogs in Machines: Thomas Huxley and Epiphenomenalism." *Journal of the History of the Behavioural Sciences* 46 (3): 276–99.

Grist, Matt. 2009. *Changing the Subject: How New Ways of Thinking about Human Behaviour Might Change Politics, Policy and Practice*. London: RSA.

Gros, Frédéric. 2014. *A Philosophy of Walking*. London: Verso.

Grosz, Elizabeth. 2004. *The Nick of Time: Politics, Evolution, and the Untimely*. Durham, NC: Duke University Press.

Grosz, Elizabeth. 2010. "Feminism, Materialism, and Freedom." In *New Materialisms: Ontology, Agency, and Politics*, edited by Diana Coole and Samantha Frost, 139–57. Durham, NC: Duke University Press.

Grosz, Elizabeth. 2011. *Becoming Undone: Darwinian Reflections on Life, Politics and Art*. Durham, NC: Duke University Press.

Grosz, Elizabeth. 2013. "Habit Today: Ravaisson, Bergson, Deleuze and Us." *Body and Society* 19 (2–3): 217–39.

Gutting, Gary. 2014. "Archaeology." In *The Cambridge Foucault Lexicon*, edited by Leonard Lawler and John Nale, 13–19. Cambridge: Cambridge University Press.

Hadot, Pierre. 1995. *Philosophy as a Way of Life*. Translated by Michael Chase. Oxford: Blackwell.

Haggard, Patrick. 2008. "Human Volition: Towards a Neuroscience of Will." *Nature* 9:934–45.

Hardt, Michael, and Antonio Negri. 2000. *Empire*. Cambridge, MA: Harvard University Press.

Hardt, Michael, and Antonio Negri. 2006. *Multitude: War and Democracy in the Age of Empire*. London: Penguin Books.

Harris, Michele, ed. 2012. *A Decision to Discriminate: Aboriginal Disempowerment in the Northern Territory*. East Melbourne: Concerned Australians.

Hawkes, Helen. 2014. "How to Train a High-Flying Brain." *Australian Financial Review*, November 14, 2014.

Hawkins, Gay. 2021. "Governing Litter: Habits, Infrastructures, Atmospheres." In *Assembling and Governing Habits*, edited by Tony Bennett, Ben Dibley, Gay Hawkins, and Greg Noble, 81–96. London: Routledge.

Heiner, Brady Thomas. 2009. "Reinhabiting the Body Politic: Habit and the Roots of the Human." *Differences: A Journal of Feminist Cultural Studies* 20 (2–3): 64–102.

Héran, François. 1987. "La second nature de l'habitus: Tradition philosophique et sens commun dans le langage sociologique." *Revue française de sociologie* 28 (3): 385–416.

Hoffmann, Melody L. 2016. *Bike Lanes Are White Lanes: Bicycle Advocacy and Urban Planning*. Lincoln: University of Nebraska Press.

Holmwood, Michael. 2022. "'Class Is Always a Matter of Morals': Bourdieu and Dewey on Social Class, Morality, and Habit(us)." *Cultural Sociology*, online ahead of print. https://doi.org/10.1177/17499755221108135.

Horkheimer, Max. 2005. "On Bergson's Metaphysics of Time." *Radical Philosophy* 131:9–19.

Hume, David. 1975. *Enquiries concerning the Human Understanding and concerning the Principles of Morals*. Oxford: Clarendon.

Hunter, Ian. 2001. *Rival Enlightenments: Civil and Metaphysical Philosophy in Early Modern Germany*. Cambridge: Cambridge University Press.

Huxley, Thomas Henry. 1874. "On the Hypothesis That Animals Are Automata, and Its History." *Fortnightly Review* 22:555–80.

Ignatieff, Michael. 1978. *A Just Measure of Pain: The Penitentiary in the Industrial Revolution*. London: Macmillan.

Isin, Engin, and Evelyn Ruppert. 2020a. *Being Digital Citizens*. 2nd ed. London: Rowman and Littlefield.

Isin, Engin, and Evelyn Ruppert. 2020b. "The Birth of Sensory Power: How a Pandemic Made It Visible?" *Big Data and Society* 7 (2). https://doi.org/10.1177/2053951720969208.

Jackson, Mark. 2013. *The Age of Stress: Science and the Search for Stability*. Oxford: Oxford University Press.

James, William. (1890) 2007. *The Principles of Psychology*. Vol. 1. New York: Cosimo.

Jones, Caroline A. 2016. *The Global Work of Art: World's Fairs, Biennials, and the Aesthetics of Experience*. Chicago: University of Chicago Press.

Joyce, Patrick. 2003. *The Rule of Freedom: Liberalism and the Modern City*. London: Verso.

Kant, Immanuel. (1790) 1987. *Critique of Judgement*. Translated by Werner S. Pluhar. Indianapolis: Hackett.

Kant, Immanuel. (1798) 2006. *Anthropology from a Pragmatic Point of View*. Translated by Robert L. Louden. Cambridge: Cambridge University Press.

Karsenti, Bruno. 2010. "Imitation: Returning to the Tarde-Durkheim Debate." In *The Social after Gabriel Tarde*, edited by Matei Candea, 44–61. London: Routledge.

Kay, James Phillips. 1832. *The Moral and Physical Conditions of the Working Classes Employed in the Cotton Manufacture in Manchester*. London: James Ridgway.

Klein, Lawrence E. 1994. *Shaftesbury and the Culture of Politeness: Moral Discourse and Cultural Politics in Early Eighteenth-Century England*. Cambridge: Cambridge University Press.

Kotva, Simone. 2015. "Gilles Deleuze, Simone Weil and the Stoic Apprenticeship: Education as a Violent Training." *Theory, Culture and Society* 32 (7–8): 101–21.

Lahire, Bernard. 2011. *The Plural Actor*. Translated by David Fernbach. Cambridge, UK: Polity.

Lamarck, Jean-Baptiste. 1963. *Zoological Philosophy: An Exposition with Regard to the Natural History of Animals*. Translated by H. Elliot. New York: Hafner.

Latour, Bruno. 2002. "Gabriel Tarde and the End of the Social." In *The Social in Question: New Bearings in History and the Social Sciences*, edited by Patrick Joyce, 117–32. London: Routledge.

Latour, Bruno. 2013. *An Inquiry into Modes of Existence*. Translated by Catherine Porter. Cambridge, MA: Harvard University Press.

Latour, Bruno, and Vincent-Antonin Lépinay. 2009. *The Science of Passionate Interests: An Introduction to Gabriel Tarde's Economic Anthropology*. Chicago: Prickly Paradigm.

Laurie, Victoria. 2000. "Monks, Mammon, and Mystery." *Australian Magazine*, June 3–4, 20–23.

Leary, David E. 2013. "A Moralist in the Age of Scientific Analysis and Skepticism: Habit in the Life and Work of William James." In *A History of Habit: From Aristotle to Bourdieu*, edited by Tom Sparrow and Adam Hutchinson, 177–208. Lanham, MD: Lexington Books.

Lefebvre, Henri. 1971. *Everyday Life in the Modern World*. Translated by Sacha Rabinovitch. London: Allen Lane, Penguin.

Lépinay, Vincent-Antonin. 2007. "Economy of the Germ: Capital, Accumulation and Vibration." *Economy and Society* 36 (4): 526–48.

Leshem, Dotan. 2015. "Embedding Agamben's Critique of Foucault: The Theological and Pastoral Origins of Governmentality." *Theory, Culture and Society* 32 (3): 93–113.

Leys, Ruth. 1980. "Background to the Reflex Controversy: William Alison and the Doctrine of Sympathy before Hall." *Studies in the History of Biology* 4:1–66.

Leys, Ruth. 2011. "The Turn to Affect: A Critique." *Critical Inquiry* 37 (3): 434–72.

Locke, John. 1965. *An Essay concerning Human Understanding*. Vol. 1. London: Dent.

Locke, John. 2007. *Some Thoughts concerning Education*. Mineola, NY: Dover.

Lorenzini, Daniele. 2019. "The Emergence of Desire: Notes toward a Political History of the Will." *Critical Inquiry* 45:448–70.

Lukács, Georg. 1977. *History and Class Consciousness*. Translated by Rodney Livingstone. London: Merlin.

MacMullan, Terence. 2009. *Habits of Whiteness: A Pragmatist Reconstruction*. Bloomington: Indiana University Press.

Magee, Liam, and Ned Rossiter. 2021. "Habits of Data and Labour in Warehousing." In *Assembling and Governing Habits*, edited by Tony Bennett, Ben Dibley, Gay Hawkins, and Greg Noble, 132–48. London: Routledge.

Maine de Biran, Pierre. 1929. *The Influence of Habit on the Faculty of Thinking*. Translated by Margaret Donaldson Boehm. Westport, CT: Greenwood.

Malabou, Catherine. 2000. "The Future of Hegel: Plasticity, Temporality, Dialectic." *Hypatia* 15 (4): 196–220.

Malabou, Catherine. 2005. *The Future of Hegel: Plasticity, Temporality, Dialectic*. Abingdon, UK: Routledge.

Malabou, Catherine. 2008. *What Should We Do with Our Brain?* New York: Fordham University Press.

Malabou, Catherine. 2012. *Ontology of the Accident: An Essay on Destructive Plasticity*. Cambridge, UK: Polity.

Malabou, Catherine. 2016. "'You Are (Not) Your Synapses': Toward a Critical Approach to Neuroscience." In *Plasticity and Pathology: On the Formation of the Neural Subject*, edited by David Bates and Nima Bassiri, 20–34. Berkeley: Townsend Center for the Humanities, University of California.

Malabou, Catherine. 2019. *Morphing Intelligence: From IQ Measurement to Artificial Brains*. New York: Columbia University Press.

Marx, Karl. 1970. *Capital: A Critique of Political Economy*. Vol. 1. Translated by Samuel Moore and Edward Aveling. London: Lawrence and Wishart.

Marx, Karl. 1973. *Grundrisse: Foundations of the Critique of Political Economy*. Translated by Martin Nicolaus. Harmondsworth, UK: Penguin Books.

Massumi, Brian. 2002. *Parables for the Virtual: Movement, Affect, Sensation*. Durham, NC: Duke University Press.

Massumi, Brian. 2014. *The Power at the End of the Economy*. Durham, NC: Duke University Press.

Maudsley, Henry. 1884. *Body and Will: Being an Essay concerning Will in Its Metaphysical, Physiological, and Pathological Aspects*. New York: D. Appleton.

Mbembe, Achille. 2003. "Necropolitics." *Public Culture* 15 (1): 11–40.

Mbembe, Achille. 2017. *Critique of Black Reason*. Durham, NC: Duke University Press.

McCall, Corey. 2014. "Conduct." In *The Cambridge Foucault Lexicon*, edited by Leonard Lawler and John Nale, 68–74. Cambridge: Cambridge University Press.

McKittrick, Katherine. 2011. "On Plantations, Prisons, and a Black Sense of Place." *Social and Cultural Geography* 12 (8): 947–63.

McKittrick, Katherine. 2016. "Diachronic Loops/Deadweight Tonnage/Bad Made Measure." *Cultural Geographies* 23 (1): 3–18.

Menand, Louis. 2021. *The Free World: Art and Thought in the Cold War*. New York: Farrar, Straus and Giroux.

Merleau-Ponty, Maurice. 2002. *The Phenomenology of Perception*. Translated by Colin Smith. London: Routledge.

Michaud, Éric. 2019. *The Barbarian Invasion: A Genealogy of the History of Art*. Translated by Nicholas Huckle. Cambridge, MA: MIT Press.

Mill, John Stuart. 1967. *A System of Logic, Ratiocinative and Inductive: Being a Connected View of the Principles of Evidence and the Methods of Scientific Investigation*. London: Longmans.

Mill, John Stuart. 1969. *"On Liberty," "Representative Government," "The Subjection of Women": Three Essays*. Oxford: Oxford University Press.

Miner, R. C. 2013. "Aquinas on Habitus." In *A History of Habit: From Aristotle to Bourdieu*, edited by Tom Sparrow and Adam Hutchinson, 67–88. Lanham, MD: Lexington Books.

Mirzoeff, Nicholas. 2011. *The Right to Look: A Counterhistory of Visuality*. Durham, NC: Duke University Press.

Morel, Benedict. 1857. *Traité des dégénérescence physiques, intellectuelles, et morales de l'espèce humaine*. Paris: J. B. Balliere.

Moreton-Robinson, Aileen. 2009. "The Good Indigenous Citizen: Race War and the Pathology of Patriarchal White Sovereignty." *Cultural Studies Review* 15 (2): 61–79.

Morrison, Bronwyn. 2017. "Inebriate Institutions." In *A Companion to the History of Crime and Criminal Justice*, edited by Jo Turner, Paul Taylor, Karen Corteen, and Sharon Morley, 109–11. Bristol, UK: Policy Press.

Nakata, Martin. 2007. *Disciplining the Savages, Savaging the Disciplines*. Canberra: Aboriginal Studies Press.

Neilson, Brett, and Ned Rossiter. 2019. "Theses on Automation and Labour." In *Data Politics: Worlds, Subjects, Rights*, edited by Didier Bigo, Engin Isin, and Evelyn Ruppert, 187–206. London: Routledge.

Ngai, Sianne. 2012. *Our Aesthetic Categories: Zany, Cute, Interesting*. Cambridge, MA: Harvard University Press.

Ngo, Helen. 2017. *The Habits of Racism: A Phenomenology of Racism and Racialized Embodiment*. Lanham, MD: Lexington Books.

Noble, Greg, and Megan Watkins. 2003. "So How Did Bourdieu Learn to Play Tennis? Habitus, Consciousness and Habituation." *Cultural Studies* 17 (3–4): 520–38.

Ojakangas, Mika. 2012. "Michel Foucault and the Enigmatic Origins of Bio-politics and Governmentality." *History of the Human Sciences* 25 (1): 1–14.

O'Keefe, Brian. 2016. "Deleuze on Habit." *The Comparatist* 40:71–93.

Oliver, Simon. 2005. "The Sweet Delight of Virtue and Grace in Aquinas's *Ethics*." *International Journal of Systematic Theology* 7 (1): 52–71.

Osborne, Thomas, and Nikolas Rose. 1999. "Governing Cities: Notes on the Spatialisation of Virtue." *Environment and Planning D: Society and Space* 17 (6): 737–60.

Otis, Laura. 1994. *Organic Memory: History and Body in the Late Nineteenth and Early Twentieth Centuries*. Lincoln: University of Nebraska Press.

Panagia, David. 2019. "On the Political Ontology of the *Dispositif*." *Critical Inquiry* 45 (Spring): 714–46.

Parisi, Luciana. 2017. "Instrumentality or the Time of Human Thinking." *Technosphere*, September 18, 2017.

Parisi, Luciana. 2019. "Critical Computation: Digital Automata and General Artificial Thinking." *Theory, Culture and Society* 36 (2): 89–121.

Patton, Paul. 2014. "Gilles Deleuze (1925–1995)." In *The Cambridge Foucault Lexicon*, edited by Leonard Lawler and John Nale, 588–94. Cambridge: Cambridge University Press.

Pedwell, Carolyn. 2017a. "Habit and the Politics of Change: A Comparison of Nudge Theory and Pragmatist Philosophy." *Body and Society* 23 (4): 59–94.

Pedwell, Carolyn. 2017b. "Transforming Habit: Revolution, Routine and Social Change." *Cultural Studies* 30 (1): 93–120.

Pedwell, Carolyn. 2021. *Revolutionary Routines: The Habits of Social Transformation.* Montreal: McGill-Queen's University Press.

Perec, Georges. 2011. *"Things: A Story of the Sixties" and "A Man Asleep."* Translated by David Bellos and Andrew Leak. London: Vintage Books.

Petterson, Christina. 2012. "Colonial Subjectification: Foucault, Christianity and Governmentality." *Cultural Studies Review* 18 (2): 89–108.

Phillips, D. C. 1971. "James, Dewey, and the Reflex Arc." *Journal of the History of Ideas* 32 (4): 555–68.

Pick, Daniel. 1989. *Faces of Degeneration: A European Disorder, c.1848–c.1918.* Cambridge: Cambridge University Press.

Pickering, Andrew. 2010. *The Cybernetic Brain: Sketches of Another Future.* Chicago: University of Chicago Press.

Piketty, Thomas. 2020. *Capital and Ideology.* Translated by Arthur Goldhammer. Cambridge, MA: Belknap Press of Harvard University Press.

Pitts-Taylor, Victoria. 2010. "The Plastic Brain: Neoliberalism and the Neuronal Self." *Health* 14 (6): 635–52.

Pollard, Sydney. 1965. *The Genesis of Modern Management.* London: Edward Arnold.

Porter, Jane. 2018. *The Perfection of Desire: Habit, Reason, and Virtue in Aquinas's "Summa Theologiae."* Milwaukee: Marquette University Press.

Posteraro, Tano. 2016. "Habits, Nothing but Habits: Biological Time in Deleuze." *The Comparatist* 40:94–110.

Proust, Marcel. 1966. *Remembrance of Things Past: Swann's Way, Part One.* Translated by C. K. Scott Moncrieff. London: Chatto and Windus.

Radstone, Susannah, and Katharine Hodgkin, eds. 2003. *Regimes of Memory.* London: Routledge.

Rand, Sebastian. 2011. "Organism, Normativity, Plasticity: Canguilhem, Kant, Malabou." *Continental Philosophy Review* 44 (4): 341–57.

Ratnapalan, Laavanyan. 2008. "E. B. Tylor and the Problem of Primitive Culture." *History and Anthropology* 19 (2): 131–42.

Ravaisson, Félix. 2008. *Of Habit.* London: Continuum.

Redell, Petra Carlsson. 2014. *Mysticism as Revolt: Foucault, Deleuze, and Theology beyond Representation.* Aurora, CO: Davies Group.

Rees, Tobias. 2011. "So Plastic a Brain: On Philosophy, Fieldwork in Philosophy and the Rise of Adult Cerebral Plasticity." *BioSocieties* 6 (2): 263–67.

Reséndez, Andrés. 2016. *The Other Slavery: The Uncovered Story of Indian Enslavement in America*. Boston: Houghton Mifflin Harcourt.

Ribot, Théodule Armand. (1882) 1997. *Diseases of the Will*. Translated by Merwin-Marie Snell. Washington, DC: University Publications of America.

Ribot, Théodule Armand. 1890. *The Psychology of Attention*. London: Longmans, Green.

Ricoeur, Paul. 2007. *Freedom and Nature: The Voluntary and the Involuntary*. Translated by Erazim V. Kohak. Evanston, IL: Northwestern University Press.

Rivers, William Halse Rivers. 1913. "Survival in Sociology." *Sociological Review* 6 (4): 293–305.

Rose, Nikolas. 1996. "Authority and the Genealogy of Subjectivity." In *Detraditionalisation: Critical Reflections on Authority and Identity*, edited by Paul Heelas, Scott Lash, and Paul Morris, 294–327. Oxford: Blackwell.

Rose, Nikolas. 1999. *Powers of Freedom: Reframing Political Thought*. Cambridge: Cambridge University Press.

Rose, Nikolas, and Joelle M. Abi-Rached. 2013. *Neuro: The New Brain Science and the Management of the Mind*. Princeton, NJ: Princeton University Press.

Rosenthal, Caitlin. 2018. *Accounting for Slavery: Masters and Management*. Cambridge, MA: Harvard University Press.

Rowson, Jonathan. 2011. *Transforming Behaviour Change: Beyond Nudge and Neuromania*. London: RSA.

Sartre, Jean-Paul. 1967. *Critique de la raison dialectique*. Paris: Gallimard.

Savage, Mike. 2021. *The Return of Inequality: Social Change and the Weight of the Past*. Cambridge, MA: Harvard University Press.

Schilling, Heinz. 1995. "Confessional Europe." In *Handbook of European History, 1400–1600: Latin Middle Ages, Renaissance and Reformation*, vol. 2, *Visions, Programs and Outcomes*, edited by Thomas A. Brady Jr., Heiko A. Oberman, and James D. Tracy, 641–82. Leiden: E. J. Brill, 1995.

Schuller, Kyla. 2018. *The Biopolitics of Feeling: Race, Sex, and Science in the Nineteenth Century*. Durham, NC: Duke University Press.

Schuller, Kyla, and Jules Gill-Peterson. 2020. "Introduction: Race, the State and the Malleable Body." *Social Text* 38 (2): 1–17.

Schwendener, Martha. 2020. "Why Philip Guston Can Still Provoke Such Furor, and Passion." *New York Times*, October 2, 2020, C5.

Scott, Charles E. 2014. "Genealogy." In *The Cambridge Foucault Lexicon*, edited by Leonard Lawler and John Nale, 165–74. Cambridge: Cambridge University Press.

Seigel, Jerrold. 2005. *The Idea of the Self: Thought and Experience in Western Europe since the Seventeenth Century*. Cambridge: Cambridge University Press.

Shah, Shriddha. 2017. "Body, Habit, Custom and Labour." *Social Change* 47 (2): 189–99.

Shapiro, Gary. 2003. *Archaeologies of Vision: Foucault and Nietzsche on Seeing and Saying*. Chicago: University of Chicago Press.

Sharpe, Christina. 2016. *In the Wake: On Blackness and Being*. Durham, NC: Duke University Press.

Simmel, Georges. 1950. "The Metropolis and Mental Life." In *The Sociology of Georges Simmel*, edited and translated by Kurt H. Wolff, 409–24. New York: Free Press.

Sinclair, Mark. 2011a. "Is Habit 'the Fossilised Residue of a Spiritual Activity'? Ravaisson, Bergson, Merleau-Ponty." *Journal of the British Society for Phenomenology* 42 (1): 33–52.

Sinclair, Mark. 2011b. "Ravaisson and the Force of Habit." *Journal of the History of Philosophy* 49 (1): 65–85.

Sinclair, Mark. 2018. "Habit and Time in Nineteenth-Century French Philosophy: Albert Lemoine between Bergson and Ravaisson." *British Journal for the History of Philosophy* 26 (1): 135–51.

Slifkin, Robert. 2021. "Ugly Feelings." *Artforum* 59 (4).

Smith, Mark M. 1996. "Time, Slavery and Plantation Capitalism in the Ante-bellum American South." *Past and Present* 150:142–68.

Smith, Mark M. 1997. *Mastered by the Clock: Time, Slavery and Freedom in the American South*. Chapel Hill: University of North Carolina Press.

Smith, Roger. 1992. *Inhibition: History and Meaning in the Sciences of Mind and Brain*. Berkeley: University of California Press.

Solnit, Rebecca. 2014. *Wanderlust: A History of Walking*. London: Granta Books.

Sparrow, Jeff. 2022. "Friday Essay: A Slave State—How Blackbirding in Colonial Australia Created a Legacy of Racism." *The Conversation*, August 5, 2022.

Spencer, Baldwin, and Frank J. Gillen. 1899. *The Native Tribes of Central Australia*. London: Macmillan.

Spencer, Herbert. 1996. *The Principles of Psychology*. London: Routledge/Thoemmes.

Stedman Jones, Gareth. 1976. *Outcast London: A Study in the Relationship between Classes in Victorian Society*. Harmondsworth, UK: Penguin Books.

Steinmetz, George. 2013. "Toward Socioanalysis: The Traumatic Kernel of Psychoanalysis in Neo-Bourdieusian Theory." In *Bourdieu and Historical Analysis*, edited by Philip S. Gorski, 108–30. Durham, NC: Duke University Press.

Stocking, George W., Jr. 1982. *Race, Culture, and Evolution: Essays in the History of Anthropology*. Chicago: University of Chicago Press.

Stocking, George W., Jr. 1987. *Victorian Anthropology*. New York: Free Press.

Stoker, Bram. 2011. *Dracula*. London: HarperCollins.

Stump, Eleonore. 2003. *Aquinas*. London: Routledge.

Sullivan, Shannon. 2000. "Reconfiguring Gender with John Dewey: Habit, Bodies and Cultural Change." *Hypatia* 15 (1): 23–42.

Sullivan, Shannon. 2004. "From the Foreign to the Familiar: Confronting Dewey Confronting Racial Prejudice." *Journal of Speculative Philosophy* 18 (3): 193–202.

Sullivan, Shannon. 2006. *Revealing Whiteness: The Unconscious Habits of Racial Privilege*. Bloomington: Indiana University Press.

Sweetman, Paul. 2003. "Twenty-First Century Dis-ease? Habitual Reflexivity or the Reflexive Habitus." *Sociological Review* 51 (4): 528–49.

Tanke, Joseph J. 2009. *Foucault's Philosophy of Art: A Genealogy of Modernity.* New York: Continuum.

Tarde, Gabriel. 1903. *The Laws of Imitation.* Translated by Elsie Clews Parsons. New York: Henry Holt.

Thaler, Richard, and Cass Sunstein. 2008. *Nudge: Improving Decisions about Health, Wealth and Happiness.* London: Penguin Books.

Thompson, E. P. 1991. "Time, Work-Discipline and Industrial Capitalism." In *Customs in Common,* 352–403. London: Penguin Books.

Thompson, Mary V. 2019. *"The Only Unavoidable Subject of Regret": George Washington, Slavery and the Enslaved Community at Mount Vernon.* Charlottesville: University of Virginia Press.

Tönnies, Ferdinand. 1961. *Custom: An Essay on Social Codes.* Translated by A. Farrell Borenstein. New York: Free Press of Glencoe.

Tully, James. 1993. "Governing Conduct: Locke on the Reform of Thought and Behaviour." In *An Approach to Political Philosophy: Locke in Contexts,* 179–241. Cambridge: Cambridge University Press.

Tylor, Edward Burnett. 1867. "On Traces of the Early Mental Condition of Man." *Notices of the Proceedings at the Meetings of the Royal Institution of Great Britain* 5:83–93.

Tylor, Edward Burnett. 1871. *Primitive Culture.* 2 vols. London: John Murray.

Tylor, Edward Burnett. 1994. "Review of Max Müller, *Lectures on the Science of Language.*" In *The Collected Works of Edward Burnett Tylor,* 7:394–435. London: Routledge/Thoemmes.

Ure, Andrew. 1835. *The Philosophy of Manufactures, or An Exposition of the Scientific, Moral and Commercial Economy of the Factory System.* London: Charles Knight.

Ussishkin, Daniel. 2017. *Morale: A Modern British History.* Oxford: Oxford University Press.

Valverde, Mariana. 1998a. *Diseases of the Will: Alcohol and the Dilemmas of Freedom.* Cambridge: Cambridge University Press.

Valverde, Mariana. 1998b. "Governing Out of Habit." *Studies in Law, Politics and Society* 18:217–42.

Vidal, Fernando. 2009. "Brainhood, Anthropological Figure of Modernity." *History of the Human Sciences* 22 (1): 5–36.

Von Leyden, W. 1981. *Hobbes and Locke: The Politics of Freedom and Obligation.* London: Palgrave Macmillan.

Vrettos, Athena. 1999/2000. "Defining Habits: Dickens and the Psychology of Repetition." *Victorian Studies* 42 (3): 399–426.

Walusinski, Olivier. 2020. "The Concepts of Heredity and Degeneration in the Work of Jean-Martin Charcot." *Journal of the History of the Neurosciences* 29 (3): 299–324.

White, Melanie. 2005. "The Liberal Character of Ethnological Governance." *Economy and Society* 34 (3): 474–94.

White, Melanie. 2013. "Habit as a Force of Life in Durkheim and Bergson." *Body and Society* 19 (2–3): 240–62.

Wilderson, Frank, III. 2003. "Gramsci's Black Marx: Whither the Slave in Civil Society?" *Social Identities: Journal for the Study of Race, Nation and Culture* 9 (2): 225–40.

Wolf, Johannes. 2017. "The Art of Arts: Theorising Pastoral Power in the English Middle Ages." PhD diss., University of Cambridge.

Wolfe, Patrick. 1999. *Settler Colonialism and the Transformation of Anthropology: The Politics and Poetics of an Ethnographic Event*. London: Cassell.

Wormald, Thomas. 2014. "Sculpted Selves, Sculpted Worlds: Plasticity and Habit in the Thought of Catherine Malabou." MA thesis, University of Western Ontario.

Yin, Henry H., and Barbara J. Knowlton. 2006. "The Role of the Basal Ganglia in Habit Formation." *Nature Reviews Neuroscience* 7 (6): 464–76.

Young, Iris Marion. 2005. *On Female Bodily Experience: "Throwing like a Girl" and Other Essays*. New York: Oxford University Press.

Young, Robert M. 1970. *Mind, Brain, and Adaptation in the Nineteenth Century*. Oxford: Clarendon.

Zieger, Susan. 2008. *Inventing the Addict: Drugs, Race, and Sexuality in Nineteenth-Century British and American Literature*. Amherst: University of Massachusetts Press.

Zieger, Susan. 2020. "Back on the Chain Gang: Logistics, Labour, and the Threat of Infrastructure." Lecture presented at the Institute for Culture and Society, Western Sydney University.

Zieger, Susan. 2021. "'Shipped': Paper, Print, and the Atlantic Slave Trade." In *Assembly Codes: The Logistics of Media*, edited by Matthew Hockenberry, Nicole Starosielski, and Susan Zieger, 34–51. Durham, NC: Duke University Press.

# INDEX

Callard, Felicity, 141, 144
Cameron, David, 142
Camic, Charles, 22–23, 143–44
Canguilhem, Georges, 87, 215n2, 216n8
Cannon, Walter, 220n6
capacity/capacities, 4, 106, 143–44, 180, 218n14; for attentiveness, 187; Dewey on, 26, 161; of factory workers, 49–50; for freedom, 3, 129–34; habit as, 207–8; intelligence as, 207; for reflection, 75, 77, 179; for repetition, 191
capital: circuits of, 12, 15, 48, 67, 197–98; cultural, 166, 177–78; germ, 14, 68
*Capital* (Marx), 49
capitalism, 27, 50, 194, 197
Carlisle, Clare, 7–8, 111–12, 217n1, 218n9, 222n2; on power, 21–22
Carpenter, W. D., 81
Cassian, Jean, 105
Catholic Church, 3–4, 106, 108, 216n1, 218n9. *See also* pastoral government/ governance
causality, 13, 104, 116, 118
celibacy, 106, 217n8
cerebral intervals, 116–17, 122
chain gang (coffle), 54–5, 214n9
chain of habit, 3, 19, 39, 100; breaking the, 120–21, 146
children: factory discipline and, 51–52, 76; habit and, 45, 66–68; sexual abuse and, 204, 223n9
choice, 98–99, 117, 120–21, 128, 222n6; choice architectures, 142–43; choice of the necessary, 181
Christianity, 13, 96–98, 192, 216n2, 222n2. *See also* pastoral government/gover- nance; theology, Christian
Chun, Wendy, 136, 197
citizens/citizenship, 201–2
city life, rhythms of and habit, 82–86, 95, 216n7
"civilized people," 58–59, 61, 66–67, 163–64
Civil War, American, 54–55
Claparède, Edouard, 153

class (social), 4, 150–51, 157–58; middle, 60, 89, 158, 213n3, 219n7; working, 23, 51, 83, 85, 181
cleft habitus, 181–82
climate change, 2, 10–11, 206–7
clock time, 48, 52–53, 120, 138–39, 214nn5–6
Clough, Patricia, 223n7
Cold War, 194
Cole, Henry, 83, 85
Collini, Stefan, 85
colonialism, 64–68, 157, 182, 204–5
commodities, 23, 54, 159, 163
communities/communal, 18, 99, 108, 201–5
competency/competencies, 5, 36, 62, 91, 198
computational media, 198–99
conditionability, 154–55, 207–8
conduct, 93–96, 151, 184–85, 190–91, 208; of conduct, 5, 15–16, 75, 80, 95, 108–10, 188, 201; counterconducts, 16, 99, 107–10, 113, 123, 201, 217n10; Dewey on, 161, 166–67, 179; Foucault on, 98; training and, 212n6
conscience, 34, 94, 102, 107, 190
consciousness, 11, 23, 60, 78, 95, 119, 127, 135, 214n11; choice and, 121; will and, 117–18
*consuetudo*, 8, 37–38, 99–100, 103, 105, 212n4, 217n4
consumption, 2, 21, 193, 196–97, 202, 206–7
Cooley, Heidi Rae, 202
Cooper, Rosalind, 200–201
Cope, Edward Drinker, 59–61, 114–15, 214n11
cosmic memory, 122–23
cotton factory system, 48, 50, 56
counterconduct, 16, 99, 107–10, 113, 123, 201, 217n10
countercultural, 51
COVID-19 pandemic, 199, 215n23
Crary, Jonathan, 26, 42, 50, 197–98, 217n1
critical race theory, 2, 10–11, 171–72
critique of everyday life, 12, 21, 23–26, 188, 212n5
Crossley, Nick, 175
Cryle, Peter, 29–30, 42

equilibrium, 152; of modernity, 162–67; of personhood, 124–25, 165; of plasticity, 148

education, 76–77, 117, 158, 161–62, 175, 177–78, 216n1. *See also* training
egalitarianism, 108, 129–31
Eliot, George, 61–62, 137
embodied/embodiment, 25, 90–91, 103, 109, 122, 174, 179–80, 201
emergency governance, 69, 202–5
empirical disciplines, 1, 8–10, 13, 43–44, 151, 160, 207
*Empiricism and Subjectivity* (Deleuze), 25, 189, 207
Engels, Friedrich, 36, 50, 133
English (language), 8–9, 19–20, 25–26, 211n1 (intro.)
Enlightenment, 149, 202
*Enquiry* (Hume), 189–90
epigenetics, 154
epistemology, 31, 37, 43–44, 90, 173
equilibrium: machinic, 152–53; psychological, 81, 155, 167
eugenics, 30
Evans-Pritchard, E. E., 214n5
everyday habits, 23–24, 201, 203, 206–7
*Everyday Life in the Modern World* (Lefebvre), 24
evolution/evolutionary theory, 3, 7, 10, 57, 59–61, 115–16, 125, 138, 214n11, 219n17; American School of Evolution, 15, 58; in the blacksmith's arm example, 47; organic memory and, 126–27; race and, 66–67; variation and, 114, 126, 128–29
*Experience and Nature* (Dewey), 163
experiential knowledge, 37, 71
exploitation, 14–15, 36, 48, 58, 68–69, 107

factory system, 15, 50–52, 197, 214n4; labor, 36, 48–51, 53, 56; mechanization in, 6, 53
Fanon, Frantz, 172
Faucher, Nicolas, 99–100

Fearing, Franklin, 71, 174
Felski, Rita, 25, 211n2
feminism, 2, 10–11, 16–17, 25; difference and, 112–14, 128–29; egalitarian, 129–31
Ferguson, Adam, 49–50
flexibility, 219n2; reflexive, 143–46
Foucault, Michel, 4, 12, 21–22, 103, 186, 194, 218n14; archaeological analyses, 27, 33–35, 67–68, 195, 212n9; on discipline, 29, 48–49; genealogical analyses, 33–35, 97, 195, 212n9; on habit, 27–31; Malabou on, 149, 156; on mysticism, 108–9, 113, 123; on normalization, 28–29, 112; on pastoral government, 29, 32–33, 96, 97–98, 101, 216n2; on power, 26–27
France, 88, 189
freedom, 3, 11, 43–45, 51, 106, 125–35, 213n18, 220n6; and autonomy, 134–35, 143–44; Bourdieu on, 175–79; of choice, 98–99, 124; "guided," 113, 217n2 (chap. 5), 219n5; habit and, 98–99, 104–5; Locke on, 77–78; politics of, 129, 180, 221n13
free will, 71–72, 92, 94
French (language), 211n1 (intro.), 218n6
Freud, Sigmund., 6, 170–71, 214n17
Fullager, Simone, 131–32
*Future of Hegel, The* (Malabou), 148

"gapped time," 43–44, 114, 134–36, 149, 179, 180, 186, 191–92, 197
gender, 4, 114–22, 128, 150–51, 181, 218n14; feminism and, 2, 10–11, 16–17, 25, 129–31; queer theory and, 2, 131
genealogical analysis, principles of, 33–35, 97, 195, 212n9
generations/generational, 106–7, 125–26, 187–88; transgenerational inheritances, 30, 47, 62, 88, 115, 164
Genovese, Eugene, 15, 48–49, 52–53
germ capital, 14, 68
Giddens, Anthony, 39–40, 143
Gillen, Frank J., 65, 214n17
Gill-Peterson, Jules, 151
Goodlad, Lauren, 213n3
Google Ngram, 8–9, 211n1 (intro.)

governance/government, 2, 12, 19, 199, 215n23, 223n7; agency and, 41; algorithmic, 4, 18, 186, 201–2, 223n7; biopolitical forms of, 127, 150–51; of emergencies, 69, 202–5; freedom and, 213n18; plasticity and, 140–46; power of, 34, 108–9. *See also specific forms of government*

governmentality: algorithmic, 4, 18, 186, 201–2, 223n7; Foucault on, 97–98, 101–2; liberal, 72, 142–43, 207

grace acquired via habit, 8, 12, 32, 39, 92, 96, 98, 102–3, 105, 113, 118–19, 192

Grosz, Elizabeth, 16, 112–14, 125; on habit and becoming, 130–34; sexual selection and, 128–29; the "wayward tradition" and, 12, 43, 136, 222n2

*Grundrisse* (Marx), 49, 196

Guattari, Félix, 147, 195

"guided freedom," 113, 217n2 (chap. 5), 219n5

Guston, Philip, 37–38, 212n12

Gutting, Gary, 34

habit: the acquisition of grace and, 8, 13, 32, 39, 92, 96, 98, 102–3, 105, 113, 118–19, 192; becoming and, 114–22, 129, 138, 222n3; liberating potential of, 3, 39, 44, 111–12, 123, 125, 136; positive conception of, 4–7, 12–14, 25, 45, 104. *See also specific topics*

habit archive, 14–15, 22, 37–43, 110

habit as a "second nature," 7, 96, 102–3, 119, 128–29, 190, 196

habit as repetition of the same, 6–7, 15, 18, 36, 66, 182–83

habit-memory, 119–21, 124, 130, 135, 177

habit-obedience, 104–8

habit of acquiring habits, 12, 26, 132, 135–36, 186, 190, 207

habit-repetition, 19–20, 22–27, 44

*Habits of New Norcia, The* (documentary), 107, 217n9

habit's pathways: aquatic versions, 16, 121–22, 137–38; the blacksmith's arm, 47, 60, 114–15, 133, 213n2; metaphors for, 4–7, 46–47, 58, 62, 86–93, 115, 220n6; as

roadways, 54–56; the "routineer's road," 167–69, 179, 220n6

Habitual Drunkards Act (1898), 88

habituation, 41, 89, 104, 145, 152–53, 174, 176

habitus, 8, 38–39, 174–83, 212n4, 217n4; archaic, 17, 160, 181–83; bodily, 156–58; cleft, 181–82; modern, 161–62, 182

"habitus interruptus," 140, 146–53

Hadot, Pierre, 43, 122

Haggard, Patrick, 71–72

Hall, Marshall, 79

Hardt, Michael, 101, 162

Hegel, G. W. F., 139, 148, 211n1 (intro.)

Heidegger, Martin, 211n2

Heiner, Brady Thomas, 101

Héran, François, 212n4

heredity/hereditary, 7, 30–31, 49, 62, 88, 91, 93, 106, 114–15

hesitation as prelude to habit change, 6, 111–12, 115–17, 147, 157, 159, 168

*hexis*, 8, 99–100, 103, 105, 217n4

hierarchy: of impressibility, 32, 59, 60–61; monastic, 103–4

hiker figure, 5, 18, 76, 111, 167, 185–87

historical anamnesis, 180, 183

history: of habit, 3, 8–12, 14–15, 20–21, 27–31; of the life sciences, 47; Nietzsche on, 34–35; of reflex action, 71–73, 138; of sociology, 22, 39; two states of (Bourdieu), 179–80, 182–83

Hobbes, Thomas, 212n10

homeostasis, 220n6

Horkheimer, Max, 16, 123–24

human-animal relations, 20, 32, 43, 54, 126–28

*Human Nature and Conduct* (Dewey), 26, 164, 168

humans, 60, 127–28, 141; agency, 196, 198; as distinct from animals, 42–43, 102–3, 120–21, 138; nature, 168–69, 221n7

Hume, David, 14, 19–20, 27–28, 39, 71, 186, 189–91, 207

Huxley, T. H., 73–74, 126

imitation, 39, 67–68, 119, 192; unconscious, 23, 123

impressibility, 57–61, 150

machines/machinic, 49–52, 152–53, 156; agency, 151–52, 196
machinofacture, 52, 124, 196, 198
MacMullan, Terence, 220n2, 220n4
Magee, Liam, 197
Maine de Biran, Pierre, 3, 12–13, 95–96, 189, 221n9; Ravaisson and, 112–13, 217n1; Tarde on, 215n22
Malabou, Catherine, 16–17, 136, 137–38, 207, 219n4; on aesthetics, 146–50, 157–58; on neural plasticity, 140–49, 156; "wayward way" tradition and, 151–52
Malebranche, Nicolas, 7
malleability, 150–51, 156–57
managed mindfulness, 41, 43, 139, 141–42, 206–7
management, 57, 59, 83, 97; labor, 51, 53; of neuro-reflexivity, 146; of personhood, 140
*Man Asleep, A* (Perec), 24
Margulies, Daniel, 141, 144
Martin, Valerie, 205
Marx, Karl, 49–51, 124, 193, 196, 214n4
masculine domination, 181–83
Massumi, Brian, 20, 147, 222n6
materialism, 113, 134–35, 147–48
matter, 218n4, 218n14; agency of, 133, 135
*Matter and Memory* (Bergson), 124
Maudsley, Henry, 73, 88, 90, 110, 118; habit and degeneration, 92–95
Mbembe, Achille, 56, 203
McKittrick, Katherine, 54
mechanical: repetition, 12–13, 19, 188; reproduction, 124, 135
mechanization, 6, 53
media, 198–99; digital, 21, 135–36; new, 89, 136, 197
medieval Europe, 3–4, 16, 38–39, 106–8
memory, 101, 114–23, 219n17; habit, 119–21, 124, 130, 135, 177; time and, 190. *See also* organic memory
Merleau-Ponty, Maurice, 37, 162, 221n9; embodied habits, 172–76
metaphysics, 113–14, 117, 123–24, 163, 188; Christian, 26–27; of interiority, 74–75

Michaud, Éric, 151
middle class, 60, 89, 158, 213n3, 219n7
milieu(s), 61, 165, 177, 213n3, 216n8; governing via, 15, 72–73, 82–87
Mill, John Stuart, 39, 65, 84, 85–86, 213n15, 218n7
*Mill on the Floss, The* (Eliot), 61, 137
mind-body-environment relations, 140, 206–7
mind-body relations, 71–74, 80, 198
Miner, Robert, 104–5
Mirzoeff, Nicholas, 214n7
miscegenation, 66–67
modern habitus, 161–62, 182
modernity/modernism, 24–25, 162–63, 179; capitalist, 51; reflexive, 143–44; technologies of, 89
monks, moralized clothing of, 37, 105
morality, 190, 192, 205, 220n5
Morel, Benedict, 88, 90
Moreton-Robinson, Aileen, 204–5
*Morphing Intelligence* (Malabou), 16–17, 139, 151, 158
*Multitude* (Negri, Hardt), 162
music: atonal, 156, 157, 219n7; figures of habit and, 36, 173–74
mystics/mysticism, 222n4, 99, 108–9, 123–24; authority of, 16, 18, 113–14, 122, 193, 222n4

Native Americans, 171, 215n18
natural selection, 58, 62, 126, 128–29
nature, human, 168–69, 221n7
necropolitics, 203–4
negative conception of habit, 3, 8, 11–12, 36, 45, 101, 187–88; overturned in *Difference and Repetition*, 21, 25–26
Negri, Antonio, 101, 162
Neilson, Brett, 196
neoliberalism, 144, 222n6
nervous system, 5, 7, 11, 62–63, 72–73, 80–81, 91–94; impressibility of, 58; James on, 46, 48; reflex arc and, 20
neural plasticity, 16–17, 140–49, 153–54, 156
neurasthenia, 36–37

white privilege, habits of, 2, 17, 161–62, 169–72, 182, 221n8

white supremacism, 37, 56, 169–72, 212n12

Whytt, Robert, 36, 173–74

Wilderson, Frank, III, 56

will, 7, 11, 82–86, 91–92, 117–18, 127; in Christian theology, 99–101, 103; Dewey, 40; free, 71–72, 92, 94; power of, 73, 75

*Will to Knowledge, The* (Foucault), 31–32

Wolf, Johannes, 108

Wolff, Christian, 147–49

women: degeneration and, 88; everyday life and, 13, 23–25, 35, 211n2; impressibility and, 60–61; walking routines, 88

Woolf, Virginia, 181

working-class, 23, 51, 83, 85, 181

worms, habits of, 127

Wright of Derby, Joseph, 50–51, 197–98

Yin, Henry, 70–71

Young, Robert, 90

Zieger, Susan, 54–55, 89